SOCIAL WORK AND LAW

PARENTS AND CHILDREN

AUSTRALIA
The Law Book Company Ltd.
Sydney: Melbourne: Brisbane

CANADA AND U.S.A.
The Carswell Company Ltd.
Agincourt, Ontario

INDIA
N.M. Tripathi Private Ltd.
Bombay

ISRAEL
Steimatzyky's Agency Ltd.
Jerusalem: Tel Aviv: Haifa

MALAYSIA: SINGAPORE: BRUNEI
Malayan Law Journal (Pte.) Ltd.
Singapore

NEW ZEALAND
Sweet and Maxwell (N.Z.) Ltd.
Wellington

PAKISTAN
Pakistan Law House
Karachi

SOCIAL WORK AND LAW

PARENTS
AND
CHILDREN

Brenda M. Hoggett, M.A.

of Gray's Inn and the Northern Circuit, Barrister,
Senior Lecturer in Law, University of Manchester

LONDON
SWEET & MAXWELL
1977

Published in 1977 by
Sweet & Maxwell Ltd. of
11 New Fetter Lane, London.
Photoset by Red Lion Setters, London.
Printed in Great Britain by
Fletcher & Son Ltd., Norwich

ISBN 0 421 21410 4

Preface

This book is about the relationship between parents and their children and what can go wrong with it. It is such a large and complex subject that I have unfortunately had to limit it to the law in England and Wales, although I realise that for the child care practitioner Scotland and Northern Ireland are not the separate entities which they are to the lawyer. It is also a subject which is developing so rapidly that it is hard to keep up to date. I have tried to state the law as it is at Easter 1977, but Parliament has already passed the Adoption Act 1976, consolidating all the adoption legislation referred to in the text, and may well do the same for the child care legislation in this session. As the Adoption Act is not yet in force I have left the text unaltered, but a Comparative Table shows where its sections are derived from, for future reference.

In trying to understand the problems of the child care practitioner for whom this book is largely designed, I have been greatly helped by the staff and students on the social work courses for which I have taught the subject, and I should like to thank them all. Miss Margaret Heywood, Director of the course leading to the extra-mural Diploma of Social Work, has given me much encouragement and much to think about. Doctor Frank Bamford, Senior Lecturer in Community Paediatrics, and the Manchester unit of the National Society for the Prevention of Cruelty to Children have been good enough to let me see their side of the problems of child abuse. My colleagues in the law, particularly Professor P.M. Bromley of Manchester and Mr. Stephen Cretney of Oxford, have helped me to understand the complexities of recent legislation. I am grateful to everyone: it is certainly no one's fault but my own if I have got it wrong.

BRENDA HOGGETT

Easter 1977

Contents

TABLE OF CASES

References are given to the most accessible reports of cases referred to in text. Abbreviations used:

TABLE OF STATUTES

TABLE OF STATUTORY INSTRUMENTS

REFERENCES AND FURTHER READING

Sources which are relevant virtually throughout the book are listed first. References and other sources are listed under the chapter where they appear or are most relevant.

SOURCES RELEVANT THROUGHOUT

H.K. Bevan, *The Law Relating to Children* (Butterworths 1973).

P.M. Bromley, *Family Law*, 5th ed. (Butterworths 1976).

Clarke Hall and Morrison's *Law Relating to Children and Young Persons*, 9th ed. by Margaret Booth (Butterworths 1977).

S.M Cretney, *Principles of Family Law*, 2nd ed. (Sweet and Maxwell 1976).

J. Goldstein, A. Freud and S.J. Solnit, *Beyond the Best Interests of the Child* (Free Press 1973).

J.D. McClean, *The Legal Context of Social Work* (Butterworths 1975).

Sweet and Maxwell's *Family Law Statutes*, 2nd ed. by Sweet and Maxwell's Legal Editorial Staff with J. Terry (Sweet and Maxwell 1976).

P. Seago and A. Bissett-Johnson, *Cases and Materials on Family Law* (Sweet and Maxwell 1976).

J. Terry, *A Guide to the Children Act 1975* (Sweet and Maxwell 1976).

CHAPTER 1

P. Adams, *Children's Rights: Towards the Liberation of the Child* (Panther 1972).

Committee on the Age of Majority (Chairman: Mr. Justice Latey), Report, Cmnd. 3342 (H.M.S.O. 1967).

M.C. Dutchman-Smith, "Parental Rights in Education" (1975) 119 *Solicitors' Journal* 158.

J.M. Eekelaar, "What are Parental Rights?" (1973) 89 *Law Quarterly Review* 210.

M.D.A. Freeman, "Child Law at the Crossroads" (1974) 27 *Current Legal Problems* 165.

J.C. Hall, "The Waning of Parental Rights" [1972B] *Cambridge Law Journal* 248.

Justice, *Parental Rights and Duties and Custody Suits* (Stevens 1975).

P.H. Pettit, "Parental Control and Guardianship" in R.H. Graveson and F.R. Crane, *A Century of Family Law 1857-1957* (Sweet and Maxwell 1957).

Practice Direction: Home Office Assistance to Prevent Unauthorised Removal of Infant [1963] 3 All E.R. 66.

P.D.G. Skegg, "Consent to Medical Procedures on Minors" (1973) 36 *Modern Law Review* 370.

P.D.G. Skegg, "A Justification for Medical Procedures Performed without Consent" (1974) 90 *Law Quarterly Review* 512.

H. Street, *Torts*, 6th ed. (Butterworths 1976).

CHAPTER 2
See also references in Chapters 9 and 10.

M.D.S. Ainsworth, "Further Research into the Adverse Effects of Maternal Deprivation," in J. Bowlby, *Child Care and the Growth of Love*, 2nd ed. (Penguin Books 1965).

M.D.S. Ainsworth, R.G. Andry, R.G. Harlow, S. Lebovici, M. Mead, D.G. Prugh and B. Wootton, *Deprivation of Maternal Care: Reassessment of its Effects* (World Health Organisation 1962).

J. Bowlby, *Maternal Care and Mental Health* (World Health Organisation Geneva 1951), revised and republished as *Child Care and the Growth of Love*, 2nd ed. (Penguin Books 1965).

J. Bowlby, *Attachment and Loss*, Vol. 1: Attachment (Penguin Books 1969).

J. Bowlby, *Attachment and Loss*, Vol. 2: Separation: Anxiety and Anger (Penguin Books 1973).

Care of Children Committee (Chairman: Miss M. Curtis), Report, Cmd. 6922 (H.M.S.O. 1946).

A.M. Clarke and A.D.B. Clarke, *Early Experience — Myth and Evidence* (Open Books 1976).

D.H.S.S., *The Family in Society: Dimensions of Parenthood* (H.M.S.O. 1974).

J.S. Heywood and B.K. Allen, *Financial Help in Social Work: a Study of Preventive Work with Families under the Children and Young Persons Act 1963* (Manchester University Press 1971).

R. Holman, *Trading in Children — A Study of Private Fostering* (Routledge and Kegan Paul 1973).

M.L. Kellmer Pringle, *The Needs of Children* (Hutchinson 1974).

M. Mead, *Male and Female* (first published 1950, Penguin Books 1962).

P. Morgan, *Child Care: Sense and Fable* (Temple Smith 1975).

M. Rutter, "Parent-Child Separation: Psychological Effects on the Children" (1971) 12 *Journal of Child Psychology and Psychiatry* 233-260.

M. Rutter, *Maternal Deprivation Reassessed* (Penguin Books 1972).

N. Timms, *Casework in the Child Care Service*, 2nd ed. (Butterworths 1969).

N. Timms, *The Receiving End: Consumer Accounts of Social Help for Children* (Routledge and Kegan Paul 1973).

CHAPTER 3

F. Bates, "The Changing Position of the Mother in Custody Cases: Some Comparative Developments" (1976) 6 *Family Law* 125.

C.J. Buttle, "Divorce — A Consideration of the Work of the Divorce Court Welfare Officer" (1975) 6 *Social Work Today* 327.

G. Cross, "Wards of Court" (1967) 83 *Law Quarterly Review* 200.

J. Dominian, *Marital Breakdown* (Penguin Books 1968).

J. Eekelaar, *Family Security and Family Breakdown* (Penguin Books 1971).

E. Elston, J. Fuller, N. Murch, "Judicial Hearings of Undefended Divorce Petitions" (1975) 38 *Modern Law Review* 609.

E. Ferri, *Growing Up in a One-Parent Family* (N.F.E.R. Publishing Company 1976).

E. Ferri and H. Robinson, *Coping Alone* (N.F.E.R. Publishing Company 1976).

Finer Report, Committee on One-Parent Families (Chairman: Mr. Justice Finer), Report, Cmnd. 5629 (H.M.S.O. 1974).

H.A. Finlay and S. Gold, "The Paramount Interest of the Child in Law and Psychiatry" (1971) 45 *Australian Law Journal* 82.

R. Fletcher, *The Family and Marriage in Britain*, 3rd ed. (Penguin Books 1973).

V. George and P. Wilding, *Motherless Families* (Routledge and Kegan Paul 1972).

Goldstein, Freud and Solnit — *see* Sources relevant throughout.

E. Griew and A. Bissett-Johnson, "Supervision Orders in Matrimonial and Guardianship Cases" (1975) 6 *Social Work Today* 322.

Home Office, Memorandum of Guidance for Divorce Court Welfare Officers (H.M.S.O. 1968).

Justice 1975 — *see* Chapter 1.

M. King, "Maternal Love — Fact or Myth?" (1974) 4 *Family Law* 61.

Law Commission, Reform of the Grounds of Divorce — The Field of Choice, Cmnd. 3123 (H.M.S.O. 1966).

Law Commission, Arrangements for the Care and Upbringing of Children (section 33 of the Matrimonial Causes Act 1965) (Report by Mr. John Hall of St. John's College, Cambridge), Published Working Paper No. 15 (1968).

Law Commission, Financial Provision in Matrimonial Proceedings, Report, Law Com. No. 25 (H.M.S.O. 1969).

Law Commission, Matrimonial Proceedings in Magistrates' Courts, Working Paper No. 53 (H.M.S.O. 1973).

Law Commission, Matrimonial Proceedings in Magistrates' Courts, Report, Law Com. No. 77 (H.M.S.O. 1976).

O.R. McGregor, L. Blom-Cooper and C. Gibson, *Separated Spouses* (Duckworth 1970).

N. Michaels, "The Dangers of a Change of Parentage in Custody and Adoption Cases" (1967) 83 *Law Quarterly Review* 547.

S. Maidment, "Access Conditions in Custody Orders" (1975) 2 *British Journal of Law and Society* 182.

S. Maidment, " A Study in Child Custody" (1976) 6 *Family Law* 195 and 236.

B. Mortlock, *The Inside of Divorce* (Constable 1972).

Rutter 1971 — *see* Chapter 2.

M. Wynn, *Fatherless Families* (Michael Joseph 1964).

CHAPTER 4

V. Bean, "In Whose Best Interests?" (1976) 6 *Family Law* 116.

P. Bean, "The Challenge of Social Enquiry Reports" (1974) 4 *Family Law* 25.

M. Berlins and G. Wansell, *Caught in the Act* (Penguin Books 1974).

W.E. Cavenagh, *Juvenile Courts, The Child and the Law* (Penguin Books 1967).

W.E. Cavenagh, *The Juvenile Court* (Barry Rose 1976).

Committee on Children and Young Persons (Chairman: Viscount Ingleby), Report, Cmnd. 1191 (H.M.S.O. 1960).

N. Davies and A. Knopf, *Social Enquiry Reports and the Probation Service, Home Office Research Studies 18* (H.M.S.O. 1973).

D.H.S.S., *Intermediate Treatment: a guide for the Regional Planning of new forms of treatment for children in trouble* (H.M.S.O. 1972).

D.H.S.S., *Intermediate Treatment Project, Development Group Report* (H.M.S.O. 1973).

D.H.S.S., *Youth Treatment Centres* (H.M.S.O. 1971).

D. Ford, *Children, Courts and Caring* (Constable 1975).

P. Ford, *Advising Sentencers* (Blackwells 1972).

B. Harris, "Children's Act in Trouble — An Appreciation of the Children and Young Persons Act 1969 in Operation" [1972] *Criminal Law Review* 670.

Home Office Circular No. 31/1964, Notes on the Judges' Rules, *printed in* Archibold's *Criminal Pleading Evidence and Practice*, 39th ed. (Sweet and Maxwell 1976).

Home Office, *The Child, The Family and the Young Offender*, Cmnd. 2742 (H.M.S.O. 1965).

Home Office, *Children in Trouble*, Cmnd. 3601 (H.M.S.O. 1968).

Home Office, *Part I of the Children and Young Persons Act 1969: A Guide for Courts and Practitioners* (H.M.S.O. 1970).

Home Office, Letter to the Editor (1974) 4 *Family Law* 32.

Home Office, *Observations on the 11th Report of the House of Commons Expenditure Committee*, Cmnd. 6494 (H.M.S.O. 1976).

House of Commons Expenditure Committee, 11th Report session 1974-75, The Children and Young Persons Act 1969, 1974-75 H.C. 534 (H.M.S.O. 1975).

J.D. McClean, "Another View" (following Harris *above*) [1972] Crim. L.R. 684.

A.M. Morris, "Children's Hearings in Scotland" [1972] Crim. L.R. 693.

O.M. Stone, "Children Without a Satisfactory Home — A Gap Family Law must Fill" (1970) 33 *Modern Law Review* 649.

J. Temkin, "The Child, The Family and the Young Offender — Swedish Style" (1973) 36 *Modern Law Review* 569.

J.A.F. Watson and P.M. Austin, *The Modern Juvenile Court* (Shaw and Sons 1975).

D.J. West, *The Young Offender* (Duckworth 1967).

D.J. West, *Who Becomes Delinquent?* Second Report of Cambridge Study in Delinquent Development (Heinemann 1973).

Widgery Committee, Departmental Committee on Legal Aid in Criminal Proceedings (Chairman: Mr. Justice Widgery), Report, Cmnd. 2934 (H.M.S.O. 1966).

CHAPTER 5
See also references in Chapter 4.

Bevan 1973 — *see* Sources relevant throughout.

J. Berry, *Social Work with Children* (Routledge and Kegan Paul 1972).

M. Borland (ed.), *Violence in the Family* (Manchester University Press 1976).

J. Carter (ed.), *The Maltreated Child* (Priory Press 1974).

R.L. Castle and A. Kerr, *A Study of Suspected Child Abuse* (National Society for the Prevention of Cruelty to Children 1972).

W.E. Cavenagh, "Battered Baby Cases in the Courts" (1974) 138 *Justice of the Peace* 30.

Committee of Inquiry into the Care and Supervision provided in relation to Maria Colwell (Chairman: T.G. Field-Fisher Q.C.), Report (H.M.S.O. 1974).

Committee of Inquiry into the Provision and Co-ordination of Services to the Family of John George Auckland (Chairman: P.J.M. Kennedy Q.C.), Report (H.M.S.O. 1975).

Concerning Child Abuse: Papers presented by the Tunbridge Wells Study Group on Non-Accidental Injury to Children (Churchill, Livingstone 1975).

D.H.S.S., Circular LASSL (74) 13/CMO (74) 8, Memorandum on Non-Accidental Injury to Children (1974).

D.H.S.S., Local Authority Circular (76) 20, Children Act 1975: Implementation — Separate Representation in Certain Care and Related Proceedings (sections 64 (Part) and 65) (1976).

R.E. Helfer and C.H. Kempe (ed.), *The Battered Child* (University of Chicago Press 1968).

J.G. Howells, *Remember Maria* (Butterworths 1974).

M. Kellmer Pringle, "In Place of One's Own — A Look into the Future," in J. Seglow, M. Kellmer Pringle and P. Wedge, *Growing Up Adopted* (National Foundation for Educational Research 1972).

C.H. Kempe and R.E. Helfer (ed.), *Helping the Battered Child and His Family* (Blackwell 1972).

C. Low, "The Battering Parent, the Community and the Law" (1971) 3 *Applied Social Studies* 65.

Maria Colwell Inquiry Report, *see* Committee etc.

J. Renvoize, *Children in Danger* (Routledge and Kegan Paul 1974, Penguin Books 1975).

A.E. Skinner and R.L. Castle, *78 Battered Children: A Retrospective Study* (National Society for the Prevention of Cruelty to Children 1969).

S.M. Smith, *The Battered Child Syndrome* (Butterworths 1975).

J. Stark, "The Battered Child — does Britain need a Reporting Law?" [1969] *Public Law* 48.

CHAPTER 6

D. Barber, *Unmarried Fathers* (Hutchinson 1975).

Board for Social Responsibility of the National Assembly of the Church of England, *Fatherless by law?* (Church Information Office 1966).

M. Bones, *Family Planning Services in England and Wales* (H.M.S.O. 1973).

Committee on Statutory Maintenance Limits (Chairman: Miss J. Graham-Hall), Report, Cmnd. 3587 (H.M.S.O. 1968).

E. Crellin, M.L. Kellmer Pringle and P. West, *Born Illegitimate: Social and Educational Implications* (National Foundation for Educational Research 1971).

B. Dodd, "The Scope of Blood Grouping in the Elucidating of Problems of Paternity" (1969) 9 *Medicine, Science and the Law* 56.

Ferri 1976 — *see* Chapter 3.

Finer Report 1974 — *see* Chapter 3.

J.F. Josling, *Affiliation, Law and Practice*, 3rd ed. (Oyez Publishing 1971).

Law Commission 1966 — *see* Chapter 3.

Law Commission, Blood Tests and the Proof of Paternity in Civil Proceedings, Law Com. No. 16 (H.M.S.O. 1968).

R. Lister, *As Man and Wife? A Study of the Cohabitation Rule* (Child Poverty Action Group 1973).

O.R. McGregor, L. Blom-Cooper and C. Gibson — *see* Chapter 3.

L. Mair, *Marriage* (Penguin Books 1971).

M.M. Mayo, "Legitimacy for the A.I.D. Child" (1976) 6 *Family Law* 19.

National Council for the Unmarried Mother and Her Child (now National Council for One-Parent Families), *Forward for the Fatherless* — memorandum for the Finer Committee on One-Parent Families.

J. Neville Turner, *Improving the Lot of Children Born Outside Marriage: A Comparison of Three Recent Reforms: England, New Zealand and West Germany* (National Council for One-Parent Families).

J. Pochin, *Without a Wedding Ring: Casework with Unmarried Parents* (Constable 1969).

E.C. Ryder, "Property Law Aspects of the Family Law Reform Act 1969" (1971) 24 *Current Legal Problems* 157.

C. Smith and D.C. Hoath, *Law and the Underprivileged* (Routledge and Kegan Paul 1975).

Supplementary Benefits Commission, S.B.A. Paper No. 5, *Living together as husband and wife* (H.M.S.O. 1976).

V. Wimperis, *The Unmarried Mother and Her Child* (George Allen and Unwin 1960).

CHAPTER 7

Ferri 1976 — *see* Chapter 3.

Finer Committee — *see* Chapter 3.

Law Commission, Second Report on Family Property: Family Provision on Death, Law Com. No. 61 (1974).

Rutter 1971 — *see* Chapter 2.

CHAPTER 8

Crellin, Kellmer Pringle and West 1971 — *see* Chapter 6.

Ferri 1976 — *see* Chapter 3.

B. Maddox, *The Half Parent: Living with Other People's Children* (Andre Deutsch 1975).

D. Marsden, *Mothers Alone: Poverty and the Fatherless Family* (Penguin Books 1969).

Stockdale Report, 1972 — *see* Chapter 11, Departmental Committee on the Adoption of Children.

CHAPTER 9

See also references in Chapters 2 and 10.

Association of British Adoption and Fostering Agencies, *Practice Guide to the Children Act* 1975.

S.M. Cretney, "Children in Care: The Real Issues" (1970) 33 *Modern Law Review* 696.

D.H.S.S., *Youth Treatment Centres* (H.M.S.O. 1971).

D.H.S.S. and Welsh Office, Children in Care in England and Wales — March, 1974, Cmnd. 6147 (1975).

D.H.S.S., Local Authority Circular (75) 21, "Children Act: Main Provisions and Arrangements for Implementation."

D.H.S.S., Local Authority Circular (76) 15, "Children Act 1975: Programme for Implementation in 1976/77," Annex A: Guidance on the "Time Limit" Provisions (sections 29, 30, 56, 57 and 58 (Part)) which are planned to come into force on November 26, 1976.

D.H.S.S., Scottish Education Department and Welsh Office, Working Party on Fostering Practice, *Guide to Fostering Practice* (H.M.S.O. 1976).

D.H.S.S., Social Services for Children in England and Wales 1973-75, 1976-77 H.C. 68 (H.M.S.O. 1977).

R. Dinnage and M. Kellmer Pringle, *Foster Home Care: Facts and Fallacies* (Longmans 1967).

R. Dinnage and M.K. Kellmer Pringle, *Residential Child Care: Facts and Fallacies* (Longmans 1967).

J.M. Eekelaar, "Children in Care and the Children Act 1975" (1977) 40 *Modern Law Review* 121.

M.D.A. Freeman, "Children in Care — The Impact of the Children Act 1975" (1976) 6 *Family Law* 136. — *see* Sources relevant throughout.

Goldstein, Freud and Solnit 1973 — *see* Sources relevant throughout.

J. Heywood, *Children in Care: The Development of the Service for the Deprived Child* (Routledge and Kegan Paul 1959).

J. Packman, *Child Care: Needs and Numbers* (Allen and Unwin 1969).

J. Packman, *The Child's Generation: Child Care Policy from Curtis to Houghton* (Blackwell 1975).

J. Rowe and L. Lambert, *Children Who Wait* (Association of British Adoption Agencies 1973).

R. White, The case for Retaining a Child in Voluntary Care" (1976) 6 *Family Law* 141.

CHAPTER 10

See also references in Chapters 2 and 9

G. Adamson, *The Care-Takers* (Bookstall Publications 1973).

"Alternatives to 'Parental Right' in Child Custody Disputes involving Third Parties" (1963-64) 73 *Yale Law Journal* 151.

Bowlby 1951 — *see* Chapter 2.

D.H.S.S. 1976 — *see* Chapter 9.

V. George, *Foster Care: Theory and Practice* (Routledge and Kegan Paul 1970).

Goldstein, Freud and Solnit — *see* Sources relevant throughout.

R. Holman, "The Place of Fostering in Social Work" (1975) 5 *British Journal of Social Work* 3.

R. Jenkins, "Long Term Fostering" (1969) 15 *Case Conference* 349.

R.A. Parker, *Decision in Child Care: a Study of Prediction in Fostering* (Allen and Unwin 1966).

Rowe and Lambert 1973 — *see* Chapter 9.

O. Stevenson, *Some-one Else's Child*, new ed. (Routledge and Kegan Paul 1968).

R. Thorpe, "Mum and Mrs. So and So" (1974) 4 *Social Work Today* 691.

G. Trasler, *In Place of Parents* (Routledge and Kegan Paul 1960).

E.A. Weinstein, *The Self Image of the Foster Child* (Russell Sage Foundation 1960).

CHAPTER 11

Advisory Councils on Child Care, *Guide to Adoption Practice* (H.M.S.O. 1970).

Association of British Adoption Agencies, *The Guardian-ad-litem*.

Association of Child Care Officers, Monograph No. 3, *Adoption — The Way Ahead*.

S.M. Cretney, "Children Act 1975 — Effects of the Act on Property Law" (1976) 126 *New Law Journal* 7.

C. Davies, "The Departmental Committee on the Adoption of Children and the Tug of War Cases" (1973) 36 *Modern Law Review* 245.

Departmental Committee on the Adoption of Children (Chairman: Sir W. Houghton, decd., then Judge F.A. Stockdale), Report, Cmnd. 5107 (1972).

Departmental Committee on the Adoption of Children, Working Paper (H.M.S.O. 1970).

I. Goodacre, *Adoption Policy and Practice* (Allen and Unwin 1966).

J.F. Josling, *Adoption of Children*, 7th ed. (Oyez Publishing 1972).

M. Kellmer Pringle, "In Place of One's Own — A Look into the Future," in J. Seglow, M. Kellmer Pringle and P. Wedge, *Growing Up Adopted* (National Foundation for Educational Research 1972).

M.L. Kellmer Pringle, *Adoption: Facts and Fallacies* (Longmans 1967).

M. Kornitzer, *Adoption and Family Life* (Putnam 1968).

A. McWhinnie, *Adopted Children: How They Grow Up* (Routledge and Kegan Paul 1967).

N. Michaels, "The Dangers of a Change of Parentage in Custody and Adoption Cases" (1967) 83 *Law Quarterley Review* 547.

L. Raynor, *Adoption of Non-white Children* (Allen and Unwin 1970).

L. Raynor, *Giving Up a Baby for Adoption* (Association of British Adoption Agencies 1971).

J. Rowe, *Parents, Children and Adoption: A Handbook for Adoption Workers* (Routledge and Kegan Paul 1966).

J. Rowe, *Yours by Choice: A Guide for Adoptive Parents*, revised ed. (Routledge and Kegan Paul 1968).

A. Samuels, "Adoption Reform" (1973) 36 *Modern Law Review* 278.

J. Seglow, M.L. Kellmer Pringle and P. Wedge, *Growing Up Adopted* (National Foundation for Educational Research 1972).

P. Selman, "Patterns of Adoption in England and Wales since 1959" (1976) 6 *Social Work Today* 194.

Stockdale Committee *see* Departmental Committee.

J. Triseliotis, *In Search of Origins* (Routledge and Kegan Paul 1973).

Introduction

Most people would probably still define a "normal" family unit as a husband and wife and the children of their marriage. Even if moral and religious restrictions on sexual relationships between adults are much weaker, this unit is still regarded as providing the ideal upbringing for children. All children have physical needs which must at first be supplied by someone else if they are to survive at all, and it is scarcely surprising that society looks first to the natural mother to supply those needs and to the natural father to protect and support both mother and child while she is doing so. Equally it is now recognised that all children have complex emotional and psychological needs, which are probably best supplied if they are brought up throughout their childhood by a couple who are warmly and deeply committed both to one another and to their children. Marriage is thus assumed to be the best means of achieving both these ends. Society is indeed becoming much more interested in the welfare of children, principally but not entirely for humanitarian reasons. Stable, happy children will grow up into stable, happy adults, ready to reproduce the "normal" family unit, and it is thought that the stability and continuity of society itself depends upon the stability of its smallest unit, the family. These assumptions may all be challenged by those who think them devices for perpetuating social structures and sexual stereotypes of which they disapprove, but few would deny that this is indeed the "normal" family at present promoted by both society and the law.

Moreover, most of the legal problems confronting the child care practitioner arise either because of some crisis in, or because of some deviation from, such a "normal" upbringing. Thus any event which necessitates the separation of a child from one or both of his parents, or even some lesser degree of official intervention in the family, is clearly a crisis of great importance both to social work and to the law. Part II of this book will therefore be devoted to the legal controls which operate when four of the most common of these crises happen to a child — when his parents have for some reason to arrange for someone else to look after him, when his parents' own relationship is breaking up, when his parents are treating him badly, and when he himself is getting into trouble with the law. However, the actual crisis is rarely the end of the story, for as a result the child's upbringing is bound to be abnormal; there are also some abnormalities arising from events which are not in themselves legal crises, such as illegitimacy or the death of a parent; in either case, people or authorities other than the child's own parents may acquire an interest in his future and conflicts can easily arise. Many, but by no means all, of these can be resolved in accordance with what is best for the child, but the subject is so complex that it seems simplest to divide it according to the relationship between the adult or agency involved and the child, whatever the circumstances in which that relationship may have arisen. Thus Part III will be devoted to the claims and responsibilities of unmarried parents, of guardians over orphaned children, of step-parents, of local authorities over the children in their care, and of relatives and other foster-parents caring for other people's children. The final chapter will be devoted to the most final step of all, adoption.

Obviously, several of these people or agencies may be involved in the future of one unfortunate child who has already suffered the crisis of separation. It may be necessary to consult several chapters in order to see the complete picture in any individual case, but each should present a relatively clear-cut factual situation to which the law's response can be described and evaluated. However, in this field as in most others, the law can never be more than a tool for enabling the authorities to make the best of a bad job, for a child who has been brought up in anything other than a "normal" family has by definition been deprived of what society regards as his "best" interests. It seems a logical introduction, therefore, to ask what the law has to say about the relationship of parent and child within this normal family, and in particular to see what the rights and responsibilities of the parent may be.

Part I
The "Normal" Family

1 Parental Rights and Duties

It is much easier to define a "normal" family — a husband and wife and the children of their marriage — than it is to define the rights and responsibilities of the people in it. Although modern statutes often mention parental rights, powers or duties, the law does not provide us with a neat little list of them. There is only a patchwork of legislation and decided cases on particular points. In any event, legal relationships between parents and children can never be quite like those between adults, for the whole object of the relationship is to govern the upbringing of someone who is not only too young to bring himself up but also too young to force others to do it for him. Parental rights have thus largely depended on the degree of practical power which parents enjoy over their children coupled with the extent to which other people or authorities will either recognise or limit that power, while parental responsibilities depend largely on the ability of other people or authorities to oblige the parents to adopt acceptable standards of child care. The present state of the law can only be understood after some account of how it has developed.

1. *The Historical Development*

The common law took the easy way out of the problem. For a great many economic, physiological, social and religious reasons, a husband enjoyed considerable practical power over both his wife and their youthful progeny, and the courts eventually recognised this to the extent of translating it into "rights" which they would enforce against the wife, the child and the outside world in almost every case. They recognised that fathers had concomitant obligations, but they were baffled by the problem of enforcing them: the child was too young to do so, the mother was regarded as one person with her husband and thus unable to challenge him, and the outside agencies which might have been given the right to interfere simply did not exist, even supposing that the courts would have welcomed the idea. A few limits were recognised, for the child would come of age at 21 and gain his freedom; the father never became entitled to his child's property and although he might have management powers the child could sue him for "wasting" it; the criminal law would punish the more serious forms of ill-treatment; and if the father were grossly unfit the courts might be persuaded to decline to enforce his claim to possession (the best known example being the case of the poet Shelley, whose atheism and amorality were thought serious disqualifications for fatherhood). However, in most cases the courts would enforce the father's wishes about the upbringing, education and religion of his legitimate minor children, even if this involved removing an eight-month-old baby from his mother (*R.* v. *De Manneville*, 1804) or forcing a 17-year-old to accept the father's choice of religion (*Re Agar-Ellis*, 1883). Moreover, he could rule his children from the grave, by appointing a guardian who, though rather more subject to the courts' control, would take precedence over the mother. Illegitimate children, on the other hand, being born outside the recognised family unit, belonged to no one.

Little by little the law was changed. The first important steps were towards giving the courts power to hear applications from the mother. In 1839, legislation gave her the right to apply for custody of children up to seven, and for access to children of any age, provided that she had not committed adultery. In 1873, the age limit was raised to 16 and the adultery exclusion removed (although it still exercised a powerful influence in practice), and a separation deed allowing the mother to have custody was declared enforceable against the father. In 1886, the age limit went up to 21, the mother was given guardianship rights after the father's death and limited rights to appoint a guardian after her own death. Finally, in 1925, courts were expressly told to ignore the question of whether the father's rights were technically superior to those of the mother (or even vice versa), and their rights to act as and appoint guardians were also made equal. Meanwhile, the courts had been acquiring increasing powers to intervene in the relationship of marriage itself. In 1857, a new court was given power to dissolve a valid marriage, and the powers of the old ecclesiastical courts to annul invalid ones or to relieve the parties of the duty to live together were transferred to the same court. By 1895, magistrates' courts had acquired various powers to grant separation and maintenance orders to wives who needed a quicker and cheaper solution. In both cases, the courts were permitted to make custody orders about the children of the marriage.

These procedural developments were by no means the whole story. In the first place, they only applied where there was a parental dispute or a death. Until then, the father remained the sole natural guardian of his children with the ultimate power to take most important decisions. The mother could only challenge him by splitting up the family or by asking the court to take over the child's guardianship by making him a ward of court. Respectable married women were understandably annoyed that their legal powers over their own children were less than those of the widow, the divorced or separated woman, or, worst of all, the unmarried mother. Thus the Guardianship Act of 1973 now specifically provides that "In relation to the custody or upbringing of a minor, and in relation to the administration of any property belonging to or held in trust for a minor or the application of income of any such property, a mother shall have the same rights and authority as the law allows to a father, and the rights and authority of mother and father shall be equal and exercisable by either without the other" (s. 1(1); this does not, of course, apply to illegitimate children). If they disagree, either may apply to a court for its direction (s. 1(3)).

Secondly, of course, having acquired all these various powers to intervene, the courts required a principle upon which to arbitrate parental disputes. At first, they may have remained more sympathetic to the father's wishes, not only because of his common law rights but also because Victorian judges believed that he was usually the best judge of what was best for his own child. However, they did develop the principle that the child's welfare could *override* such considerations, and gradually they came to consider that welfare *before* everything else. Quite what point the courts had reached by 1925 may be disputed, but in that year statute put the matter beyond doubt in what is now section 1 of the Guardianship of Minors Act 1971 and the most important principle of child law today:

"Where in any proceedings before any court ... (*a*) the custody or upbringing of a minor; or (*b*) the administration of any property belonging to or held on trust for a minor, or the application of the income thereof, is in question, the court, in deciding that question, shall regard the welfare of the minor as the first and paramount consideration, and shall not take into consideration whether from any other point of view the claim of the father ... in respect of such custody, upbringing, administration or application is superior to that of the mother, or the claim of the mother is superior to that of the father."

The position as between mother and father of a legitimate child is thus quite clear (the way in which that principle is applied in practice is discussed in Chapter 3). By placing the child's welfare first it clearly also places considerable limits on the exercise of parental powers and authority, once either parent is prepared to challenge the other. Furthermore, once the parents separate, the courts are also able to define and enforce their respective financial obligations towards the child.

More complicated inroads into the simplicity of the common law have been made by giving various people and bodies *outside* the family unit powers to intervene in it in the interests of the children. These powers are many, various and by no means a coherent body of doctrine, but they may be roughly divided into three categories.

In the first are procedures which enable individual non-parents to ask for some or all of the incidents of parenthood to be transferred to them. This has always been theoretically possible if the court can be persuaded to make the child its own ward and to delegate every-day care to the applicant. Modern statutes have increased the possibilities, but these vary according to the applicant's status, whether step-parent, relative, or unrelated foster parent. However, once the case can be got before them, the courts have now made it clear that the child's welfare is also the "first and paramount consideration" in custody disputes between parents and non-parents (the vital decision of *J.* v. *C.*, 1970, is discussed in Chapter 10). This obviously represents a revolution in the traditional concept of parental "rights" and may well be in advance of some public and even professional opinion. Furthermore, since 1926 it has been possible for children to be adopted. Although adoption normally requires the parents' agreement, this may sometimes be dispensed with, and once granted the order transfers the child almost completely and irrevocably from one family to another.

In the second category are the statutory responsibilities of local authorities. These may simply involve some control over the arrangements made by parents for other people to look after their children or some limitation on the employment of school-age children. These certainly limit parental freedom of action, but they pose little threat to their more important rights. Alternatively, the authority may be able to undertake the care of a child at his parents' request. This much-needed service usually has no effect upon the parents' claims, save in respect of matters of day-to-day decision while the authority is looking after the child, but there are some circumstances in which the parents may be prevented from recovering him and these certainly invade parental "rights." Furthermore, the authority may be ordered by a court to care for or supervise a child whose home circumstances, upbringing, education or behaviour have been found unsatisfactory; and there are also emergency powers to remove children to a "place of safety" for a short time. These are not only important qualifications to the parents' rights but also a considerable inducement to observe parental responsibilities. However, in all these situations, the grounds for official intervention are clearly defined; it is not enough, as it is in an ordinary custody dispute, to show that the action is justified because it will be the best for the child's welfare. While it is no doubt right that society should not be too eager to interfere in the family unit of which it so whole-heartedly approves, it is this discrepancy which is largely responsibe for much of the confusion and complexity of the law about child care. So much depends upon who is involved and what procedure is being invoked.

The final category covers criminal offences which have been designed to protect children from a wide variety of evils, from dangerous or over-taxing employment, from the purchase of alcohol, cigarettes, fireworks and the like, from sexual exploitation and so on. Most of these are only indirect and marginal limitations on parental freedom, for they are more concerned with limiting the freedom of employers, retailers, and sexual offenders, and are largely outside the scope of this book. However, the offences which are designed to protect children from various forms of neglect or ill-treatment, or to ensure that they are properly educated, place vital limits on the power of the parent or the person who is bringing up a child and oblige them to fulfil their responsibilities.

2. *Parental Powers and Duties Today*

There are now so many limitations from so many different quarters upon the otherwise absolute power that a parent might enjoy over his young children that it is difficult to talk of parental "rights" at all. One can only look at the varying legal processes which may operate upon a number of important incidents of parenthood and childhood.

(i) *Caring for a child*

(a) The "right to possession"

Society does not seek to choose the ideal parents for each child, as it automatically assumes (for reasons which have been indicated in the Introduction) that his natural parents, if they are married to one another, are ideal. Thus their claim to the new-born baby is highly respected by the law; although it would be theoretically possible to make him a ward of court and ask the court to give him to someone else, it is extremely unlikely that the court would grant this unless the natural parent either had no interest in the child or was totally unfit to look after him; however, although most of the grounds for care or place of safety proceedings relate to what has happened to the child in question and must thus wait until the child has gone home, there are two grounds which relate to what *might* happen to him because of what has already been done to another child; thus it may even be possible to prevent a mother taking her baby home from hospital.

Once the child goes home, the parents' right to possession

will be respected until some crisis (discussed in Part II) interrupts his actual possession. Such a crisis may involve a court order which will deprive one or both of the parents of that right (for example, a custody order following their separation, or a care order following their ill-treatment of the child or his own delinquency), although such orders can always be later varied or revoked. However, if the parents have simply arranged for someone else, whether an individual or an agency, to look after their child, they will retain the right to possession and thus the right to reclaim him; but this is increasingly subject to qualification, partly because they may not always be able to enforce it, partly because an agency may be able to delay returning the child or even take over parental rights itself, and partly because even individual caretakers have some steps which they can take to counteract the parents' claims. As already explained, all these procedures have their own particular principles and rules, and generalisation is impossible. Although all are based on a fundamental respect for the child's welfare above all else, there are so many difficult practical problems that each claim must be considered individually (and it is the purpose of Part III to do so).

If a parent is deprived of the actual or legal possession of his child, it might be thought that he had at least a right to visit him; but the extent to which the law respects that right depends upon whether it is an individual (such as a spouse or custodian) or an agency (such as a local authority) which is looking after the child, and again generalisation is impossible.

Indeed, the child himself may have a voice. Although the age of majority is now 18, the courts recognise that the degree of practical power exercisable by parents (or indeed most other care-givers) diminishes considerably before that age (*Hewer* v. *Bryant*, 1970). Thus the traditional remedy to enforce the parental right to possession, apart from simply taking him away, is habeas corpus; but as this merely frees a person from unlawful detention by a third party, it cannot force an unwilling child who has reached a certain age to return home; this "age of discretion" seems to be 14 for boys and 16 for girls. The parents could alternatively make the child a ward of court, but unless there were some element of moral danger, fortune hunting or the like, the court would be unlikely to coerce a 16-year-old who had, for example, left home and found both a job and a place to live. The only other possibility would be care proceedings, which are available up to 17, but not only would one of the specific grounds have to be proved — the order would also deprive the parents of their right to possession (it would however give the police power to recapture an absconder). Moreover, in an ordinary custody dispute between adults, the courts will rarely make an order against the wishes of a 16-year-old, and will usually take the wishes of a much younger child into account.

Thus the parents' claim to possession, which used to be virtually undeniable, is now severely limited, not only against third parties, but also against the child himself. However, actual possession of a child obviously carries with it most of the important powers and responsibilities of parenthood. Apart from the recognition that many of those powers decrease as the child grows older, the law undoubtedly sets some more specific limits on the matters discussed below.

(b) Discipline

The power to control a child's everyday behaviour ought surely to go hand-in-hand with the power to look after him. This is undeniable if the person looking after him also has the legal "right to possession"; more difficult is the situation where the person with legal rights has delegated care to someone else, whether child-minder, foster parent, local authority, or, perhaps most importantly, school. To what extent can the parent limit that person's powers? The parent's instructions may well be effective where care is delegated to a private foster parent or school, for in theory the recipient can refuse to take the child unless the parent agrees to give him a free hand, and the parent can choose someone whose views coincide with his. With state schools, however, not only has the local education authority a statutory duty to provide them, but the parent has a statutory duty to use them unless he can afford an alternative. Their disciplinary powers therefore probably arise from statutory authority rather than parental delegation, and are limited by the L.E.A.'s rules rather than the parents' instructions. The same is probably true where a child is received voluntarily into local authority care, for although the parent has no duty to place him there, the authority clearly has statutory responsibility for his care (the Community Homes Regulations appear to be drafted on this basis, for they make no distinction between compulsory and voluntary care).

This is only a problem where the person wishes to impose something, such as corporal punishment or detention, which might be an actionable wrong (a "tort") against the child, or even a criminal offence, if done without lawful authority. No one has unlimited authority to impose corporal punishment on a child, and a parent may not only run the risk of prosecution for excessive punishment, but also of having the child taken away because of ill-treatment (see Chapter 5). To be lawful, punishment must be imposed for a reason, and be reasonable in relation both to that reason and to the age, understanding and physique of the particular child. It is sometimes suggested that no adult should ever be allowed to hit a child, for any power to do so is very susceptible to abuse and creates the wrong impression of acceptable child care practices. However, the courts seem to find little difficulty in making sensible distinctions, and any ban would be more difficult to enforce than are the present limits. These would probably command more general acceptance than would total prohibition.

(c) Medical treatment

Most medical and dental procedures would also be actionable wrongs against the child if performed without lawful authority. It is often assumed that such authority consists of the consent of the person with parental rights, so that not only can a parent prohibit operations, blood transfusions, and the like, but he can also authorise treatment without reference to the child's wishes. This assumption must be questioned, and in any event there are means of counter-acting the parent's wishes.

First, the Family Law Reform Act 1969 provides that the consent of a 16-year-old is as effective as if he were 18, without the need for parental consent (s. 8(1)). A 16-year-old can also be informally admitted for psychiatric treatment without reference to his parents (Mental Health Act 1959, s. 5(2)). Secondly, the 1969 Act does not affect the validity of any other consent (s. 8(3)), and a younger child who is capable of understanding what is proposed may very well be able to give an effective consent. Indeed it is surely doubtful whether a parent's consent would always be effective if the child were actively opposed to the treatment, for example, where a mother wished her 14-year-old girl to have an abortion. Thirdly, consent is not the only lawful authority for medical treatment (see *Skegg*, 1974), and life-saving procedures can certainly be carried out without it; indeed, practitioners are more likely to be vulnerable to legal action if they do *not* carry them out than if they do. Similarly, as with discipline, authorities with statutory responsibilities to care for children surely have statutory authority to arrange at least routine and essential medical treatment even if they do not have parental rights (again, both the Community Homes Regulations and the Boarding-out Regulations are drafted on this basis). Examination in suspected child abuse cases may well be another example.

After all, legal action by the child in all those cases is extremely unlikely to be taken, let alone to succeed. A parent might seek an injunction forbidding a doctor to operate without consent, but the court would surely exercise its discretion in accordance with the welfare principle, and once an operation has been performed, the parent has no right to sue for damages unless the child himself can sue (see (iii) (c) below). However, any interested person who either wishes to obtain clear legal authority to act without consent or to prevent a parent imposing treatment on a child may seek to make the child a ward of court. Thus in *Re D.* (1976), an educational psychologist wished to challenge the decision of the mother and paediatrician that an 11-year-old girl should be sterilised. She suffered from a rare congenital handicap which might affect her capacities as a mother and was fast approaching puberty. The judge held that this was a proper use of the wardship procedure, which is designed to protect all children. The court can take over the child's guardianship, and although care and control will be delegated to the most suitable person, all the major decisions can be taken by the court in accordance with the welfare principle. Here it was decided that sterilisation was *not* in this child's best interests.

Alternatively, it may be possible to bring care proceedings, which are cheaper and more convenient; but they must be brought by the right applicants, and although the grounds would be relatively easy to prove, the object could only be achieved by a care order. This transfers all parental "powers and duties" to the local authority, and although this ought to include whatever power a parent does have to decide medical treatment, there may be a difficulty where the parent's decision resulted from religious conviction for the authority cannot impose a different religion on the child.

(d) Travel abroad

Anyone wishing to take a child abroad should have, or have permission from the person with, the right to his possession. Thus the Crown requires the consent of (now) either parent before issuing a passport to a child under 16. A more serious problem is that it may be urgently necessary to prevent the child's removal, even though the parent has the right to possession; for example, where a father may "kidnap" the children to prevent the mother getting custody, or where a mother with custody proposes to emigrate and deprive the father of all effective contact. Thus not only do High Court and county court custody orders normally provide that the child shall not be taken abroad without the court's consent (and it is recommended that magistrates' courts should be able to do the same), but both the High Court and the divorce court can prohibit a child's removal whether or not any proceedings have been started, and even without notifying the other party in advance. Where there is a real risk of disobedience, the Home Office will take precautions at ports and airports to prevent the child leaving.

On the other hand, local authorities have a mysterious power to arrange the emigration of any child in their care (apart from one committed there in divorce and similar proceedings) whether or not they have parental rights. However, as the Secretary of State and, usually, the child must consent, and the parents must be consulted, there is probably little risk of abuse (Children Act 1948, s. 17).

(e) Day-to-day obligations

Here again, the obligations which go hand-in-hand with caring for a child can only be defined in the light of the legal tools available should things go wrong. In many cases where parents or others are finding it difficult to cope adequately, the informal guidance and support of social workers (Children and Young Persons Act 1963, s. 1), coupled with help in obtaining welfare benefits and perhaps day-care facilities may be both the best and the sufficient response. In others, the parent may agree that reception into care (Children Act 1948, s. 1) is for the time being the best solution (see Chapters 2 and 9).

Sometimes, however, intervention may be necessary whether or not the family agrees, and the possible steps are discussed in Chapter 5. Thus parental responsibilities can be defined by reference to the grounds upon which care or place of safety proceedings can be taken to allow the authorities to supervise or remove the child, and by reference to the circumstances in which a caretaker may be prosecuted. Care and place of safety proceedings are technically brought against the child himself, and so his exact legal relationship with the people looking after him is immaterial. Prosecutions for the most important criminal offence ("cruelty to a child" under section 1 of the Children and Young Persons Act 1933) can be brought against anyone of 16 or over who has "custody, charge or care"; thus although it is harder for parents with "custody" to evade their obligations, the obligations implied by the offence are imposed on all actual caretakers.

These official responses were devised because children are not only too young to look after themselves but also too young to take action to force others to do so. However, it seems clear that a child can sue a parent who commits an actionable wrong against him, although in practice this is only likely where he has been injured by the parent's careless driving, for then the insurance company will pay (the Congenital Disabilities (Civil Liability) Act 1976 has made it impossible for a disabled child to sue his own mother for wrongs committed before he was born, except when she was driving a car). Thus, while parents must certainly refrain from deliberately or carelessly injuring their children, the extent to which this imposes positive obligations to take steps which they would not have to take for adults has not been worked out in litigation. This is perhaps just as well, but it does leave the position of schools and other substitute parents undesirably vague.

(ii) *Developing his mind*

(a) Education

Originally a father or guardian could decide whether his child should be educated at all, and then impose his choice, even up to university level, upon the child, the mother and anyone looking after the child for him. He did not, of course, have the right to force a particular institution to accept his child. Nowadays, the position is entirely different.

First, where the child is of compulsory school-age, the parent is deprived of his right *not* to educate him, because a parent, guardian and indeed every person who has actual custody of such a child has a duty to cause him to receive efficient full-time education suitable to his age, ability and aptitude, either by regular attendance at school or otherwise (Education Act 1944, s. 36). The local education authority can require that person to convince them that this is being done, and if unconvinced can order him to enter the child at a particular school (s. 37). Disobedience is a criminal offence, unless the person can convince the court that the child is being properly educated (ss. 37(5) and 40). That person also commits a crime if a registered pupil fails to attend regularly, the only excuses being leave of absence, sickness or other "unavoidable" cause, religious observance, and failure of the education authority to make adequate arrangements where the school is not within walking distance (ss. 39 and 40). More importantly perhaps, care proceedings may be taken if a school-age child is not being properly educated (this is discussed in Chapter 5).

In return, the local education authority has a duty to provide sufficient and suitable schools to meet the needs of the children in its area (s. 8). It must also "have regard to the general principle that, so far as is compatible with the

provision of efficient instruction and training and the
avoidance of unreasonable public expenditure, pupils are to
be educated in accordance with the wishes of their parents" (s.
76). Within certain limits, however, it is the judge of what is
suitable, and the parent cannot force the authority to provide
whatever he chooses (*Watt* v. *Kesteven County Council*, 1955).
Thus parental choice depends either, as in the past, on the
ability of the parent to pay, or, nowadays, on the flexibility of
public provision. The parent no longer has the right to choose
nothing.

Secondly, parents may now be deprived of some or all of
their parental rights, and with them the right to choose
education. Care orders made because the child is not being
educated properly are an example. Custody orders (see
Chapter 3) are another, and the child's welfare is always the
first and paramount consideration in disputed custody cases,
although parental wishes and continuity of education are
obviously factors to be taken into account. The court may even
decide to separate the right to decide upon matters such as
education, religion and property from the day-to-day care of
the child, in what is known as a "split order" at present. This is
perhaps most likely in relatively well-off families where the
father may be expecting to pay for, and have a voice in,
private education. Indeed, education is one matter on which
mother and father might easily disagree while still living
together; such disputes can now be referred to a court for
decision (Guardianship Act 1973, s. 1 (3)), but unless the
mother has her own resources, there may be little the court can
do to make her wishes, however desirable, financially possible;
this may be a particular problem where the father is unwilling
to allow an able 16-year-old to stay on at school, unless local
authority assistance is sufficient.

Last, financial problems apart, it is perhaps unlikely that a
court would force a parental decision upon a child who had
reached 16. He will, however, find it easier to leave school than
to obtain his parents' support on the course of his choice,
although even this is not impossible.

(b) Religion

In disputes between parents or other adults, or between

parent and child, religion must be closely analagous to education; the welfare principle, coupled with the courts' general attitude to older children, should apply. The law governing official intervention is however entirely different.

First, there is no parental duty to provide religious instruction or to insist on religious observance, and so the authorities cannot intervene if there is none. They can however take action if the parents' choice of religion does some positive harm to the child so as to bring the case within the grounds for care proceedings or prosecution; sincere religious belief in such circumstances is no defence. Secondly, however, the authorities are generally under some obligation to respect the religion of a child who comes into their care, and of course this will normally have been determined by the parents. This is reflected both in the Boarding-out Regulations and the Community Homes Regulations, and where an authority allows a child to go out of care to someone other than a parent or guardian. Furthermore, even if the authority has parental rights under a section 2 resolution or care order, it has no right to cause him to be brought up in a religion *other* than the one in which he would otherwise have been brought up. Last, although a parent can no longer impose a religious condition upon her agreement to adoption, an adoption agency is under a duty, as far as practicable, to respect her wishes when choosing a placement for the child. Thus the law treats the child's religion with considerable respect.

(iii) *Finances*

(a) The child's own property

Parents have no claim to property or money which belongs to their children, but they do have power to administer both assets and income. Should disputes arise, and here again this is a matter upon which mother and father might well disagree without separating, the court would be guided by the welfare principle, and, probably, by reluctance to allow a parent in modern times to interfere with an older child's disposition of his own earnings (see again, *Hewer* v. *Bryant*, 1970). If a parent acted fraudulently or negligently in relation to his child's possessions, the child would be able to sue him.

In practice, few difficulties are encountered, save perhaps with earnings. If a child has any substantial property, it is almost certain to be held upon trust for him, and there are complex rules governing the powers and duties of trustees, who need not be the child's parents.

(b) Parents' financial obligations

The obligations of day-to-day care will obviously involve a parent, or anyone else, in expense, which may be compensated to a greater or lesser extent by state benefits (such as child benefit or family income supplement or guardian's allowance), or by a boarding-out allowance, or by maintenance payments. With one exception, however, only natural parents can be *ordered* to make financial provision for their children (the exception is a non-parent who has treated or accepted a child as a member of his family). Moreover, such orders can only be made in matrimonial or custody cases (see Chapter 3) or in the new custodianship jurisdiction (see Chapter 10) or when a child goes into care (see Chapter 9). At present, they are not designed to enforce the parent's financial obligations while the family remains united. Thus although orders can sometimes be made or continued after the child is 18, when he may even be able to apply for or enforce them himself, they can only be ancillary to some proceedings started by adults when the family is in some way divided.

(c) Compensation for interference with parental rights

There used to be several actions which a parent might bring to obtain damages for interference with his rights. Now that most disputes about a child's future are governed by the welfare principle (or by specific statutory powers), the idea that someone who is found to have been acting in the child's best interests might nevertheless have to pay damages for interference with parental rights is surely unacceptable, and most of these actions have been abolished. However, there remains an action which a father can bring against someone who wrongfully injures his child, for example, in a road accident. This is quite separate from the child's own action for his injuries, and is technically based on interference with the father's right to his child's services. Nowadays, the courts would scarcely enforce such a "right" against the child, but the action against third parties can be a useful recognition that parents can be put to considerable expense by wrongful injuries to their children.

(iv) *Leaving the nest*

(a) When can a child leave home?

This question has already been discussed (see (i)(a) above). The law provides no hard and fast answer, for it depends upon whether the courts would be prepared to do anything about it.

(b) When can the child marry?

Marriages under 16 are void. If the child is 16 but under 18, and not a widow or widower, marriage law requires that his parents should give their consent; but as it says little about how the parties' age or parental consent should be proved, allows certain marriages at very short notice, and in some cases overlooks the use of false names, it is by no means impossible to get married without it; the marriage is then quite valid, although there may be criminal penalties. Nor is the law at all clear about whose consent is required; the Marriage Act of 1949 provides a complicated list (see Sched. 2), which includes both parents of a legitimate child while they are living together; if they are separated by agreement, court order or divorce, it is the parent with custody; but if one parent has deserted the other, it is the desert*ed* parent, whether or not the child is with him; if both have been deprived of custody by a court order, it is the person who has been granted it, but it is not clear whether this includes a local authority having parental powers under a care order. (Nor is it clear whether this is one of the "parental rights and duties" which may be transferred under a "section 2 resolution.") It is sometimes possible to dispense with the consent of an incapable or inaccessible parent, and even if the required consents are not forthcoming the couple can apply to the magistrates' court, county court or High Court for permission to marry. As almost all applications are made in the magistrates' courts, it is not known upon what principles they operate. Thus the parents' rights are by no means as strong as might be expected. Their only other course is to make the child a ward of court and ask the court to forbid the marriage, for then the couple could be punished for contempt if they disobeyed; but while a court might well be prepared to forbid a hasty young marriage, it would hesitate to make matters even worse by punishing the young couple if they nevertheless managed to get married.

(c) Giving him up

The right to surrender one's parental rights is hardly a right at all, and so the common law drew the conclusion that it was impossible. Nowadays it is still impossible to surrender parental rights by mere agreement (Children Act 1975, s. 85(2)), except when a husband and wife are separating (Guardianship Act 1973, s. 1(2)) and even then a court may decline to enforce the agreement if it is not in the child's best interests. There are however many procedures for removing some or all of a parent's rights. Of these, only adoption requires his positive agreement, but in many others he may have no actual objection to the order or resolution.

More important is the degree of choice which a parent may exercise when his child has to be looked after by others, and the general tendency of the law is to restrict individual discretion in favour of the presumably more expert discretion of child-care and adoption agencies. Thus it is intended to outlaw most private placements for adoption (see Chapter 11), local authorities and voluntary organisations provide most of the substitute care service (see Chapter 9), private fostering is subject to some control and in practice very little choice (see Chapter 2), and the only areas where the degree of legal interference in parental choice is minimal are substitute care in the child's own home (see Chapter 2) and the appointment of guardians to act after the parent's death (see Chapter 7).

The rest of this book will be devoted, in one way or another, to the legal problems arising out of the various methods of "giving him up."

Part II
Crises in the Family

2 Substitute Care

A parent may want or need someone else to look after his child for a great many different reasons and in theory there are many different ways in which he may choose to arrange it. All, however, raise the same legal questions. To what extent does the law seek to control the making of those arrangements? And once made, what effect may they have on the relationship between parent and child? The object of this chapter is to answer the first question; the second depends entirely upon who is seeking to establish some relationship in opposition to the parents, and thus is discussed in the chapters on local authorities or relatives and foster parents. Adoption is of course the ultimate alternative arrangement, and its highly specialised requirements have been collected in the final chapter.

There are always potential dangers in the separation of a child from his parents, whether this is voluntary or involuntary, although these depend very largely upon the reason for the separation and the quality of the substitute care provided. Thus as well as imposing controls upon most of the arrangements which parents may choose to make, the law also imposes a duty on local social services authorities to try and prevent its happening at all. They must "make available such advice, guidance and assistance as may promote the welfare of children by diminishing the need to receive children into or keep them in care or to bring them before a juvenile court" (Children and Young Persons Act 1963, s. 1). The law thus imposes few limitations on the provision of casework support to families with children, although it should be associated with the need to keep children out of care. It also reflects current views on the best way of bringing up children, although it should surely not be taken to mean that it is *always* better to keep children out of care or to return them to their natural families. Furthermore, authorities are empowered (but not obliged) to further the same objectives by providing assistance in kind or, in exceptional circumstances, in cash. As unsatisfactory home conditions and homelessness are two quite common grounds for reception into care, this seems to allow authorities to provide help with furniture, fuel supply, hire-purchase, rent or mortgage arrears, or by guaranteeing a mortgage. Yet the long-term relief of poverty should surely be the responsibility of the social security and supplementary benefits schemes, and not of an agency which is primarily concerned with personal services. However, those schemes have quite strict statutory limits, whereas the local authorities' discretion is extremely vague. This has led to its use for purposes far beyond the crisis intervention originally contemplated, and although flexibility is welcome, it can lead to confusion and resentment if one authority can be persuaded to do what another cannot. Luckily the controls on substitute care are rather more specific, although they may be equally variable in success.

1. *Substitute Care at Home*

Most normal, caring parents who need to provide substitute care for their children, whether because they are working, or ill, or having another baby or simply going out, would no doubt prefer this to happen in the child's own home. Some child care experts have given the impression that it is potentially damaging for any young child to be deprived of almost constant daily care by his mother, at least until the age of about three (*Bowlby*, 1951; but see *Kellmer Pringle*, 1974). Others have however pointed out the lack of any evidence that this is so (*Rutter*, 1971, 1972; *Morgan*, 1975), even on a long-term basis, provided that the substitute care is good and reasonably stable. The extremes of respect for exclusive maternal care are certainly confined to modern western society (see *Mead*, 1950), and it is noteworthy that care in the home is the one type of substitute care over which there are no direct legal controls whatsoever. Whether it is for a day, a night, a week or many months, and whether it is provided by a relative, a friend, an au-pair girl or a trained nanny, there is no provision for notification, registration or supervision (the situation is expressly excluded from the controls on private fostering). Few would suggest that there should be.

There is however some sanction, for the parents may be guilty of the criminal offence of wilfully neglecting a child under 16 "in a manner likely to cause him unnecessary suffering or injury to health" (Children and Young Persons Act 1933, s. 1(1), discussed in Chapter 5), if they leave him unattended or with someone who is too young or otherwise unsuited to protect him from harm. There are no hard-and-fast guide-lines on this. A teenage child is unlikely to be caused suffering or injury if he is left alone for an evening, nor are younger children likely to suffer if a responsible teenager babysits. But views can obviously differ about when to draw the line and a little more detail might not come amiss. A social worker who suspects that an offence is being committed can apply for a search warrant under section 40 of the 1933 Act (these warrants are fully discussed in Chapter 5).

2. *Day-care outside the home*

To many, day-care outside the home would seem the next best alternative. If the care is properly suited to the child's needs and he can retain a good relationship with his parents, there is again little evidence of damage. Indeed, day-care is often a good way of relieving stress in the home and enabling parents to cope. Because demand always seems to exceed supply, however, and because that demand almost always relates to pre-school children, there is a considerable risk that the people or places which agree to take children in will neither appreciate their needs nor be able to cater for them properly. The law therefore attempts to provide some control by means of registration, which is essentially similar whether the child is beng minded in a private house or attending a nursery or play group.

(i) *Child-minders*

Anyone who *for reward* (in cash or in kind) receives children *under five* into her house to be looked after for the day (or even a part or parts of the day if it amounts to more than two hours), or for any longer period of not more than six days, may apply for registration with the local social services authority (Nurseries and Child-Minders Regulation Act 1948, s. 1(1) and (2)). It is an offence to receive a child in such circumstances, even once, without being registered, but only if the child-minder is not a relative (s.4(2); "relative" means grandparent, brother, sister, uncle or aunt, including those related by adoption or marriage as well as by blood, and the father of an illegitimate child and people related through him, s.13(2)). Although registration is of the person and not of the place, if the minder moves house she is not regarded as registered to receive children in her new home until she notifies the local authority (s.4(3)). A person authorised by a local authority may apply to a magistrate for a warrant to enter and inspect any home where he has reasonable cause to believe that children are being received in contravention of section 4 (s.7(2)). It is not an offence in itself for the parent to place a child with an unregistered minder but he could be guilty of aiding and abetting the minder's offence, or even, in an extreme case, of neglect.

The local authority can refuse registration if the applicant, or anyone to be employed in looking after the children, is unfit, or if the premises are unsuitable because of their condition or equipment or any reason connected with their situation, construction or size, or because of the other people there (s.1(4)). Otherwise, the authority must register the applicant (s.1(2)) and issue a certificate of registration (s.3), but it may impose conditions limiting the maximum number of children (bearing in mind the other children she may have) and requiring precautions against exposure to infectious disease (s.2(2) and (3)). These conditions may be revoked or varied at any time (s.2(6)) and it is an offence not to comply with them (s.4(2)). There is no duty on the local authority to supervise registered child-minders, but a person authorised by the authority may at all reasonable times enter a registered minder's home and inspect it and the children (s.7(1)). If he suspects contravention of the conditions he may get a warrant (s.7(2)). It is an offence to obstruct him (s.7(4)). The authority may cancel the registration if the conditions are not complied with or if circumstances exist which would justify a refusal to register in the first place (s.5). There is a right of appeal to a magistrates' court against the refusal or cancellation of registration and against any conditions imposed (s.6).

These provisions may be adequate in themselves but they are largely unenforceable. Their scope is not widely known, and it is just those people who are unlikely to be thought suitable by the local authority who will not apply for registration. It would require many more social workers adequately to police it, for unlike most crimes the "victim" will be too young to complain. Some authorities therefore offer amnesties to illegal minders to encourage them to seek expert help, or even employ child-minders themselves. Certainly the provision of more public day-care facilities will be the only complete answer to the problem.

(ii) *Nurseries*

Nurseries are usually regarded as more satisfactory than child-minding, not because it is necessarily preferable to have a young child cared for with many others in an institutional setting, but because places are much easier to police than are people, and thus higher standards may more readily be imposed. Local social services authorities may of course provide day nurseries and local education authorities may provide nursery schools, but lack of resources tends to limit these to areas of high priority. Private facilities are covered by the 1948 Act.

A person receiving or proposing to receive children (of any age up to 16 and whether or not for reward) into premises which are not wholly or mainly used as a private dwelling, to be looked after for more than two hours a day or for not more than six days, may apply for registration of the premises (s.1(1) and (2)). The offence is however committed by the *occupier* of any unregistered premises where such children are received (s.4(1)). The provisions relating to refusal of registration (s.1(3), certificates (s.3), cancellation of registration (s.5), entry and inspection (s.7(1) and (2)), and appeals (s.6) are much the same as for child-minders. The conditions which may be imposed are however more extensive (s.2(1)(3)(4)), for they can also cover the number and qualifications of the staff, the safety and maintenance of the premises and equipment, the arrangements for feeding the children and their diet, medical supervision for the children and the keeping of records.

Premises which are adequately covered by other controls are of course exempted from the Act. These include all schools for children over five (even though the children are received to be looked after and not educated), nursery schools which are maintained or assisted by the local education authority or aided by government funds or recognised or approved by the Secretary of State, play-centres maintained or assisted by the local education authority, hospitals, nursing homes, voluntary children's homes and any home or institution maintained by a public or local authority (s.8 and Children Act 1958, s.2).

There are also provisions designed to prevent overlap between anything in the 1948 Act and the other child protection legislation (ss.9 and 10).

3. *Private Fostering*

Day-care facilities are still in very short supply, especially in some areas, and from the parents' point of view often have disadvantages such as restricted opening times or high charges. Nowadays parents who can neither look after their children themselves nor arrange suitable day-care are likely to think first of the local authority or perhaps a voluntary organisation. But there are some whose reasons for requiring substitute care may not be thought acceptable under section 1 of the Children Act 1948 (see 4 below), a prime example being Commonwealth citizens who have come here to study. There are others, and middle-class mothers of illegitimate children may be an example, who for good or bad reasons would prefer to make their own arrangements. For these, the solution has to be private fostering. Here again, demand exceeds supply and the practice appears to be very largely confined to the under-fives, so that the risks are both obvious and more severe than in cases where the child can retain daily contact with his parents. Indeed, the horrors of Victorian baby-farming cases led quite early to the imposition of legal controls, but these now compare most unfavourably with the protection available to children in public care.

The controls are not based on registration (perhaps because private fostering is thought more likely to be a "one-off" occurrence), but on letting the local authority know what is happening, so that it may supervise the placement and remove the child if necessary, or even prohibit it in advance. They are contained in the Children Act 1958, as amended by the Children and Young Persons Act 1969 and shortly to be re-amended by the Children Act 1975.

(i) *Definition of "foster child"*

The Act protects children under 16 (and those placed before that age whose fostering continues after it, s.13) whose care and maintenance are undertaken by someone who is not his relative (the definition is the same as in the Nurseries and Child-Minders Regulation Act 1948), guardian (which must mean legal guardian, see Chapter 7) or custodian (see Chapter 10) (s.2(1)). There is no longer any need for "reward," so that children whose parents never arranged to pay, or, as seems quite common, fail to pay the sums agreed, are now covered. The Act excludes all children who are fostered for no more than six days (s.2(3A)(*a*)), although not all such children will be protected by the child-minding legislation; it also excludes those who are fostered for no more than 27 days, if the foster parent does not foster on a regular basis (s.2(3A)(*b*)); a regular foster parent is one who during the past year has had one or more children to whom she was neither related nor a guardian for a total of three months or for three separate periods each of more than six days; the object is to exclude any "one-off" fostering arrangement of less than a month, which as the Act would otherwise cover children going to stay with friends for the holidays is sensible, but to enable regular foster parents to be supervised after a week.

The Act also excludes children who are being looked after by anyone in a place where a parent, adult relative or guardian is living (s.2(3)(*a*)) and children who are thought adequately protected by other means. These are: children in the care of local authorities or voluntary organisations (s.2(2)); children in voluntary homes (s.2(3)(*b*)), or in hospitals, nursing homes (s.2(3)(*d*)), or residential homes for the mentally disordered (s.2(4)), or in any home or institution provided by a public or local authority (s.2(3)(*e*)); children who are in the care of any person in compliance with a probation or supervision order, or who are subject to compulsory powers under the Mental Health Act 1959 (s.2(4)); and children who have been placed for adoption by an adoption agency or who are otherwise protected under the adoption legislation (s.2(4A)). Children in boarding schools where they are receiving full-time education are also excluded (s.2(3)(*c*)), but if they stay there for more than two weeks during the school holidays, the local authority must be notified and can exercise its normal powers (s.12).

(ii) *Notification*

At present the onus of notifying the local social services authority lies solely on the foster parent. She must give notice between four and two weeks *before* the placement, unless the child was received in an "emergency" or became a "foster child" while already in her care, in which case she must notify within 48 hours *after* the event (s.3(1)). However, if she has already given notice about one foster child and has not ceased to foster since then, she need not at present give notice of each new arrival (s.3(2A)). The local authority already knows what she is doing and it was, wrongly, assumed that supervision would be adequate to detect new children. The foster parent also has to notify changes of address (s.3(3)), death of any foster child (s.3(4)), and, at present, giving up fostering in general unless she intends to take it up again within 27 days (s.3(5A) and (5B)). The Children Act 1975 will however require foster parents to notify each new arrival and each departure (s.95(4)). The Act will also break new ground by requiring the *parent* to notify private fostering arrangements (s.96). Failure to notify is of course an offence (Children Act 1958, s.14(1)(*c*)), but quite apart from the limitations of the present system, particularly the lack of detail required, there is every reason to believe that many placements are not notified at all. A dual obligation may at least make it more likely.

(iii) *Regulation of placements*

The authority may prohibit a specific placement, or any placement in a particular place, or any placement with a particular person at any place in its area (s.4(3A)), if it thinks that the premises or the person are unsuitable, or a particular placement would be detrimental to the child (s.4(3)). This is only effective if the authority knows about the proposed placement in advance, yet at present many specific placements need not be notified at all (see above) and many of those that must are notified later as "emergencies."

A few people are actually disqualified from taking foster children at all unless the local authority consents. These are people who have had children removed from their care under this Act, the Children and Young Persons Act or the Adoption Act; people who have been refused or had cancelled registration for themselves or their premises under the Nurseries and Child-Minders Regulation Act; people who have been deprived of parental rights under a "section 2 resolution"; and people who have been convicted of one of the many offences against children listed in Schedule I to the Children and Young Persons Act 1933 (s.6(1)). No one else can take a foster child if there is such a person living or employed on the same premises (s.6(2)).

The authority can also impose conditions on foster parents, as to the number, age and sex of any foster children, the accommodation and equipment provided, medical arrangements, the number, qualifications and experience of anyone employed in looking after the children, giving particulars of the person in charge, record-keeping, fire precautions, and giving extra particulars about the children themselves (s.4(2)).

The foster parent can appeal to the juvenile court against a prohibition or condition (s.5), but it is an offence to contravene them (s.14(1)(*a*)) or to take a child when disqualified (s.14(1)(*d*)). All this is however a far cry from the careful selection procedures for local authority foster parents. As Holman (1973) has pointed out, parents have freedom to place their children with almost anyone, yet the conditions of supply and demand give them very little choice, and many placements are made with people whom the local authority

would consider unsuitable (it is not a disqualification to have
been turned down as a local authority foster parent). Nor is
there any means of ensuring that the same care is taken over
the actual transfer of the child; some are simply "dumped"
without prior warning after a casual arrangement between the
adults.

(iv) *Supervision*

The local authority has a duty to satisfy itself as to the well-
being of every foster child in its area, whether or not it has
been notified of his existence. The present duty to supervise is
however extremely imprecise, for the authority is only required
to see that the children are visited from "time to time" as it
thinks appropriate, and that such advice is given "as to the
care and maintenance" of the children as appears to be needed
(s.1). This is backed up by the power of the worker who is
authorised to visit to enter and inspect any premises in the area
in which foster children are to be or are being kept (s.4(1));
and to seek a magistrates' warrant to enter premises by force if
there is reasonable cause to believe that a foster child is being
kept there and entry has been or seems likely to be refused or
the occupier is absent (s.4(2)). Furthermore, any refusal to
allow visiting of a foster child or inspection of premises is
automatically reasonable ground for a suspicion of neglect or
ill-treatment, so that a warrant to enter and remove the child
may be obtained under section 40 of the Children and Young
Persons Act 1933 (s.8); the warrant also allows removal of the
child if the suspicions are found to be true. (Section 40 is fully
discussed in Chapter 5.)

Refusal to allow visiting may thus be adequately covered by
the law, but a much more serious problem is the limited nature
of the supervision at present required. Despite the fact that
most of the children are under five, and many of the foster
parents would have been considered unsuitable by the local
authority, visits are in practice much less frequent than they
are to children boarded-out by local authorities, sometimes as
little as once a year (*Holman*, 1973). There is no duty to insist
on regular medical examination. Furthermore, the purpose of
the visit is generally to secure the well-being of the children

and to offer advice about their "care and maintenance," yet inadequate physical care does not seem to be a major problem. The real difficulty is that these foster parents are having to cope with all the problems of the fostering relationship without adequate casework preparation or support. That relationship is in practice less secure than that of a local authority foster parent, for although there are ways of preventing it, the parent can usually come and remove the child without prior warning or guidance from a social worker. Yet the foster parents will receive little, if any, advice about this aspect of their role as temporary though loving caretakers. Most will wish to behave just like substitute mothers, which is contrary to received social work opinion on fostering (although it may be a comment on that opinion). Thus Holman (1973) identified "role uncertainty" as a major, and potentially harmful, characteristic of private fostering.

The Children Act 1975 goes a little way towards solving these problems, for it will enable the Secretary of State to make detailed regulations about the frequency of visits by social workers (s.95). This, coupled with the need to notify each new placement, may make it easier for social workers to help foster parents towards a better understanding.

(v) *Removal*

Apart from applying for a warrant after a social worker has been refused entry to visit (see above), a local authority may apply to a juvenile court for permission to remove a child to a place of safety if he is being looked after, or is about to be received, by someone who is unfit to have him or who is disqualified or prohibited from having him, or in any premises or environment likely to be detrimental to him (s.7). If there is imminent danger to the child's health, the social worker who has been authorised to visit may make an emergency application under the section to a single magistrate. The court or magistrate may authorise the removal of the child (and, if the foster parent has contravened a specific prohibition, all her foster children, s.7(3)) for a specified period of up to 28 days. If he needs to be detained longer, the authority must bring him before a juvenile court (Children and Young Persons Act

1963, s.23). The usual purpose of removal, however, will be to try and restore him to a parent, relative or guardian, and thus the authority must if practicable inform the parent or guardian (1958 Act, s.7(5)). Alternatively, the child may be received into local authority care even though the normal grounds for doing so do not exist (s.7(4)).

Here again, it is more difficult to remove private foster children from unsatisfactory foster homes than it is in local authority cases (see Chapter 9). Furthermore, when local authority places are in short supply a social worker may hesitate to suggest removal of a child who will then have to go into care, particularly as it is very likely that he would not have been eligible in the first place.

(vi) *Return*

Fostering as such gives the foster parent no legal rights over the child, for a parent cannot surrender these by mere agreement (Children Act 1975, s.85(2)). In theory, however, a determined foster parent could seek to retain the child either by making him a ward of court or, when the new procedure is introduced, by applying for custodianship (both of these are discussed in Chapter 10), and in both cases the child's welfare would prevail over parental rights; there are also circumstances in which an adoption application would forestall removal of the child (this is discussed in Chapter 11). In practice, unless a private foster parent is both knowledgeable and resourceful, the child will be less well protected from arbitrary removal by his parents because there is no agency to intervene between parent and foster parent.

The only major research project on private fostering covered only cases which were known to the local authorities (*Holman*, 1973). Even then it suggested that although private foster children are a more vulnerable group than those in public care they receive much less help, both from the law and from the practice of that law. Private fostering could only be banned altogether, even if this were thought desirable, if local authorities could be required either to receive into care all children for whom parents wished to arrange alternative care or to provide many more, and more flexible, day-care facilities. This is a pipedream, but both the law and social workers could do much more to help private foster parents, who provide an essential service for which the demand shows no sign of decreasing.

4. *Local Authority Care*

Private fostering may be inevitable, but it will always be difficult to police, particularly at the most crucial point of the initial placement. The most effective solution is the provision of a better alternative. Thus when the Curtis Committee (1946) recommended that local authorities should establish specialist children's departments, the opportunity was taken to oblige them to provide not only for destitute, abandoned or maltreated children, but also for a great many other children whose parents needed to arrange, usually temporary, alternative care. The rights and duties of (now) local social services authorities towards all the children in their care are considered in detail in Chapter 9, but it is appropriate to this chapter to consider the main characteristics of reception into care under section 1 of the Children Act 1948.

(i) *Limited eligibility*

The cost of providing a public child care service of high quality is almost bound to exceed what the "customers" can afford. Thus local authorities are only under a duty, and indeed only permitted, to take children who fall within the criteria laid down. First, the child must be under 17 (although once in care he may remain until he is 18). Secondly, it must appear to the local authority either (a) that he has neither parent nor guardian or has been and remains abandoned by his parents or guardian or is lost, or (b) that his parents or guardian are for the time being or permanently prevented by reason of mental or bodily disease or infirmity or other incapacity or any other circumstances from providing for his proper accommodation, maintenance or upbringing. Thirdly, it must appear to the local authority that its intervention under this section is necessary in the interests of the welfare of the child (s.1(1)).

The references to parents or guardian apply to all people

who are for the time being parents or guardians (s.9). "Parent"
means both parents of a legitimate, legitimated, or adopted
child, but only the mother of an illegitimate child (s.59(1));
but if anyone has been awarded custody of the child by court
order, that person is parent or guardian to the exclusion of
anyone else (s.6(2)). These definitions can cause problems
where the mother of an illegitimate child, or a mother who has
custody following a divorce, places the child in care even
though the father is both able and willing to take over: the
answer depends either on the authority's interpretation of its
duty to allow a "relative or friend" to take over the child or on
the courts' willingness to make or alter custody orders while a
child is in care (both are discussed in Chapter 9). Guardian
means a legally appointed guardian (see Chapter 7).

The section gives considerable discretion to the local
authority, which can presumably not be forced by the parent
to take any particular child. Interpretations of those
circumstances which "prevent" a parent from providing
adequate care and of those cases where the authority's
intervention is "necessary" can obviously vary and most
authorities will have their own guide-lines. By far the most
frequent reason for a child to come into care under section 1 is
the short-term illness of a parent, followed by the mother's
desertion leaving the father unable to cope, unsatisfactory
home conditions, confinement, homelessness and illegitimacy.
Other reasons, which are common enough to appear in the
statistics but much less common than these, are abandonment,
long-term illness or imprisonment of a parent, death of a
mother, and last, having no parent or guardian. Authorities
seem to be more prepared to take over where the father is left
alone than if the mother is, perhaps because they are more
often asked to do so; they would surely be less than sympathetic
to a married woman who wished to go out to work or to study,
and these are major reasons for turning to the private market.

(ii) *Expert placement*

The main feature of local authority care which should make
it better for the children, but may deter some parents, is that
once the child is in care, the decisions about how he is to be

looked after lie solely with the local authority. This has, or
should have, at least three advantages. First, the authority has
a much wider range of alternative accommodation available
than could possibly be obtained on the open market. Secondly,
the legal controls over each of those alternatives are far more
substantial and, presumably, far more effective in achieving
their object of protecting the child, who is by definition so
much more vulnerable than ordinary children; the most
startling comparison, of course, is between the provisions of
the Children Act 1958 on private fostering and those of the
Boarding-Out of Children Regulations (see Chapter 9) on
public fostering. Thirdly, the decisions are being made, and
the arrangements monitored, by workers who, whatever their
much-publicised individual shortcomings, should be much
more skilled in handling the task than the parents themselves.

However, some parents could be pardoned for thinking that
the section gives too much discretion to the social workers to
whom they have voluntarily surrendered their children. Thus
although the local authority must give first consideration to
the need to safeguard and promote the child's welfare, it must
also find out the child's views and give appropriate weight to
them; there is no duty to discover, let alone to take into
account, the parents' views, or even to keep them informed of
their child's whereabouts or allow them to visit. All these are of
course required by good practice, but the law might give them
greater encouragement, particularly in view of the likelihood
that the child will return.

(iii) *Return*

As with all the other types of substitute care discussed in this
chapter, section 1 is designed for parents who want to use the
service provided. They will not want to use it, however great
their need, if they feel that they will run a greater risk of losing
their children than they would if they made private
arrangements. Such fears would defeat the whole object of
the public service. Thus section 1 expressly states that, like a
private foster parent, a local authority which receives a child
into care under the section does not *thereby* acquire any right
to keep the child once a parent or guardian wishes to take over

his care. However, the local authority should be able to make long-term assessments of the individual needs of each child in care. Increasing recognition that return to the natural parents is not always the best solution has led to powers to delay returning children who have been in care for six months and even, in certain circumstances to pass a resolution under section 2 of the Act taking over the parents' rights (see Chapter 9). The result is that whereas the private foster child is dependent on the resourcefulness of his foster parents and the courts' interpretation of his best interests, the local authority child is largely dependent on the social workers' skills and attitudes. It is interesting to speculate on which is best.

5. *Care by a Voluntary Organisation*

Most voluntary organisations caring for children were set up to provide the same service as that now provided by local authorities and for the same reasons. Their legal position is remarkably similar (and most of the relevant provisions can be found in Chapter 9). Thus while there is obviously no equivalent of section 1 of the 1948 Act to empower or oblige them to take certain children, they will obviously be guided by the terms of their foundation. Once a child has been accepted, it is again for the organisation to select the appropriate care, although their alternatives are more limited. Most will be accommodated in the organisation's homes, which may be either voluntary homes or assisted or controlled community homes. Some will be boarded out with foster parents, in which case the Boarding-Out of Children Regulations will apply with a few additional safeguards. Equally, the organisation obviously acquires no rights in the child simply because the parents have placed him in its care. If the parents wish the child to be returned to them, the organisation is at present in much the same position as a private foster parent (see Chapter 10); however, the Children Act 1975 has already given it the same power to insist on delay before a returning child who has been in its care for six months (s.56(2)) as has a local authority. It will also eventually be possible for a local authority to pass a resolution transferring to a voluntary organisation the parental rights and duties over a child in its care (ss.60-63); these will have the same grounds and much the same effect as those which may be passed in respect of children in local authority care. Provided that the organisation's standards are high, therefore, a child in its care will receive much the same protection as a child who has been received into the care of a local authority.

3 Marriage Breakdown

Many suspect that marriage breakdown is increasing dramatically. The divorce rate is certainly doing so, but this is partially explained by legal changes, which have enabled a higher proportion of broken marriages to be dissolved and have made the process simpler and less disagreeable, and by legal aid, which has made divorce available to those who cannot afford it. Domestic cases in magistrates' courts have scarcely increased at all, and this may well be because more people can turn immediately to the divorce court. It is still not known how many marriages break down without the parties' resorting to litigation at all.

However, even if the extension of the grounds for divorce does not in itself make breakdown more likely, there are certain features of modern life which do. There is no longer a preponderance of women in the marrying age groups, so that most young people are able to find a mate if they wish. They also do so at an earlier age, and the youth of the bride is significantly associated with the risk of breakdown. People live longer, so that spouses are less likely to die young and relationships are at risk for longer. Smaller, consciously planned families have released women earlier from the dependence of child-bearing and rearing and given them other things to think about. Perhaps most importantly, much greater emphasis is now placed on the happiness which each spouse may expect from a marriage. It could even be suggested that a higher rate of marriage breakdown reflects a better attitude than there was in the days when marriage was the only respectable career for a woman (*Fletcher*, 1973; *Mortlock*, 1972).

There must nevertheless be considerable concern about the effects of this situation upon the children involved. Although many divorced people remarry, women seem less likely to do so than men and their "chances" seem to decrease the more children they have (*Finer Report*, 1974); prolonged one-parent status often brings financial stringency, housing problems and downward social mobility, and these all tend to be worse where the marriage was broken by divorce rather than death (*Finer Report*, 1974; *Ferri*, 1976). There is also a significant link between marriage breakdown and delinquency, emotional disturbance, and poorer educational achievement in the children (*Rutter*, 1971; *Ferri*, 1976). As might be expected, however, it seems to be parental bitterness and disharmony, rather than the actual separation, which is largely responsible, for children who lose a parent by death or who later form a good relationship with a substitute for the absent parent do much better. There is also some evidence that "staying together for the sake of the children" without any improvement in relations does more harm than good.

If the parents do separate, some decision has to be reached about the children, and although custody disputes are remarkably rare (*Maidment*, 1976), the courts are frequently involved. Thus the various legal procedures available to the parents who break up will first be listed, followed by an account of the orders which may be made relating to the children involved, and finally by some discussion of the principles upon which the courts seem to operate in disputed cases.

1. *The Procedures on Marriage Breakdown*

(i) *Divorce*

This is now the most popular, because it dissolves the marriage, leaves each party free to remarry, and gives the courts wide powers to deal with "ancillary" financial problems and the children's future. However, the sole ground for divorce is that the marriage has irretrievably broken down and this can only be established by proving one or more of five facts: that one party has committed adultery and the other finds it intolerable to live with him; that one has behaved in such a way that it is not reasonable to expect the other to live with him; that one has deserted the other for at least two years; that they have lived apart for at least two years and both agree to a divorce; and that they have lived apart for at least five years, irrespective of the wishes or behaviour of the other spouse, although if that spouse can prove that divorce would cause her grave financial or other hardship, she may be able to resist a decree (Matrimonial Causes Act 1973, ss. 1, 2 and 5). Thus unless the petitioner can prove one of the first two facts, there must be a considerable period of separation beforehand. Divorce cases are heard in specially designated divorce county courts, unless the petition is defended or for some other reason they are transferred to the Family Division of the High Court.

(ii) *Judicial separation*

This is also heard in the divorce court, and should not be confused with a matrimonial order in the magistrates' courts. The court's ancillary powers are the same as they are on divorce, but the decree merely relieves the parties of their duty to live together while leaving the marriage intact. One of the five facts necessary for divorce must be proved, but it is not necessary to show that the marriage has irretrievably broken down (Matrimonial Causes Act 1973, ss. 17 and 18). A spouse who does not want, or cannot yet obtain, either a divorce or a judicial separation could apply to the divorce court on the ground that the other was not properly maintaining her or the children (Matrimonial Causes Act 1973, s. 27), but this is very rarely done.

(iii) *Matrimonial proceedings in magistrates' courts*

More commonly, a spouse who does not want, or cannot yet obtain, a divorce applies to the magistrates' court for a matrimonial order, usually because she wants maintenance, but sometimes because she wants an order relieving her of the duty to live with her husband; the court then has extensive powers to deal with the children's future. At present, however, orders for the spouse can only be obtained if she can show that the other has committed a "matrimonial offence" of which the most commonly alleged are desertion (for which there is no minimum period), persistent cruelty, wilful neglect to provide reasonable maintenance for a wife or child, and adultery (see

Matrimonial Proceedings (Magistrates' Courts) Act 1960, s. 1); the complainant herself must be free of matrimonial fault. This approach is now out of step with that in the divorce court, where fault in the strict legal sense is increasingly irrelevant, and it is proposed to make the powers of magistrates' courts more flexible (see *Law Commission*, 1976).

(iv) *Guardianship of Minors Act proceedings*

Parents who are unable or unwilling to litigate about their marriage may still wish to litigate about their children. While husband and wife are living together, they can refer disputes about the children's upbringing to a court under section 1(3) of the Guardianship Act 1973; on separation, they can apply for custody, access or maintenance for a child under section 9 of the Guardianship of Minors Act 1971. These applications can only be made by parents but may be made either to the local magistrates' or county court or to the High Court.

(v) *Wardship proceedings*

An alternative method of litigating solely about children is to make them wards of court. The power of the High Court in effect to assume the guardianship of children who are in need of its protection stems from the ancient notion that the King was father of his people. Although no doubt formerly used mainly to preserve the property of young orphans (hence the supposed preoccupation with preventing heiresses from marrying), these powers can be used for any purpose to protect a child. One example is the action taken to prevent sterilisation of an 11-year-old girl which has already been mentioned (*Re D.*, 1976). As any interested person may attempt to make a child a ward of court, the procedure is perhaps more important for relatives and foster parents (see Chapter 10), who do not have the wide range of alternatives open to natural parents and even step-parents. Parents may however use wardship, either because they are in dispute and consider the High Court's powers more effective, or because they wish to protect their child from harm; the most usual example is an unwise marriage, but in one highly unusual case a step-father nearly succeeded in preventing the publication of a book about a child's dead father, on the ground that if she read it its revelations would almost certainly cause her grave emotional harm (*Re X*, 1975); he failed in the Court of Appeal, not because the wardship jurisdiction is not wide enough, but because in such a case it must be balanced against the freedom of the press.

The immediate effect of any application to make a child a ward of court is that he becomes a ward automatically. It is thus possible to preserve the existing position, and orders to prevent removal from the country or other drastic steps can be obtained very quickly. However, the court can always "deward" the child, and this will happen automatically 21 days after an application unless by then some further step has been taken in the action, so that matters should not be dragged out indefinitely. However, save in emergencies where it can act extremely quickly, the court's procedure tends to be slow; this is largely because it is so careful; it will almost invariably involve lawyers, and the Official Solicitor is usually asked to represent the child. Sometimes, however, the wrong decision arrived at quickly is better for a child than the right decision arrived at slowly.

There is of course nothing to prevent a husband and wife separating without ever going to court and there is reason to believe that, at least until the recent changes made divorce a great deal more attractive, many couples did so. Some may enter into a separation or maintenance agreement. Provided that the normal rules on the formation of contracts are observed, these agreements are legally enforceable, although if they are written the courts have wide powers to vary the financial arrangements which they contain (Matrimonial Causes Act 1973, ss. 34 and 35); it is never possible for a spouse to contract out of the right to apply to a court for financial provision. Similarly, while such agreements may well provide for who is to have custody of the children (Guardianship Act 1973, s. 1 (2)), the court can always decline to enforce it if it is not in the child's best interests.

2. *The Orders Available*

In all these proceedings, the courts have very similar powers to make orders about the children's future. There are however some considerable differences of detail, and although the Law Commission has recommended that these should be tidied up (1976), it will be necessary to point them out under each type of order.

(i) *The duty to consider the children's future*

In guardianship and wardship proceedings, which are essentially about the children, it should be impossible to overlook their interests. Divorce and matrimonial cases are essentially about the parties' marriage, and in a large proportion there may be no dispute about the children at all. Marriage breakdown can however have such terrible consequences for the children involved that the law now imposes a positive duty upon courts to consider their welfare, whatever the parents have decided.

Before making a decree of judicial separation or making absolute a decree of nullity or divorce, the court must discover all the relevant "children of the family" (Matrimonial Causes Act 1973, s. 41). A "child of the family" is not only a legitimate, legitimated or adopted child of the marriage, but also *any* other child who has been *treated* by *both* parties as a child of their family, apart from one officially boarded-out by a local authority or voluntary organisation (1973 Act, s. 52(1)). The obvious example is a step-child, who may be treated as a member of the family whether or not the husband knew that he was not the father, but privately fostered children or orphans being cared for by relatives are also covered. The essential criterion is that the child was regarded and treated by both as a member of their common household, so that it is his home as much as anyone else's which is breaking up. For the purpose of this duty, however, the relevant children of the family are all those under 16, those of 16 but under 18 who are still being educated or trained (even if, like apprentices, they also have a job), and any others of whatever age whom the judge orders to be included because there are special circumstances, such as handicap.

If there are any such children, the court must examine the proposals for their future, which must be set out in a special document accompanying the petition, and must also be discussed personally with the judge (the new procedure for granting divorces without formal hearings now applies to almost all undefended cases). The court must then be able to declare that the arrangements proposed are satisfactory, or the best that can be devised in the circumstances, or that it is impracticable for the parties before the court to make any arrangements (an example might be where the children were in care under a section 2 resolution). Occasionally, the court may decide that there are special circumstances making a decree desirable even though such a declaration cannot yet be made, but if so the parties must undertake to bring the future of the children before the court within a specified time. In most cases, however, if the court will not make a declaration the parties do not get their decree

This sounds excellent, but there are obvious problems. The new private discussion should improve on the brief enquiry made during formal divorce hearings, but is almost bound to be superficial. If this reveals some cause for concern, the judge may adjourn the matter for a welfare officer's report but judges vary considerably in the matters which arouse their concern and in their readiness to ask for reports (see *Law Commission*, 1968); examples are where the petitioner has not seen the children for some time and thus cannot tell the judge much about them, or where very young children are with their father, or where children have been split up, or where there are obvious stress factors such as handicap or health or housing problems. But even if the judge is unhappy with what is proposed, he can only force the parents to think again. He cannot force an unwilling parent to make alternative arrangements and the alternative of committing the children to care will usually be even worse. Once the decree has gone through, the only means of ensuring that the approved arrangements are adhered to is to make a supervision order, which would surely be impracticable in every case.

A similar concern about the children whatever their parents' attitude is reflected in the courts' powers to make orders about their custody and maintenance even though the divorce or other decree is not granted (see below). Magistrates' courts similarly have power to make orders about the children once they have begun to hear a matrimonial complaint and irrespective of its eventual outcome. There is no elaborate procedure as in the divorce court, but if the magistrates do have power to make orders about children, they must not make a final decision on the matrimonial complaint until they have decided whether and how to exercise those powers (Matrimonial Proceedings (Magistrates' Courts) Act 1960, s. 4(1)). Unless custody is disputed, however, they are highly unlikely to call for a welfare officer's report or to be alerted to any cause for concern. At present, moreover, the definition of "child of the family" in these proceedings is slightly different from that in divorce. As well as any child of both parties to the marriage, it only includes the child of *one* party who has been *accepted* as a member of the family by the other (1960 Act, s. 16(1); the relevant definition appears to have been inadvertantly repealed by the Children Act 1975 but presumably the courts will continue to interpret the phrase in the same way for the time being); it has been held that a husband cannot "accept" a child whom he wrongly believes to be his; acceptance means in effect agreeing to take a child on, rather than behaving in a particular way towards him. This anomaly should soon be changed.

(ii) *Custody orders*

A court hearing divorce, nullity or judicial separation proceedings may make such order as it sees fit for the custody and education of any child of the family under 18, whether or not it also grants the decree; alternatively it may direct proceedings to be taken to make the children wards of court, but this is rare (Matrimonial Causes Act 1973, s. 42(1)). A divorce court which is simply asked to make a maintenance order before any other proceedings have been started, may also make a custody order, but only if and for as long as it makes an order for the spouse (1973 Act, s. 42(2)). Magistrates' courts hearing matrimonial complaints may make provision for the legal custody of any child of the family under 16 irrespective of the outcome of the complaint (Matrimonial Proceedings (Magistrates' Courts) Act 1960, ss. 2(1)(*d*) and 4). Custody orders are of course the main object of proceedings under the Guardianship of Minors Act 1971 (s. 9), but here again at present a magistrates' court can only make them if the children are under 16, whereas other courts can go up to 18. Custody orders are not made over wards of court, but care and control will be delegated to whomever is best suited to have it.

In divorce and matrimonial proceedings, the courts have power to grant custody to someone other than the warring spouses. In the divorce court it is thus possible for some third party to intervene in the proceedings in order to ask for custody. In Guardianship of Minors Act proceedings the court also has power at present to grant custody to some third party, but of course only the mother or father have power to start the proceedings. When the custodianship procedure is introduced (see Chapter 10), the court will instead have to direct that the proceedings be treated as though the third party had applied for custodianship and will then be able to make a custodianship order in his favour even if he would not have been "qualified" to apply for custodianship in the first place.

The effect of a custody order is not precisely defined. In the Children Act 1975, "legal custody" is defined as "so much of the parental rights and duties as relate to the person of the child (including the place and manner in which his time is spent)" (s. 86) and it may be that this reflects the position under other legislation. It may thus be expected to include the rights and responsibilities of caring for a child and developing his mind discussed in Chapter 1, the right to decide whether the child can marry before 18, and the "right" for the time being to be treated as the child's "parent" for the purposes of the Children Act 1948 (see Chapter 9). As already seen, special considerations apply to taking the child abroad. A father who is deprived of custody can still object to any change in the child's surname and to any adoption. Unlike adoption, a custody order can always be revoked or varied at a later date, and it has no effect on the relationship of parent and child for such purposes as inheritance. Last, in divorce and matrimonial proceedings, orders may be made relating to children of the family whose parents are not parties to the proceedings; such orders will have no effect on the parents' rights and responsibilities.

The decision on custody is clearly the most important and so the criteria adopted by the courts will be discussed in a separate section.

(iii) *"Split" orders*

As custody is a bundle of rights and responsibilities, that bundle may be split up. There is of course no problem if the court wishes to award joint custody to two people who are living together (for example, a mother and step-father), but when parents separate the court may think it better for the children if they both retain some influence over their children's future upbringing. Where the parents are interested and concerned, and likely whatever their personal differences to make serious attempts to cooperate over their children, this is encouraged (*Jussa* v. *Jussa*, 1972). One solution is to grant them both "custody," while giving "care and control" to the one best suited to provide it; indeed, as between mother and father of a legitimate child there is no need to make a custody order at all, as both have equal rights; the court might simply wish to decide which should have day-to-day care and control (or "actual" custody). Another, rather less satisfactory, solution is to grant custody to one parent and care and control to the other; this was originally devised so that the "guilty" wife in a divorce case might continue to look after her children while their father retained overall control (*Wakeham* v. *Wakeham*, 1954); nowadays there is surely little need to deprive her of the other rights of custody, even if she shares them with the father.

However desirable these orders may be, at present the court does not always have power to make one. The problem arises because under some proceedings the court only has power to grant access to, or order maintenance payments from, someone who has been deprived of custody. It will rarely be sensible to allow a father to retain overall control if he cannot be ordered to make payments and the mother cannot be ordered to allow him to visit. This is at present the position in matrimonial proceedings in magistrates' courts, and it has been held that there is no power to make "split" orders then (*Wild* v. *Wild*, 1969). However, the parties could usually ask for a Guardianship of Minors Act summons on the spot, and it has been held that such orders can be made under that Act (*Re W.(J.C.)*, 1963), although at present the maintenance problem arises there as well. In divorce and wardship proceedings there is no problem, as the court can divide up rights and responsibilities as it sees fit. These anomalies obviously require reform.

(iv) *Access*

In all these proceedings, the court has power to grant access to either party, but in magistrates' court matrimonial proceedings at present only if that party has been deprived of custody. In other proceedings it can be combined with a split order. From the point of view of the parent who has lost day-to-day care of his child, retaining joint custody is obviously much more satisfactory than simply having access, for this is nothing more than a right to see the child at reasonable intervals. There is always room for considerable disagreement about what is reasonable, and it should depend upon the facilities available, the distances involved, the age, character and inclinations of the children, and the qualities of the parent. Staying access is likely to be reasonable if a caring and careful father has suitable accommodation and the children are old enough to go, particularly if he lives too far away to visit regularly. If the parties cannot agree, either may apply to the court for access to be defined, although it is always hoped that they will come to sensible arrangements. The court can also impose conditions (for example, that the children are met on "neutral" ground). A supervision order is sometimes seen as a suitable means, not usually of arranging a neutral supervisor of the actual meeting, but of helping the parents to reach agreement.

Views also differ about the advisability of retaining any contact with the absent parent. The welfare of the child is always the first and paramount consideration, and many consider that this would be better served by a clean break from the distressing associations of the past (see *Goldstein, Freud and Solnit*, 1973); it may also remove a damaging source of worry for the parent who is looking after them. Others feel that a complete severance of ties may do serious harm to the child's later sense of identity and personal worth, particularly if he is of the same sex and grows up closely resembling the absent parent who, he has always been told, treated his mother so badly. He may in turn see the absent parent either as a monster or as an ideal, and these unhealthy reactions might well have been avoided by some regular contact.

The courts seem to take the latter view, for they have described access as a right of the child as much as the parent (*M. v. M.*, 1973). They are also well aware that a parent who is allowed some contact with his children is more likely to respect his financial obligations towards them, although in theory the one is not a *quid pro quo* for the other. Access is thus a "right" of parenthood which the courts tend to respect unless there is very clear indication to the contrary. This makes it all the more important that the parties be encouraged to come to terms with each other, and a recent report has suggested a "visiting code" to help them to do so (*Justice*, 1975).

(v) *Supervision orders*

Supervision was originally devised as a method of following up the approved arrangements in divorce cases. Orders can now be made by any court which grants custody of a child to any person, or in divorce or wardship cases where it simply decides who is to have care of the child (Matrimonial Causes Act 1973, s. 44, Matrimonial Proceedings (Magistrates' Courts) Act 1960, s. 2(1)(*f*), Guardianship Act 1973, s. 2(2)(*a*), and for wards of court, Family Law Reform Act 1969, s. 7(4)).

In theory, there should be "exceptional circumstances" making it desirable that the child should be under the supervision of some independent person, but practice varies considerably. Orders usually result from a welfare officer's report. Whereas these are almost invariably obtained in cases of disputed custody, only the divorce court, in the course of investigating the proposed arrangements for the children, is likely to call for one in an undisputed case. This will account for the impression that divorce courts make supervision orders in 5 per cent of cases whereas magistrates only in between 1 and 2.5 per cent (*Griew and Bissett-Johnson*, 1975; no official statistics are available). Their objects are now much broader

than originally envisaged. Usually, an order is made to provide
support for the children or, more often, for the parent with
custody; sometimes it may be designed to protect children
where the court or the other parent has a nagging doubt about
the custody decision, although it was the best alternative
available; occasionally it may be hoped that the supervisor will
help the parents to co-operate with one another, for example,
over access. Thus the sort of factors which lead a court to make
an order are instability or inadequacy in the parent, poor
housing conditions, health or behaviour problems in the
children, and difficulties between the parents. The court is
unlikely, however, to reject any recommendation for supervision made in the welfare officer's report.

The supervisor may be either the court welfare officer (in
the High Court or divorce court) or a probation officer (in the
magistrates' court) or the local social services authority.
Practice varies, as does the actual supervision provided. The
various Acts do not prescribe duties for the supervisor, who can
decide for himself what is necessary. More unfortunately,
neither do they give him any specific powers to carry it out. He
cannot insist on seeing the parents, the child or the house, or
on being informed of changes of address (although the court
may put this into the order). What he can do is to ask the court
to vary the existing custody, access or maintenance arrangements; in the divorce court he can ask for such arrangements
to be made and he can also ask for a care order instead, but he
cannot do so in the magistrates' court (there also appears to be
no power to ask for these variations under the Guardianship of
Minors Act, which leaves him with no sanction at all). There is
obviously a case for both strengthening and clarifying the
supervisor's powers; in divorce proceedings, he can ask the
court for directions as to their exercise, but as no one seems to
know what they are, this is not very helpful.

The order normally has no stated duration and so lasts as
long as the custody order to which it is linked, which can be up
to 18 in the divorce court, but only 16 in the magistrates'
court. (Guardianship Act orders can neither be made nor
continue if the child is over 16.) It can of course be varied or
discharged on the application of any party or the supervisor.
There seems, however, to be nothing to prevent the court

limiting its duration, for in many cases the order may only be necessary for a short time, but apparently very few do.

(vi) *Care orders*

In all these proceedings, the court could reach the conclusion that there were exceptional circumstances making it impracticable or undesirable to entrust custody or even care and control of the child to any of the possible candidates. Provided that the child is still under 17, or in the magistrates' court under 16, the court can instead commit him to the care of the local authority (Matrimonial Causes Act 1973, s.43, Matrimonial Proceedings (Magistrates' Courts) Act 1960, s. 1 (1)(e), Guardianship Act 1973, s. 2(2)(b) and, for wards of court, Family Law Reform Act 1969, s.7(2)).

These orders are very rare: in the 12 months to March 31 1974, only 253 were made in divorce courts, 118 in magistrates' courts and 33 in respect of wards of court; the Guardianship Act provision was not yet in force. The court must give the authority an opportunity of "making representations" before any order is made. The effect of the order is ambiguous. The authority must treat the child as though he had been received into care under section 1 of the Children Act 1948 and so does not enjoy the parental rights conferred by a care order under the 1969 Act or by a section 2 resolution. It is specifically excluded from arranging for the child's emigration under section 17 of the 1948 Act, and in the divorce court or a wardship case its powers are expressly made subject to any directions given by the court (in the wardship case of *Re Y.*, 1976, the court gave directions about access to the child by his father; magistrates' courts are expressly prohibited from doing this). Contributions to the child's maintenance are also governed by the court's financial powers rather than the usual system. On the other hand, the authority must keep the child in its care notwithstanding any claim by his parents or anyone else (although it could no doubt send the child home on trial under section 13(2) of the 1948 Act). The order lasts until the child is 18 unless it is earlier discharged, and it appears that either the local authority or any party to the original proceedings can apply for this.

(vii) *Money*

Much the most comprehensive financial powers are enjoyed by the divorce court, for it is almost invariably regulating the total break-up of the family. It may order either party to make periodical payments, sometimes with security, or to provide lump sums for the other party or for the children (Matrimonial Causes Act 1973, ss.23(1) and 27(6)). These may be ordered for the children even though the divorce, nullity or judicial separation proceedings are unsuccessful (s.23(2)). If a decree is granted, however, the court also has power to order the transfer or settlement of any property owned by either spouse to or for the benefit of the other spouse or the children (s.24(1)).

The court is directed to take into account the relative financial needs and resources of both spouses and the children, the standard of living enjoyed by the family before the breakdown, and any physical or mental disability of either spouse or the children. For the spouses, it must consider their ages, the duration of the marriage, the contribution made by each to the welfare of the family (including looking after the house and caring for the family), and the potential loss of benefits such as pensions. For the children, it must consider their actual or expected education and training, and, in ordering a spouse to make provision for a child of the family who is not his own, the court must consider whether, and if so to what extent, on what basis, and for how long, he assumed any financial responsibility for the child; whether he did so knowing that it was not his; and the liability of anyone else to maintain the child (s.25).

Having considered all this, the object of the exercise is so far as practicable to place both parties and the children in the financial position in which they would or should have been had the marriage not broken down (s.25 (1) and (2)). In most cases this is quite impossible, for two households cannot live as cheaply as one, but the courts are prepared to make the fullest possible use of their powers to ensure an equitable distribution of the family assets (*Wachtel* v. *Wachtel*, 1973). The way in which the parties have behaved towards one another will be irrelevant unless the behaviour of one was so much worse than that of the other that to disregard it would offend anyone's sense of justice.

In practice one of the most important considerations is the need to preserve a home for the children. Capital or property provision is rarely ordered for the children themselves, for the courts assume that few children can expect more from their parents than support during their childhood and education (*Chamberlain* v. *Chamberlain*, 1973). They can however expect a home, and it is increasingly common for the matrimonial home to be re-settled so that it cannot be sold without the agreement of both parties until the children have finished their education (which is usually assumed to be longer in the case of middle class families). Indeed, the decision on custody can even dictate what is to happen to the house, as in a recent case where a wife left the home with the daughter on learning of her husband's affair; the two sons stayed behind, but they were unhappy, and the court decided that the children should be reunited under their mother's care. Accordingly it was ordered that the matrimonial home, which was in the husband's name, should be settled on husband and wife in equal shares, not to be sold until the youngest child had reached 17, and further that the husband should be ordered to leave the home so that the wife and children could live there (*Allen* v. *Allen*, 1974).

Having to look after young children also affects whether a wife can be expected to go out to work, and thus how much she should receive in periodical payments. The usual practice, if there is enough to go round, is to bring her income up to one-third of the joint income (*Wachtel* v. *Wachtel*, 1973). In addition there will be periodical payments for the children. These cannot usually be ordered or continued after a child reaches 18, but they may be if the child is still being educated or trained (even if he also has a job) or if there are other special circumstances (for example disability), in which cases there is no upper age limit (s. 29).

In matrimonial proceedings in magistrates' courts, the court can order weekly payments for a wife (or, in cases of impaired earning capacity, for a husband), but only if a matrimonial offence is proved and the complainant has not committed adultery (Matrimonial Proceedings (Magistrates' Courts) Act

1960, s. 2(1)(*b*) or (*c*), and 2(3)(*b*)). It can however order weekly payments for a child of the family (s. 2(1)(*h*)) whether or not the matrimonial complaint succeeds (s. 4). Such orders cannot usually be made or continued if the child is over 16, but they may be if he is receiving full-time instruction at an educational establishment, or undergoing full-time training for a trade, profession or vocation on a course which is to last at least two years, or his earning capacity is impaired through illness or mental or physical disability, but even in those cases there is an upper age limit of 21 (ss. 2(1)(*h*) and 16(1)).

Under the Guardianship of Minors Act there is of course no question of maintenance for a spouse or parent. Either mother or father (apart from the father of an illegitimate child) can, if deprived of custody, be ordered to make weekly or other periodical payments for a child (ss. 9(2) and 14(2)). Magistrates' courts cannot make orders in respect of children over 16 unless they are incapable of self-support (s. 15(2)(*a*)), and other courts cannot make orders in respect of children over 18 unless at some time that child has been the subject of an order under the Act (s. 12(2)); but orders which have already been made can continue up to 18 and even beyond; there are no educational or other criteria laid down for this, but there is an upper age limit of 21 (s. 12(1)). The provisions for ordering mother or father to pay maintenance for wards of court are essentially the same (Family Law Reform Act 1969, s. 6(2)(3) and (4)).

Apart from the bewildering variety of provisions relating to age, other discrepancies should be noted. Divorce court orders may be made payable to the child himself, no matter what his age; orders in matrimonial proceedings in magistrates' courts may be made payable directly to any child over 16; orders in guardianship or wardship proceedings may be so payable over the age of 18. This is useful, because it may reduce the parent's income tax liability and increase entitlement to means-tested benefits. Furthermore in guardianship and wardship proceedings it is clear that the child over 18 may make the application himself, although no order will be made or enforced if his parents are living together; and it has recently been held that a similar application may be made by an 18-year-old child whose parents are divorced (*Downing* v. *Downing*, 1976).

There is thus the beginnings of a right to provision which the child can enforce himself, but only if his parents are separated or divorced.

In many cases, of course, private support rights are totally inadequate to provide for the needs of broken families. Apart from child benefit, there is no automatic allowance which they can claim from the state (compare the position of widows, discussed in Chapter 7), and many must rely on means-tested supplementary benefit or, if working, on family income supplement. Both are reduced by the full amount of any maintenance paid.

The courts are not supposed to take supplementary benefit into account as a resource available to the wife and children, for otherwise the father could throw the whole burden onto the state; but neither should they reduce his income below what he could receive for himself and his new family were he on supplementary benefit himself (*Barnes* v. *Barnes*, 1972). Thus the courts increasingly recognise that the difference between what he can afford and what she and the children need may have to be made up by the state, but their official position is still less generous to the husband than is that of the Supplementary Benefits Commission. The Commission regards it as reasonable if the "liable relative" offers what is left after deduction of the requirements of himself and his new family, his full housing costs, and one-quarter of his net income or £5 a week, whichever is greater (see *Finer Report*, 1974).

The Finer Committee discovered widespread and long-term poverty among families of broken marriages. It recommended that private support procedures, which produce much bitterness and many unenforceable orders, should usually be superseded by state benefits, with the state recouping a reasonable amount from the husband by means of an "administrative order." This would have the same practical effect as nowadays where the wife assigns the benefit of any order to the Commission, so that she may collect the same allowance each week whether or not her maintenance is paid. More importantly perhaps, the Committee thought that the state should provide a Guaranteed Maintenance Allowance for all one-parent families, so that their financial position might at least be comparable to that of widows. This is however unlikely to materialise for many years, if at all.

3. *The Principles*

"Where in any proceedings before any court ... the custody or upbringing of a minor ... is in question, the court, in deciding that question, shall regard the welfare of the minor as the first and paramount consideration...." (Guardianship of Minors Act 1971, s. 1). What factors do the courts take into account when considering the welfare of children? And what other considerations apart from that "first and paramount" one may there be?

(i) *Welfare*

The courts are always saying that each custody case is an exercise of their discretion in its own individual circumstances and that there are no "rules" or even "principles" as to what is best. It is however possible to describe the sort of matters which the courts are likely to take into account.

(*a*) Most obvious is the child's physical welfare. This was the courts' major preoccupation in earlier days and even now that other factors loom larger, its mundane importance should not be over-looked. Is either party likely to neglect or ill-treat the child? How suitable is the accommodation offered? How will a working parent cope with school holidays, late afternoons, or a pre-school child? What in general is the quality of the physical care provided or offered? It is not primarily a question of which family is the better-off, for a higher income or better accommodation may well be counteracted if the parent is out at work all day. Where there is a substantial disparity in material standards the court may not be able to ignore it, but the main question under this head is whether the child's physical needs will be adequately met. In this, as in so many things, the mother usually enjoys a built-in advantage.

(*b*) The courts realised long ago that children had more than physical needs, but at first this tended to be reflected in concern for their "moral" welfare. The parents' behaviour towards one another is no longer of much significance (see (ii) below), but the effect of their behaviour on the children can be vital. The courts realise that adultery does not make a woman a bad mother, but it could have adverse effects if she were promiscuous or the children had previously been brought up on the strictest moral principles. Similarly the courts will consider the religious upbringing offered. Although they do not prefer one religion above another, they certainly prefer some religious or moral guidance to none at all, and there are a few sects which they recognise may do positive harm to the children (principally those which cut them off from ordinary life or deny them the benefits of medical treatment). Apart from those rare cases, where a child has already acquired a settled religious belief they will be reluctant to disturb it.

(c) Recently these considerations have been supplemented and even over-shadowed by concern for the child's emotional well-being. At its best, this should mean that the court investigates closely the strength of the child's attachments and the quality of the relationships surrounding him, not only with his natural parents but also with the people offered as parent substitutes. This consideration has at least led the courts to abandon the old practice of deciding custody cases on affidavit evidence; now all the adults involved should be seen as witnesses, and an attempt made to assess their character and qualities as parents. In practice, however, the courts rely heavily on their own rather stereotyped ideas of a child's emotional needs (*King*, 1974). Here again the mother enjoys a built-in advantage, for the courts tend to assume that the natural mother is best for a young child, irrespective of the real strength of the child's attachment to her. On the other hand it is sometimes assumed that the father is better for older boys.

(d) Unfortunately, the court may conclude that the person best suited to supply the child's needs is the one who is not at present looking after him. Where the parents have not been separated for long, the court is unlikely to be deterred from ordering a transfer. It would not be thought right if the parent who happened to retain the children at the separation enjoyed too great an advantage. Furthermore the court can sometimes ensure that the parent granted custody returns to the matrimonial home (see *Allen* v. *Allen*, 1974, above). The problem becomes acute when the parents have been separated for some time. Gone are the days when the court could contemplate with equanimity the transfer of a child aged seven from the only home she had ever known (*Re Thain*, 1926). Nowadays they are aware of the dangers of further disrupting an already disrupted life, particularly if the child has to change home, school, friends and surroundings as well as parents. Thus the courts frequently urge that custody disputes should be tried as quickly as possible and need not wait for the solution of other issues between the parents (*Jones* v. *Jones*, 1974). There are however no rules requiring cases to be heard according to a particular timetable (save to a limited extent in wardship) and the speed of litigation depends largely on the parties, who do not normally include the child. The whole adult world tends to forget that a child's sense of time is entirely different from their own and what may seem a short time to the court may have been an age for the child (see *Goldstein, Freud and Solnit*, 1973). Furthermore, although the courts certainly take account of the dangers of disturbing the status quo, they are quite prepared to do so if they think some other solution is in the child's "best" interests.

(*e*) What of the child himself? The High Court or the divorce court may order that he be represented, usually by the Official Solicitor, but this is rarely done. Apart from the welfare officer's report (see below), his interests will have to emerge from the competing claims of his warring parents, and it is a mistake to assume that adults who are themselves under emotional strain will necessarily present all the relevant material to the court or even be aware of it. Their lawyers' first duty is of course to their adult client, although many will urge parents to consider carefully the children's welfare when tendering their advice. How then can the child's own wishes become known? It will rarely be in his interests to be called as a witness, but in the High Court and county court the judge can interview him in private (although even then he cannot give an absolute assurance that any confidences will be respected). The magistrates cannot even do this and can only rely on the welfare officer's report. But what weight will the child's wishes carry? Even if it has jurisdiction to do so, a court will rarely, if ever, make an order which is contrary to the wishes of a child of 16. Below that age, it will take them into account, the more so the older the child, but it will also bear in mind that he may be influenced by the spite of one parent or the bribery of another. The courts are quite prepared to know better what is right for him, although in the case of an older child who is adamant they may have little choice but to agree.

(*f*) What account is taken of the views of experts? These can either take the form of an independent welfare officer's report, or of medical evidence called by the parties, and the courts' reactions to each are very different.

All courts have power to call for an independent report on all matters relevant to the child's welfare. In the High Court and divorce court this is provided by the welfare officer, who (except at the Royal Courts of Justice in the Strand, where there are full-time welfare officers) is in fact the principal probation officer for the area (Matrimonial Causes Rules 1977, r. 95). In cases under the Matrimonial Proceedings (Magistrates' Courts) Act 1960 (s. 4(2)-(5) as amended) or under the Guardianship of Minors Act (Guardianship Act 1973, s. 6 as amended) the report may be provided either by a probation officer or by an officer of the local authority. In most cases reports may be called for in advance of the actual hearing, but at present in matrimonial proceedings in magistrates' courts, the court must first come to a decision on the matrimonial complaint.

Unlike reports from the Official Solicitor when he is appointed to represent the child, these reports are not confidential. Although they no longer have to be read aloud, a copy must be given to each of the parties and if they wish to challenge anything the officer must be called to give evidence. He cannot and should not, however, be made to reveal anything which he learned in the course of trying to reconcile a matrimonial dispute between the parties, unless they both agree. Reconciliation and conciliation are of course the other main responsibilities of welfare and probation officers in the family courts; casework with the parents, to help them communicate with one another and to come to terms with their own problems, can often reduce the need for damaging disputes about the children (see *Buttle*, 1975).

The court will be looking for independent information about each of the homes offered, about the accommodation and quality of care provided, but also about the quality of relationships surrounding the child. It is obviously highly desirable therefore that the same officer should visit each home, but if they are far apart this may not be possible. The court will also want to know how the child is getting on at school, how he relates to the various people involved and others, and what he feels about the situation. Welfare officers will of course be just as cautious as judges in interpreting and assessing the child's views (see *Buttle*, 1975). There is no reason why they should not commit themselves to a definite recommendation, if they have one, and the High Court has said that magistrates should make their reasons quite clear if they are departing from it.

The courts thus place a great deal of reliance on these reports, and it is important that they should differentiate quite clearly between matters of which the officer has first-hand knowledge and matters which are merely hearsay, and also between statements of fact and expressions of opinion. A party who wishes to challenge unverified statements is placed in an unjustifiable dilemma, for he may have to choose between antagonising the court and allowing a false picture to emerge. Neither will assist the child.

The courts' attitude to medical evidence is entirely different. They cannot call for independent medical reports and so the evidence must be presented on behalf of one or both of the parties. The courts have frequently stated that otherwise healthy children should not be taken to paediatricians or psychiatrists by one party without the other's consent (*Re S.*, 1967), but solicitors who are trying to do their best for their adult clients sometimes advise this.

If medical evidence is offered, the courts treat it with great caution. If the child is suffering from some physical or mental disorder, the evidence will obviously have an important bearing on who should be looking after him, "but if one has the case of a happy and normal infant in no need of medical care ... who is taken to a psychiatrist or other medical practitioner for the sole purpose of calling the practitioner to give quite general evidence on the dangers of taking this, that or the other course ... [this] may be valuable if accepted but ... only as an element to support the general knowledge and experience of the judge in infancy matters...." (*J.* v. *C.*, 1970).

This attitude is understandable. The courts do not wish to abandon their discretion to doctors, who do rely heavily on retrospective studies of self-selected groups in offering this evidence (although they have more opportunity of learning from their mistakes than do judges). Nevertheless the criticism is a little unfair. The child may be happy and normal now, but the object of the exercise is to prevent his becoming unhappy and abnormal in the future. The judges might never have learned to respect the value of mothering or the dangers of disruption had it not been for medical evidence in the past, and they ought not to run the risk of ignoring further developments in child psychology now (see *King*, 1974).

(ii) *Other considerations*

The other consideration which is sometimes urged by the parents is their own conduct towards one another. The way in which they have behaved towards their children is obviously a vital factor in judging the children's welfare and sometimes their behaviour towards one another may be clearly relevant to their suitability as parents (particularly in the case of violence). The parties however often want the law to take their "innocence" or the other person's "guilt" into account for its own sake. It is only natural for a caring father whose wife has left him for another man to resent her claim to the children.

The law used to agree with him. While largely, though not entirely, indifferent to the father's infidelity, for many years it deliberately excluded adulterous wives from even applying for custody or access (see Chapter 1). It was not until the very end of the 19th century that the courts admitted that adultery did not necessarily make a woman a bad mother (*Re A. and B.*, 1897) and this had to be re-emphasised as late as 1951 (*Willoughby* v. *Willoughby*). Indeed, in 1962, the Court of Appeal declined to give the care of two little girls aged four and six to their mother, although they clearly thought that she could look after them better, because the "claims of justice" could not be overlooked and she had wantonly destroyed the home to go and live near her "paramour" (*Re L.*). That case suggested that the conduct of the parties might be balanced against the welfare of the children, and even that such a wife should not be given all that she wanted, because then she would have no inducement to return. Both ideas are surely wrong and the Court of Appeal has recently denounced *Re L.* in the strongest terms (*Re K.*, 1977; and *S.* v. *S.*, 1977).

The first case concerned a boy of five and a girl of two. The father was an Anglican clergyman; the mother had been a teacher of religion; but the marriage was not happy and the mother fell in love with another man. She eventually decided that she would leave the father and set up home with this man, although they would not be able to marry for many years. She did not wish to leave without the children, and so she applied for their custody before going. The father was strongly opposed to this, arguing that the children would suffer harm by being brought up by their mother and a man living together in blatant defiance of all that their father believed in, and also that as the "unimpeachable" parent his wishes should be taken into account. Nevertheless, the court held that the children should go to their mother (*Re K.*, 1977).

Such a decision would have been unthinkable 50 years ago and even now may be in advance of public opinion. The court, however, was simply applying the clear words of the legislature in section 1 of the Guardianship of Minors Act 1971 as explained by the House of Lords in the famous case of *J.* v. *C.* (fully discussed on page 217):

> "I think they connote a process whereby, when all the relevant facts, relationships, claims and wishes of parents, risks, choices and other circumstances are taken into account and weighed, the course to be followed will be that which is most in the interests of the child's welfare as that term has now to be understood. That is the first consideration because it is of first importance and the paramount consideration because it rules upon or determines the course to be followed." (Lord MacDermott).

This approach raises several questions. Although it is clearly right that the child's welfare should take precedence over all other considerations and therefore that in most cases those other considerations will fade into insignificance (for what modern judge could easily contemplate removing a two-year-old girl from a good mother who intended to live with a man whom the children knew well and liked, or think of separating the children at this crisis in their lives?), there may be cases where the welfare conclusion is not so clear cut; might not the parents' matrimonial behaviour then be taken into account as a *secondary* consideration?

Secondly, are the courts the appropriate judges of what is best for children anyway? They are not specifically trained in the subject, but on the other hand there is ample evidence that no one, however "expert," has a monopoly of righteousness in making decisions about the future of children. The courts are at least used to the impartial arbitration of disputes and are unhampered by the possibly conflicting loyalties of social workers, to whom they can turn for help with the matters which they are least able to assess. A more important disadvantage may be that, apart from this help, the court has to decide on the basis of competing claims put forward by two adults who may be too bound up in their own problems properly to appreciate those of their children. Furthermore, unless there is a supervision order, the court will be dependent upon those adults to bring the case back if there is later cause for concern. Unlike social workers, the courts rarely hear of their mistakes. A "children's ombudsman" (see *Justice*, 1975) might provide both separate representation for the child and some means of keeping his subsequent welfare under review; but quite apart from the difficulty of finding the right candidates for the job, the expense would be considerable.

Last, are the courts right to interpret the principle that the child's welfare is the first and paramount consideration as an instruction to seek the solution which is in his "best" interests? Others have pointed out that a child whose future has to be decided in litigation has already been deprived of his "best" interests (*Goldstein, Freud and Solnit*, 1973). In trying to do the impossible, the courts may not only over-estimate their own and their advisers' ability to predict what will be right in the future, but may also be too inclined to interfere in arrangements which have been working reasonably well for some time. The child will certainly have a very different idea of "some time" from that of any of the adults involved, yet he may not even be consulted about whether he wishes to be uprooted. The suggested alternative criterion of the "least detrimental alternative" for the child might be more realistic and less risky. No one, however, can pretend that these cases are easy and the courts would be the last to do so.

4 Juvenile Offenders

When an adult is thought to have behaved in a way which the law defines as criminal, the process is relatively straight-forward. He will almost always be prosecuted, usually by the police. They will bring him before the magistrates' court, which will either try him or, if the offence is serious, commit him to be tried by a judge and, if he pleads not guilty, a jury, in the Crown Court. The case will be heard in open court before press and public, and if he pleads or is found guilty he will be sentenced. The sentence is designed to protect society by deterring him and others from further offences, but it is also a punishment intended to reflect the extent of society's disapproval of his conduct. As such it will usually be related in gravity to the gravity of the offence and the offender's previous behaviour. This may sound punitive, but it also serves to limit the sentences of those who have committed a relatively minor offence but are virtually certain to do it again when released. Although it is always possible to put forward any mitigating factors relating to either the offence or the offender, and in some cases the court may choose an order which is principally therapeutic or reformative (as with the mentally disordered), this "tariff" principle tends to dominate sentencing in adult courts.

If an alleged offender is a juvenile, however, this process is modified at many points. By "juvenile" is meant a "child" under 14 or a "young person" of 14 but under 17, but unless it is necessary to distinguish between them "child" will be used for both throughout this chapter. After initial hesitations, the common law decided that children would be treated more-or-less in the same way as adult offenders, and it is only gradually and piece-meal that modifications have been introduced, often with much controversy. Those modifications can be roughly divided into four.

First, the law which defines what is criminal treats children slightly differently, for it refuses to regard the very young as responsible at all, and may be reluctant to accept the responsibility of others. Secondly, there is much more flexibility about the decision to take court action even against those whom the law does hold responsible. Thirdly, juvenile offenders are usually brought before a court whose constitution and procedure have been designed with them in mind, and not necessarily by means of a prosecution. Last, the orders which may be made are quite different from the sentences which may be imposed upon adults and more often overtly therapeutic rather than punitive. Nevertheless the process is still an uneasy and hotly debated compromise, both between treatment and punishment and between measures tailored to the individual and equality before the law.

1. *Juveniles and the Criminal Law*

Should children be expected to obey the same rules as the rest of us? The law hovers between the need to protect society from behaviour which is just as unacceptable to the victim whatever the age of the offender and a reluctance to impose sanctions upon those who do not understand the consequences of what they are doing.

Thus it is conclusively presumed that no child under 10 can be guilty of any crime (Children and Young Persons Act 1933, s. 50). They cannot therefore be prosecuted or brought before the court in care proceedings based on the "offence condition". However, if all the other requirements are fulfilled, it may be possible to succeed in care proceedings on the ground that a persistent malefactor is beyond control or in moral danger. This of course is not designed as a punishment, however he may perceive it.

A child between 10 and 14 can be found guilty of crime, but in theory it is presumed that he is incapable of committing offences until the prosecution proves otherwise (this is known as the *"doli incapax"* presumption). To rebut this, in addition to proving the offence, the prosecution must show that the child knew that it was "wrong." However, it is apparently enough to show either that he knew that it was illegal (in the sense that a police officer would take a dim view of it) or that he realised that it was morally wrong. Were this presumption commonly and strictly applied, it might well lead to the acquittal of many children, particularly those whose mental age is far lower than their chronological age or who receive little moral guidance from home (although in each case there is arguably a greater need for society's intervention in the child's own interests, but care proceedings might be more appropriate in principle). The general impression however is that the point is rarely raised in court, perhaps partly because the magistrates are not legally qualified and the precise meaning of the presumption is obscure, but also because so few juveniles are legally represented.

Furthermore, most crimes require not only the commission of an unlawful act, but also a particular state of mind, known as "*mens rea*" or a "guilty mind," while doing it. This involves foreseeing the consequences of one's actions and either intending them or being reckless as to whether they happen. Many crimes have even more specific requirements. These rules are not peculiar to children but they must often be much more difficult to prove in respect of them. However, they can easily be forgotten in a general desire to do what is best for a child who is obviously a problem but who is rarely represented by a lawyer. Many defendants, whatever their age, think that the doing of an unlawful act is enough and plead guilty, and the court may not always remember the advice of the higher courts to look with suspicion upon admissions of guilt from those of tender years.

Apart from the above, the criminal law imposes largely the same rules upon children as on us all. There are just a few crimes which can only be committed by people who have reached a certain age (for example, only people of 16 or over can be found guilty of cruelty to children under that age). In general, however, the law's concessions to youth are in procedure and treatment.

2. *Taking Juveniles to Court*

The most fundamental problem is whether a child should be brought before a court at all. Where an adult appears to have

committed a crime, the police will only exercise their
discretion not to prosecute in exceptional cases. Where a child
is involved, however, they are expected to be much more
flexible. The philosophy behind the Children and Young
Persons Act 1969, as explained in the White Paper "Children
in Trouble" which preceded it, was that instead of the almost
automatic solution of prosecution, each case should be looked
at in the light of the needs of the individual. Amelioration and
reform, rather than the marking of society's disapproval, were
to be the principal objectives, and if these could be achieved in
other ways, prosecution was to be avoided.

(i) *The aims of the Children and Young Persons Act 1969*

The Act as it appeared on the statute book was designed to
institutionalise the above objectives. First, the prosecution of
children between 10 and 14 was to be prohibited altogether
except in cases of homicide (s. 4); and the prosecution of young
people between 14 and 17 was to be restricted by requiring the
prosecution, after consultation, to consider whether the case
fell within prescribed categories where prosecution seemed the
appropriate response (s. 5, but this fell short of actually
prohibiting prosecution outside those categories). Secondly, an
alternative to prosecution was to be provided, not only for
those cases where prosecution was prohibited or restricted but
also to allow a less punitive form of proceeding in any case; this
alternative was care proceedings, in which the applicant (who
could only be a police officer or local authority whereas in
theory in most cases anyone can prosecute) had not only to
show that the child had committed an offence (homicide
however was excepted as always requiring prosecution), but
also that he was in need of care or control which he would not
receive unless the court made an order; the proceedings would
not in theory involve the stigma of prosecution and the court
would not be obliged to make an order even if the offence was
proved. Thirdly, these changes were designed to oblige the
police and other authorities to co-operate in seeking the best
solution and exploring ways in which the child and his family
could be helped without the need for court action. Last, the
Act was intended to remove the detailed decisions about the

treatment of juveniles who did appear in court from the hands of the magistrates to those of the experts in child care; this also involved a transfer of responsibility for carrying out most of the court's orders from the Home Office to the local social services authorities.

However, it is only the last of these objectives which has in fact been implemented, and even that not to the extent contemplated by the Act. The sections prohibiting or restricting prosecution have not been brought into force and, save perhaps for children under 13, are unlikely to be in the foreseeable future. Care proceedings relying on the offence condition are therefore hardly ever used, because the simpler alternative of prosecution is still available. Co-operation between the authorities remains a voluntary matter instead of being virtually necessitated by the legal complexities. The reasons for this lie partly in the grave doubts about the whole scheme which were vociferously expressed at the time when the Act was being passed, and partly in the fact that, once the Act in its truncated form came into force, many of those doubts appeared to be justified.

(ii) *The decision to prosecute*

Thus as things are the police retain their unfettered discretion on prosecution. Nevertheless, it is generally accepted that juvenile offenders require a different approach from adults, and although police attitudes and practices may differ from place to place, there remain several alternatives for them to consider.

One of these is undoubtedly to do nothing. This may be thought appropriate if there is serious doubt about whether the child is guilty of any crime, or if the offence is very trivial, or if the parents can be contacted and appear willing and able to take suitable action themselves. But the police have always to bear in mind that if certain children, particularly those from "good" homes (which is still in so many minds linked with social class), appear to be escaping official action altogether, others may feel a grave sense of injustice. A more common alternative therefore is the official "caution." This is in effect a "ticking-off" from a senior uniformed police officer, designed to tell the child and his parents that although the matter will be taken no further on this occasion it would be advisable not to do it again. Styles obviously differ.

Views on the propriety of the caution also differ. On the one hand, the experience may well deter many a child from again incurring official displeasure, and its immediacy and form may make it more effective as well as less damaging than a court appearance. However, the police will obviously not use a caution unless the child and probably his parents have admitted his guilt (they may also consider that any victim of the offence should agree, for he will thus lose the chance that the court might order the child or his parents to pay compensation, which would then have to be sought by a civil action against the child in which the parents can only be made to pay if they can be shown to have been negligent in their care of him). All too often, therefore, the child is faced with a choice between admitting it and being "let off" with a caution, or denying it and being taken to court. However scrupulous the police, there are few children who would not take the former.

Whether the child is cautioned or not, the police could also make arrangements for informal supervision if this seemed likely to be effective, either relying on the local social services authority or the school or, more probably, their own officers. Here again, whatever the merits of keeping children out of court, some have expressed doubts about the desirability of police supervision of children who have not been found guilty of any offence, particularly as the pressures to agree to that supervision cannot be overlooked.

Court action may be thought appropriate for many reasons. If the child does not admit his guilt, but the police are confident that he has done it, they are usually reluctant to let the matter go, even if a court appearance would not otherwise be indicated. If the child committed the offence in the company of others, the police will normally wish to treat them all alike to avoid allegations of bias : one of the principal arguments used by opponents of the 1969 Act was that care proceedings institutionalised unequal treatment between similar offenders from dissimilar homes, whereas it may be particularly important that children from so-called "bad" homes do not learn early in life that the authorities treat them unfairly. This criticism perhaps underestimates the extent to which the system already discriminates, both in prosecution policy and in the orders made in court, but at least in the case of joint offenders the police usually try to avoid it. This also means that if someone of 17 or over is involved, the child is unlikely to escape prosecution as the adult will not, although this would sometimes seem a reasonable basis for discrimination. Court action may also be indicated if the parents seem unable or unwilling to do anything effective themselves or to co-operate with voluntary supervision. In other cases, a single court appearance may be thought likely to have just the right deterrent effect even though the offence is not serious. Last, of course, the more serious the offence, the more likely is prosecution, for whatever their personal views the police have also public opinion to consider.

In view of all this, the police normally make much more extensive inquiries before deciding to charge a child than they would in the case of an adult. Most forces have specialist juvenile bureaux whose job it is to enquire closely into the facts of the case and, more importantly, the circumstances of the offender before making the decision. They are not required by law to consult the social services department, or the school, or any other agencies which may be involved with the family, but in some cases such liaison does take place. If either prosecution or care proceedings are decided upon, the police must inform the local authority (ss. 5(8) and (9) and 2(3)) and, if the child is 13 or over, the probation service (s. 34(2)). If care proceedings were chosen, the police would almost certainly require the co-operation of the local authority in proving the "care and control test" although it was never contemplated that local authorities would undertake the task of criminal investigation (*Home Office*, 1970). Care proceedings are in any event rarely, if ever, chosen, as already explained.

It is obviously highly desirable that the police should contact the child's parents before making any decision, or even before questioning or interviewing any child. There is no legal provision requiring them to do so, but the Home Office recommends that children should only be interviewed in the presence of a parent or guardian or, if none is available, some independent person (*Circular*, 1964). Confessions of guilt are only admissible in evidence if obtained voluntarily and so the presence of a third party is a protection for the police as well as the child, but the statement is not automatically inadmissible if no one else was present.

(iii) *Procedure before trial*

Some children may simply be summonsed to appear in court, but if a child is arrested (with or without a warrant) and cannot immediately be taken to court, his case must be inquired into by a senior police officer (s. 29(1)). That officer has a duty to release him unless it is in the child's own interests to be further detained, or there is reason to believe that he has committed a grave crime or that his release would defeat the ends of justice or (in the case of a child arrested without warrant, where the decision to prosecute may not yet have been taken) that he would fail to appear to answer to any charge that might be made. If the child is released after being arrested on a warrant, the officer must require a recognisance from the child or his parents to secure his (and if the officer thinks fit the parents') attendance at court (s. 29(2)). This is not mandatory if the arrest was without warrant, again because prosecution may not yet have been decided upon. If the child is not released the officer must arrange for him to be detained in the care of the local authority, unless this is impracticable or the child is too "unruly" (s. 29(3)).

However he is detained, he must be brought before the magistrates' court within 72 hours of his arrest, unless a senior police officer certifies that he is prevented by illness or accident (s. 29(5)).When the child or certificate is produced in court but the case is not ready to go on, the court must order his release unless either the arrest was by warrant or the court takes the same view as the officer who decided against release (s. 29(6)). In such cases the court must remand the child, but may nevertheless grant him bail. If the child is refused bail, he must normally be remanded to the care of the local authority (s. 23(1)), but if the court certifies that a young person is "so unruly a character" that this is not safe he may be committed to a remand centre if one is available and if not to prison (s. 23(2)).

The sending of young people to remand centres (in effect prison establishments) or even adult prisons is one of the most controversial topics in this whole controversial subject, for the numbers have increased alarmingly. There is great pressure for the practice to cease (*House of Commons* 1975), and the government sees the solution in grants to local authorities for the provision of secure accommodation (Children Act 1975, s. 71) and regulations prescribing the circumstances in which "unruly certificates" may be granted (s. 69) (*Home Office*, 1976). They are already forbidden for girls of 14.

The effect of a remand to the care of a local authority is discussed in Chapter 9. Whether remanded to care or prison, the juvenile has a right to apply to a judge for bail, and if he is not legally represented the court must tell him this and give him written notice of the reason for remanding him (any lawyer must be given such a notice if he asks for one) (1969 Act, s. 29(6)).

While juveniles are detained in police stations, or being taken to and from court, or waiting in court, arrangements must be made for preventing their associating with any adult defendant apart from a relative or one jointly charged with the same offence. Girls must be under the care of a woman (1933 Act, s. 31).

3. *Juvenile Courts*

(i) *Jurisdiction*

A juvenile who is prosecuted must normally be tried in the juvenile court, even if the offence is a serious one for which an adult would be tried in the Crown Court. Before the 1969 Act, young persons between 14 and 17 had the right to choose jury trial for such offences, but this was rarely exercised and has now been abolished (1969 Act, s. 6(2)). There are now only four exceptions to the rule that juveniles must be tried in the court which was specifically designed for them:

(*a*) All "homicide" charges, which presumably includes murder, manslaughter, infanticide, and perhaps causing death by dangerous driving, but not attempts. These must be tried in the Crown Court (1969 Act, s. 6(1)).

(*b*) Cases where the juvenile is charged jointly with someone of 17 or over. They must then appear in the ordinary magistrates' court (1933 Act, s. 46(1)), and if the offence is serious and the court considers it necessary in the interests of justice, the juvenile may be committed for trial in the Crown Court alongside the older accused (1969 Act, s. 6(1)).

(*c*) Cases where the magistrates before whom a young person of 14 or over is brought on a serious charge think that it ought to be possible for him to be ordered to be detained for a long fixed period (see 4(ii)(k) below). This can only be done if he is actually tried by the Crown Court and so the magistrates have power to commit a young person there with this in mind. There is no such power in the case of a child under 14, even though, if he can be tried in the Crown Court for some other reason (under (*a*) or (*b*) above), the Crown Court can then make such a detention order (1933 Act, s. 53(2)).

(*d*) Cases where an ordinary magistrates' court only learns that the accused is a juvenile during the course of the trial. They may then if they wish go on and determine the result (1933 Act, s. 46(1)).

If a juvenile is tried in an ordinary magistrates' court, he can always be remitted to the juvenile court to be dealt with and must normally be so remitted unless the magistrates decide merely to order a discharge, or fine, or parental recognisances, or endorsement of, or disqualification from holding, a driving licence (1933 Act, s. 56(1) and 1969 Act, s. 7(8)). A juvenile tried in the Crown Court must also be remitted to the juvenile court to be dealt with unless the Crown Court thinks that this would be undesirable or the case is one of homicide (1933 Act, s. 56(1)).

(ii) *Constitution*

Special courts for the trial of juvenile offenders were first set up in 1908. The object was and is to provide a tribunal which is separate from the adult courts with all their undesirable associations and in which both the judges and the procedure are better suited to the children's needs. However, all attempts at a radical departure from the ordinary courts system (see the White Paper "The Child, the Family and the Young Offender," 1965) have so far been resisted and juvenile courts remain in effect specially constituted magistrates' courts. How separate are they and how different are their judges and procedure?

The aim of keeping juvenile courts apart from adult courts is probably best realised in very large towns, where the pressure of business is sufficient to justify a specially designed court in a separate building, or in much smaller places, where it is possible to hold juvenile courts on different days albeit in the same building. The only legal requirement however is that a juvenile court must not be held in the same *room* in which an adult court has sat or will sit within an hour of the juvenile hearing (1933 Act, s. 47(2) and 1963 Act, s. 17(2)). The authorities must also make arrangements to prevent children waiting at court from associating with adult defendants unless they are relatives or jointly charged with the juvenile (1933 Act, s. 31).

The judges are of course those magistrates appointed for the area who have been specially selected to serve on the juvenile panel. In London the panel is chosen by the Lord Chancellor, but in the provinces by the local magistrates themselves, although the 1969 Act made it possible to extend the London system to the provinces (s. 61). Some care is obviously taken to choose those who are most likely to know something about children, and so magistrates should be under 50, and preferably under 40, when they go on the panel and retire from it at 65. They are now expected to undergo some training, usually in short evening or weekend courses, and some may have particularly relevant professional qualifications or experience. Nevertheless, with the exception of a few full-time salaried stipendiary magistrates, who are trained lawyers with considerable practical experience, but who do not always sit in juvenile courts, magistrates are part-time unpaid laymen. The English legal system places a high value on the commonsense, local knowledge and wide experience of lay magistrates. But views naturally differ as to whether such a tribunal is preferable to one composed of professional specialists, either in law or in the problems of juvenile delinquency and child abuse. The magistrates are of course advised on the law by their clerk, but while the actual "clerk to the justices" must now be a lawyer, the person sitting in court may be an unqualified assistant. Lay magistrates must sit in twos or threes to try cases, and in juvenile courts there should be one of each sex. Stipendiaries can sit alone, but rarely do so in juvenile cases.

(iii) *Procedure*

The procedure is basically the same as that of an ordinary magistrates' court, with some modifications. This is thought more suitable for children than is the procedure in the Crown Court, because it is quicker, simpler and less formal. These are indeed advantages if the child admits the offence, but summary trial does have drawbacks if a child denies his guilt on a serious charge. The prosecution evidence does not have to be written down and given to him or his legal advisers in advance, as it is when someone is committed for trial in the Crown Court. Thus there is not the same opportunity of examining it and discovering any evidence which may contradict it. Although prosecuting solicitors or police officers are expected to co-operate at least on the day of the hearing, this does make the task of the defence a great deal more difficult. Again, the magistrates combine the role of judge and jury, and they may decide on guilt as well as on sentence, on any legal points as well as on disputed facts, and on the admissibility of evidence. These issues are kept strictly separate in a jury trial in the Crown Court, and with the best will and advice in the world lay magistrates can find this hard to do. Whatever the disadvantages of appearing in a formal court principally designed for the trial of adults accused of serious crimes, the 16-year-old who denies a charge of attempted murder does not have quite the trial that a 17-year-old would have.

Most criticisms of juvenile courts, however, tend in the opposite direction. They are after all still courts, and conduct themselves in much the same way as do the adult tribunals. The major modifications relate to the privacy of the hearing and the publicity which may later be given to it. The law tries to diminish the trauma and stigma to the child while preserving the equally important principle of open justice. Thus the only people who may be present are those directly concerned in the case, and representatives of the press, broadcasting and news agencies (1933 Act, s. 47(2)). The child's parents can of course be required to attend at any stage, and must be so required if the court thinks it desirable, unless this would be unreasonable (1933 Act, s. 34). The general public are not admitted. Nevertheless a quite alarming number of people can take part, and the child and his parents may be confronted with a bewildering row of tables, accommodating at least two magistrates, their clerk, the probation officer, the local authority's juvenile court liaison officer, a prosecuting solicitor, and sundry police officers or ushers. He may recognise his own social worker, but rarely will he have a lawyer who might explain what is going on. Similarly, press reports and other publicity given to juvenile hearings must not disclose anything tending to identify the child himself (1933 Act, s. 49, 1963 Act, s. 57(2), and 1969 Act s. 10), but the court or Secretary of State can make an exception in order to avoid injustice to "a" child or young person. Examples may be where another child's reputation may be cleared by publishing the actual offender's name, or where the child is acquitted and publication may be necessary to clear his own name. Children appearing in other courts do not have quite the same protection, but the court always has a discretion to prohibit identifying publicity (1933 Act, s.39) and usually does so.

The actual hearing follows the same pattern as in other courts, and this is often confusing to a child or his parents who usually do not understand, for example, what is meant when they are asked to cross-examine the prosecution witnesses. The rules make some attempt to help. Thus the court has to explain the substance of the charge to the child in simple language and ask whether he admits it, rather than simply putting it to him and asking him to plead (Magistrates' Courts (Children and Young Persons) Rules 1970, rr. 6 and 7). The higher courts have said that "where the defendant is not represented or where the defendant is of tender age or for any other reasons there must necessarily be doubts as to his ability finally to decide whether he is guilty or not, the magistrate ought ... to defer a final acceptance of the plea until he has had a chance to learn a little bit more about the case, and to see whether there is some undisclosed factor which may render the unequivocal plea of guilty a misleading one" (*R.* v. *Blandford Justices, ex p. G.*, 1967). They can always allow the accused to change his plea, if this seems appropriate, at any time up to sentence (*S.* v. *Recorder of Manchester*, 1971), and in some cases should themselves take the initiative. Again, if a child is not legally represented, the court must allow his parent to help him, and if the parent cannot be found or required to attend, the court may allow any relative or other responsible person to do so (r. 5). If the child is neither legally represented nor helped, the court is allowed to translate assertions made by the child into questions for the purpose of cross-examining witnesses (r. 8(2)). This is all very well, but many parents are equally unfamiliar with the idea, and it might be more sensible if the court were always able to ask each side what it had to say and then itself devise questions on any point where they seemed to be in conflict.

Formality is always much more a matter of personalities and atmosphere than procedural rules. Some magistrates deliberately make the proceedings as formal as possible, and indeed in some cases prosecution has been decided upon as a definite deterrent after other action has failed. Even parents having trouble with their children may "build up" a court appearance as an awe-inspiring punishment and are disappointed when the court seems to bend over backwards to be kind to the child. Some magistrates reject formality in favour of a general discussion between themselves, all the participants concerned, and the family, on the best way of helping the child out of his difficulties. This approach also has its problems, for the central issue of guilt or innocence can sometimes be lost sight of in the general concern for the child's welfare.

Indeed, some courts positively dislike legal representation of children, not only because this tends to impose more formality on the proceedings (although it need not if properly handled), but also because a lawyer tends to fight for what his client regards as the best result, and this may not always be in his own long-term interests. Thus it was suggested to the Widgery Committee on Legal Aid in Criminal Proceedings (1966), that legal aid was unnecessary for juveniles, because the court always has a duty to "have regard to the welfare of the child" (1933 Act, s. 44). The Committee did not accept this, but of course the granting of legal aid remains a matter for the court before which the child appears and courts vary very substantially in their generosity.

The problem is of course to provide a setting which will explore the situation and needs of each individual child as thoroughly as possible. There may be cases where a punitive attitude is just as appropriate as a therapeutic approach, but it is virtually impossible for any court to keep both options open until it knows which is best. Equally important is a need to preserve both the appearance and actuality of fairness, for a child's sense of injustice is at least as strong as an adult's, and his future willingness to come to terms with authority and the state will depend upon how fair they seem to be in his first contacts with them.

4. *Treatment*

In criminal proceedings, once the child's guilt is established, the court has to decide what order to make. In care proceedings, of course, it would first have to decide whether the care and control test were satisfied and even then need not make an order unless it saw fit. Before deciding on an order, the court must consider all the background information relating to the child's home surroundings, general conduct, school record and medical history (r. 10(1)(*b*)). With this it usually needs help.

(i) *Home surroundings reports*

Anyone prosecuting a child or young person must give notice to the local authority for the area where he lives (or, if he lives nowhere, where the offence was committed) (1969 Act, s. 5(8) and (9)). If the child is 13 or over, notice must also be given to a probation officer for the court's area (s. 34(2)). It is then normally the duty of the local authority to make investigations and produce a home surroundings report, unless this seems unnecessary (s. 9(1)); but if the child is 13 or over, this duty falls instead on the probation service in those areas where arrangements are in force for it to do so (s. 34(3)). In any event the local authority must comply with any request from the court for information or investigations. Thus a report should usually be obtained in all but trivial cases, and certainly few courts should consider making a supervision or custodial order without one.

Any written report from a local authority, probation officer or doctor can be received and considered by the court without being read aloud (r. 10(1)(*d*)), and in any event the court can ask the child or his parents to withdraw (r. 10(1)(*e*)). But if either of these happens, the court must tell the child the substance of anything which bears on his character or conduct and seems relevant to the order, unless this is impracticable having regard to his age and understanding (r. 10(2)(*a*)); and similarly the parent must be told of any relevant information bearing on the parent's character or conduct, or the character, conduct, home surroundings or health of the child (r. 10(2)(*b*)). The object of this is to make sure that orders are not made on the basis of factual information contained in reports which the family has had no opportunity of seeing and challenging. This is an essential principle of open justice, however embarrassing it may be to a social worker for his client to realise that he has revealed damaging information. However, sometimes there may be information about the parents, or the home, or his own health, which ought not to be revealed to the child, and the rules do allow some scope for discrimination. In general, however, the best practice should surely be to give the family a copy of the report, for there are very few things that can lawfully be kept from the parents and this imposes a valuable discipline on the reporter. If the child is legally represented, there can surely be little excuse for not allowing his lawyer to see a copy.

There is no statutory form for these reports, but many authorities will give their workers guide-lines. It is usual for them to include details of the family structure and of the physical and material conditions of the home. There often follows an examination of the parents' characters, their relationships with one another and with this and other children, and of their attitude to this offence. The child's character and personality are covered in some depth, including any relevant medical (especially psychiatric) history, his school record and attendance, his work record if he is old enough, and of course his attitude to his offence and any particular circumstances in which it was committed. If he is already in care, or in some residential establishment such as a special school, it is common to include reports from there.

This reporting function can place the social worker in an ambivalent position. He is there to provide essential objective information to the court, but he will often already be involved with the child or his family. He may be reluctant to forfeit their trust by revealing certain things about them or making a "hostile" recommendation, particularly as he may also be primarily responsible for carrying out any order the court may make. He may even feel obliged to perform something of an advocate's role where a child is not represented and the worker feels that his point of view is unlikely to come across to the court. Probation officers have necessarily to reconcile these pressures, which are inherent in all their work, but local authority social workers who are less experienced in court work may find it more difficult.

(ii) *The orders available*

The choice of orders available to a court before which a juvenile has been found guilty of an offence, reflects to an unusual degree the confusion of aims in the penal system. Thus every court dealing with a juvenile has a duty to have regard to his welfare (1933 Act, s. 44), and presumably this will best be served by a "therapeutic" approach designed to encourage him to become an honest and law-abiding citizen. But welfare cannot always be the paramount consideration, for the "public interest" in the prevention of crime may require an order designed as much to prevent his offending again as to further his own interests. Moreover, it is by no means clear how far juvenile courts should attempt to make the penalty "fit the crime" on some notional "tariff" system such as is commonly applied to adults.

For this confusion the partial implementation of the 1969 Act is to some extent to blame. The very retention of prosecution for some offenders who would have escaped it had the Act been fully implemented must indicate that it is thought to have some value apart from its therapeutic effects (for if treatment were necessary, care proceedings would always be possible). More importantly, the intention behind the Act was only to retain the minor orders of absolute or conditional discharge or fine, only the last of which is punitive in design, and to replace all the others with the same orders which may be made in care proceedings and which are largely therapeutic in design. This intention has not however been fully carried out, and the pressure for change appears all in the opposite direction (*House of Commons*, 1975; *Berlins and Wansell*, 1974).

(a) Discharge

An absolute discharge means that the offence has no further consequences (see Powers of Criminal Courts Act 1973, ss. 7(1) and 13). In tariff terms it is usually only thought appropriate if the offence is trivial or the mitigation strong. Some courts may also think that in therapeutic or deterrent terms "letting the child get away with it" does more harm than good, but in some cases the shock of the court appearance may be all that is required. A conditional discharge means that there will be no further consequences provided that the child does not offend again within a specified period of up to three years (1973 Act, ss. 7(1) and 13). If he does, he may be sentenced again for the original offence (1973 Act, ss. 8 and 9), and this must be explained to him in simple language at the time of the order (s. 7(3)). This is less obviously getting away with it and does offer some encouragement to do better, although no positive help is given; it is also the next lowest on the tariff scale. But the popularity of such orders in juvenile courts must indicate either the beneficial effect attributed to a court appearance or that many children are still being needlessly prosecuted.

(b) Binding over the child or deferring sentence

It appears that the magistrates could exercise their ancient power (whether under the common law or the Justices of the Peace Act 1361 is not clear) to bind over an offender who has disturbed the peace not to do so again within a specified period. The sanction is apparently committal to custody for up to six months. There is also power (under the Powers of

Criminal Courts Act 1973, s. 1) to defer making an order for up to six months, with a view to taking his subsequent conduct into account. In each case, much the same object can usually be achieved by a conditional discharge and the powers are rarely used in juvenile courts.

(c) Fines and other payments

A fine can hardly be anything other than a punishment, although it is remarkably popular in juvenile courts, perhaps because it comes fairly low on the tariff scale. But as a punishment it has serious limitations. The maximum of £50 for a young person and £10 for a child is no doubt sensible, but there is little the court can do to ensure that it is paid. The old sanctions of committal to a remand home, attendance centre or detention centre were abolished in the 1969 Act, and so the only possibilities are attachment of earnings (if he has any), or waiting until he is 17 when he may be committed for default (but is unlikely to be), or making a fine supervision order (Magistrates' Courts Act 1952, s. 71), which may be particularly appropriate if the fine is to be paid by instalments. The order is not as elaborate as an ordinary supervision order and the supervisor's duty is to encourage him to pay, but again there is no sanction if this proves unsuccessful. The government is considering means of providing some sanction (*Home Office*, 1976) but it is difficult to see how the court can force the child himself to pay.

The court may also order the child to pay compensation to any victim of the offence (see Powers of Criminal Courts Act 1973, s. 35) and the prosecution's costs (see costs in Criminal Cases Act 1973, s. 2). There are financial limits to these powers.

The court may order the parent or guardian to pay any fine, compensation or costs awarded against a young person, and must do so if the offender is a child, unless satisfied that the parent or guardian cannot be found or did not conduce to the commission of the offence by neglecting to exercise due care or control over the offender (Children and Young Persons Act 1933, s. 55(1)). This can be enforced against the parent as if he himself had committed the offence, but many courts might rather welcome some means of ensuring that he did *not* pay the fine, rather than the other way about.

The existence of this power has however led some magistrates' courts to order local authorities to pay compensation for offences committed by children in their care. This it can sometimes do because the definition of "guardian" includes anyone who has for the time being charge of or control over the child or young person (1933 Act, s. 107(1)). However, the High Court has held that although the local authority does have "charge or control" if a child in care is accommodated in a home managed by the authority (*R.* v. *Croydon Juvenile Court Justices, ex p. Croydon London Borough Council*, 1973), it does not if he is placed in a home run by someone else (*Somerset County Council* v. *Brice*, 1973) or if he is allowed to go home (*Lincoln Corporation* v. *Parker*, 1974). Even if the authority does have "charge or control" it is only expected to behave as a good parent would and may thus not have "conduced" to the commission of the offence (*Somerset County Council* v. *Kingscott*, 1975). The High Court has frowned on any suggestion that this power should be used by magistrates to express their disapproval of authorities who do not place persistent offenders in secure homes, and has also stated that, before such an order is made, the authority should be given an opportunity of presenting its case through someone better qualified to argue the law than is a social worker.

(d) Parental recognisances

This order (see Children and Young Persons Act 1969, s. 7(7)(*c*)) is the same as that which may be made in care proceedings.

(e) Supervision order

This order was designed to replace probation, attendance centre and detention centre orders for those offenders who were thought to require some positive help short of long-term removal from home. With only minor variations, it is the same as the order which may be made in care proceedings and within the framework available leaves all the major decisions about treatment to the individual supervisor. It thus differs quite substantially from the orders which it was designed to replace.

If the offender is 13 or over, the supervisor may be either the local authority (for the area where he lives or some other authority which agrees to supervise him) or a probation officer for the court's area (1969 Act, ss. 11, 13(1) and 13(3)). If he is under 13, it must be the local authority, unless a probation officer is already working with another member of the household and the authority asks that he should also supervise this child (1969 Act, s. 13(2)). Some consider that probation officers are better suited to do this work (*House of Commons*, 1975), but the government does not share this view (*Home Office*, 1976).

The supervisor's duty is to "advise assist and befriend" the child (s. 14) and to this end the order can require the child to inform the supervisor immediately of any change of address or employment, to keep in touch with the supervisor as he directs, and to allow the supervisor to visit him at home (s. 18(2)(*b*) and Magistrates' Courts (Children and Young Persons) Rules 1970, Sched., form 43). The Probation Rules 1965 require a probation officer to keep in close touch with his client, to meet him frequently, to visit his home from time to time, and to require him to report at stated intervals (r. 35(1)); he should also keep in touch with the family if the child goes to live temporarily elsewhere (r. 35(3)); and encourage the child to make use of any statutory or voluntary agency which might contribute to his welfare, to take advantage of any suitable available social, recreational or educational facilities, and, where appropriate, to get a job (r. 36). Regular confidential reports on his progress should be made to the case committee (r. 37(1)). There are no similar rules about the conduct of supervision orders by local authorities, although presumably the same result can be achieved by administrative directions within the authority. The Secretary of State's new power to make regulations about this does not apply to orders made in criminal proceedings.

The court may also order the child to live with a named individual who agrees to this (s. 12(1)), but this is rather different from the condition of residence in a probation hostel which may be imposed in probation orders (see Powers of

Criminal Courts Act 1973, s. 2(5)). More significant are the courts' new powers to authorise "intermediate treatment." The principle of this is that the court decides whether intermediate treatment should be a possibility, and if so fixes the maximum which may be required, but the supervisor decides whether and to what extent to make use of that possibility (s. 12(2)). Schemes for providing intermediate treatment must be devised by the children's regional planning committee (s. 19(1)), and approved by the Secretary of State (s. 19(2)). The supervisor cannot direct the client to do something which is not included in the regional plan (s. 19(6)), and despite official encouragement progress has been very slow.

Intermediate treatment was intended to fill the gap between bare supervision and the drastic step of removal from home; it is designed to bring the child into contact with "a different environment, interests and experiences which may be beneficial to him" (*Intermediate Treatment Guide*, 1972) and to enable him to share them with other children who have not been before the courts. The court can allow the supervisor to give directions under either (*a*) or (*b*) below, or under both, but the total aggregate period directed cannot be more than 90 days (s. 12(3)(*a*); but the supervisor can disregard any day on which his directions have not been complied with).

(*a*) The client may be directed to live at a specified place for a single specified period of up to 90 days (s. 12(2)(*a*) and (3)(*b*)), but this must begin during the first year of supervision unless the child has failed to comply with such a requirement during that year (s. 12(3)(*b*) and (*e*)). The object may well have been to allow the supervisor to provide something of the "short, sharp shock" of removal to a detention centre, but the power is more likely to be used to provide a term in a boarding school or community home for children who are particularly disturbed or unusually deprived at home.

(*b*) The client may be directed from time to time to do all or any of the following: (i) to live at a specified place or places for a specified period or periods, (ii) to present himself to a specified person or persons at a place or places on a specified day or days, and (iii) to participate in specified activities on a specified day or days (s. 12(2)(*b*)). The aggregate of specified days cannot in all total more than 30 in any one year of supervision (s. 12(3)(*c*)). Here the object is to devise day, evening, weekend or holiday activities which will give the child new interests, new ideas and perhaps new friends. Obvious examples are outward bound centres, summer camps on farms, sporting activities, handicrafts, evening classes, scouting, youth clubs and voluntary social service. The emphasis is entirely on finding things which the child will enjoy as well as doing him good, and not at all on punishment for its own sake.

Yet here lies a problem. Great care was taken to avoid any suggestion that the court was ordering the child to do anything; it was hoped that the supervisor would be able to persuade the child that a particular activity was a good idea. Many indeed are only suitable for genuine volunteers. Thus no statutory form is laid down for the giving of directions, although it was suggested that it might be advisable to write them down so that neither party, nor any court which subsequently had to consider the case, would be in any doubt about what was required (*Home Office*, 1970). But what is to be done if the child refuses to co-operate? In one sense, any coercion may defeat the object of the exercise, yet if both the court and the supervisor have decided that the treatment is necessary should he be allowed to avoid it?

Supervision orders differ in two major respects from probation orders. First, if the child offends again while under supervision he cannot be brought back to court and re-sentenced for the original offence (compare Powers of Criminal Courts Act 1973, ss. 8 and 9). This may not matter very much, because the court can always take into account the effectiveness of the supervision order in deciding what to do about the second offence. Secondly, however, there is no specific sanction for failing to co-operate with the supervisor or to observe his directions for intermediate treatment (compare the 1973 Act, s. 6). To those points there is one exception. Provided that the order was made in criminal proceedings or on the discharge of a care order, and the client has reached the age of 17, the juvenile court (or if he is 18, the adult court) can punish him for failing to co-operate by fining him up to £20 or making an attendance centre order; it may also discharge the supervision order and sentence him again for the original offences (1969 Act, s. 15(2) and (4)). Apart from this, the only thing that a supervisor who is dissatisfied with his client's progress or co-operation can do is to ask the court to discharge the supervision order and, if the child is under 18, to substitute a care order (s. 15(1)). The court can only use this drastic solution if satisfied that the child needs the care or control it will provide (s. 16(6) (c)). Thus in criminal cases it is planned to extend fines for breach to all children and attendance centre orders to all boys; either would leave the supervision order intact. Whether this will destroy the whole concept remains to be seen.

In criminal proceedings, supervision orders last for three years or a shorter period (s. 17(a)) and need not expire when the child reaches 18. The supervisor or client (or his parents acting on his behalf) can always apply for the order to be varied by cancelling or inserting provisions for co-operation or intermediate treatment (s. 15(1) and (3); but intermediate treatment in form (a) cannot be required after the first year and no new requirements for intermediate treatment can be inserted after the client reaches 18). If the client is under 18, either party can apply for the order to be discharged, but a care order may then be substituted (s. 15(1)); and if he is over 17, the duration of a supervision order can be shortened or even extended if a shorter period than three years was originally specified (s. 15(2) and (3)(a)). If an application for discharge is refused, no one may apply again within three months without the court's consent (s. 16(9)).

Unless the order is being discharged or in some way reduced (s. 16(5)), the client must normally be before the court. A warrant may be issued if necessary to secure his attendance (s. 16(2)); once arrested he may be detained in a place of safety, but he must be brought before the court or a justice within 72 hours (s. 16(3)); the court or justice may then make an interim order or if he is over 18, remand him (s. 16(3) and (4)). Whether he has been arrested or not, the court can make an interim order if it requires more information to decide whether to make an order (s. 16(4)).

Last, the power to require psychiatric treatment should be mentioned. The court must have evidence from an approved specialist in mental disorder that the child's mental condition is "such as requires and may be susceptible to medical treatment" but does not warrant his detention in hospital under a hospital order. It may then require him for a specified period to submit to in-patient treatment at any hospital other than a special hospital, or out-patient treatment at any hospital other than a special hospital, or out-patient treatment at some specified place, or treatment by or under the direction of a specified doctor (s. 12(4)). The requirement cannot be made without the consent of a child who has reached 14 and cannot in any event last beyond the age of 18 (s. 12(5)). It cannot be inserted in an existing order which has lasted for more than three months (s. 15(1)), or without the consent of a child who has reached 14 (s. 16(7)), but if the doctor in charge thinks that a change should be made in an existing requirement, he must report to the supervisor, who must refer it to the court, which can then cancel or vary the requirement (s. 15(5)).

Apart from the provisions relating to pscyhiatric treatment, however, there is no requirement that a child should consent to be placed under supervision.

(f) Attendance centre order

This can be imposed for any offence punishable in the case of an adult by imprisonment (Criminal Justice Act 1948, s. 19). The offender is usually ordered to attend the centre for 12 hours, but the court can order less if he is under 14, or more up to a maximum of 24 (Criminal Justice Act 1961, s. 10). After the first, the duration and number of attendances are matters for the person in charge of the centre. One to three hours on alternate Saturdays is usual. The centres are provided by the Home Secretary by an arrangement with the police or local authority, and as there are not very many (and none for girls), the court can only make the order if satisfied that a suitable and reasonably accessible place is available.

The object is ambiguous. The order cannot be made if the offender has already received a custodial order, but whether it is a short, sharp punishment or a limited attempt at reformation is not clear. The former seems the more common attitude among organisers, and at least it can keep football supporters away during home matches. It is difficult to imagine that it can accomplish much more and the object of the 1969 Act was to phase it out for juveniles once intermediate treatment became available (s. 7(2)). However, this has not been done, and on the contrary it seems likely that this limited form of punishment will be retained and facilities expanded (*Home Office*, 1976).

(g) Detention centre order

This again may only be imposed for an offence punishable by imprisonment in the case of an adult and the offender must be at least 14 (Criminal Justice Act 1961, s. 4). He is ordered to be detained in a centre for three months (the Crown Court can order anything between three and six months) but up to a half may be remitted for good behaviour. The centres are again provided by the Home Secretary, and are under the overall control of the prison department. Again because places are scarce (and there are none for girls), the court must be satisfied that a suitable one is available.

These centres are even more controversial than attendance centres, for having originally been invented as juvenile substitutes for prison, their regime is rigorous and strictly disciplined. Offenders who have previously been sent to borstal or community schools should not be sent there, but time is too short for much reformative work. Indeed the likeness to prison is emphasised by the fact that the court cannot send an offender to a detention centre for the first time unless he is either legally represented, or has been refused legal aid on the ground of means, or having been told about legal aid has refused to apply for it (Powers of Criminal Courts Act 1973, s. 21). Again, the object of the 1969 Act was to phase out such orders once intermediate treatment became available (s. 7(2)), but they seem to be increasingly popular with courts who now have no other means of ensuring a period of secure detention. It has even been suggested that this "short, sharp, shock" should be available for even shorter periods (*House of Commons*, 1975), but although the government shows no signs of implementing the 1969 Act it does not favour that suggestion (*Home Office*, 1976).

(h) Care order

This again may only be imposed for an offence punishable

with imprisonment in the case of an adult (1969 Act, s. 7(7)(*a*))
or on the discharge of a supervision order (s. 15(1)). The 1969
Act provided magistrates with a single long-term custodial
order to replace the old fit person and approved school orders.
It is not only identical to the order which may be made in care
proceedings, but also specifically designed to leave all the
decisions relating to the child's accommodation and treatment
to the local authority concerned. The legal details are
therefore discussed in the chapter on Local Authorities, but
the controversy surrounding these orders must be mentioned
here.

The main problem is that courts are no longer able to insist
on a period of detention in a secure and disciplined
environment. This would not be a problem at all if local
authorities were able to send all children who needed this to
secure community homes, and if the courts and others were
able to accept that local authorities are as well qualified as
they to assess the child's needs. Unfortunately, the Act placed
additional large responsibilities on local authorities at a time
when they were also suffering the upheaval of reorganisation,
and gave them little in the way of additional resources to
discharge them. Furthermore, during the transitional period,
approved schools could clearly reject individual children, and
even now heads appear to be allowed considerable discretion,
so that some particularly difficult children have had to be sent
home because there is nowhere for them to go. More
significantly, however, people in whom the "deterrent" or
"tariff" approach to sentencing was at least as strong as the
therapeutic approach could attack local authorities for being
"soft." This was unjust, partly because of the difficulties the
authorities were labouring under, and partly because the Act's
intention had surely been to encourage the therapeutic
approach to predominate over the punitive.

Nevertheless there seems to be a widespread feeling that
while the Act works quite well for the great majority of
children, for whom delinquency is merely an incident in
ordinary development, or who can be helped quite easily to
grow out of it, it does not work well for a small but increasing
hard core of children who seriously and persistently break the
law. Pressure is growing, not only for the provision of much

more secure accommodation, which would not endanger the scheme of the Act, but also for the courts to regain some control. This would obviously, as with the suggestions on supervision orders, upset the whole division of responsibility underlying the Act. This the government is not inclined to do, although it recognises that in a few cases the court might properly wish to make its views known to the authority and to be informed of the authority's decision (*Home Office*, 1976).

It is ironic that beforehand fears were expressed that a care order might be a greater infringement of liberty than an approved school order. It lasts until 18 or 19 instead of for a fixed period of three years; and the authority can at any time decide on a secure placement even if the court would not have thought it warranted. Nevertheless the right to apply for discharge at three-monthly intervals, coupled with the pressure on places, has meant that these fears were largely unfounded, except perhaps in the minds of the children themselves.

(i) Hospital and guardianship orders under the Mental Health Act 1959

These are the same as the orders which may be made in care proceedings, but a hospital order cannot be combined with a care order.

(j) Borstal training

This can only be imposed for an offence punishable with imprisonment and the offender must be at least 15 (Criminal Justice Act 1948, s. 20). Only the Crown Court now has power to send someone to borstal immediately on finding him guilty, and thus if the juvenile or ordinary magistrates' court considers this the appropriate order, it must commit the offender to the Crown Court with such a recommendation (Magistrates' Courts Act 1952, s. 28). The committal must be to a prison, or if one is available a remand centre, and not to the care of a local authority. The Crown Court can then either send the offender to borstal or make any order which the lower court could have made.

A juvenile court can however order the removal to borstal of a child of 15 or over who is accommodated in a community home under a care order and whose behaviour is detrimental to the other children there (1969 Act, s. 31 (1) and (2)). The application must be made by the local authority with the consent of the Secretary of State. If made, the order operates like a fresh sentence of borstal training, but neither it nor the period of licence after release can last for longer than the original care order would have done (s. 31(3)). The court can order the child to be detained in a remand centre for a limited period while making up its mind (s. 31(4) and (5)).

Borstal training is of course under the control of the Home Office prison department. Training can last for anything between six months and two years and it is for the Secretary of State to decide when the trainee is ready to leave. Thereafter for a further two years he remains subject to supervision and possible recall to borstal (Prison Act 1952, s. 45). Furthermore, if he offends again within this period, the court which tries him may order his return (Criminal Justice Act 1961, s. 12).

Borstal was primarily intended as a constructive alternative to prison for 17 to 20-year-olds, although conditions and discipline vary between different institutions. It should only be used for 15 and 16-year-olds when nothing else will do and the intention of the 1969 Act was to abolish it for them as an immediate order (s. 7(1)) although retaining the possibility of removal from a community home. Again, because of the increase in juvenile crime and the problems experienced with care orders, this has not yet been done.

(k) Detention

A child or young person who is found guilty in the Crown Court of an offence for which an adult could be sentenced to 14 or more years of imprisonment (life is more) may be ordered to be detained subject to the directions of the Secretary of State for a fixed period of not longer than the maximum term of imprisonment for the offence (1933 Act, s. 53(2)). However, only young persons of 14 or more may be committed for trial in the Crown Court for no other reason than that the magistrates think that this power ought to be exercisable in his case (see

3(i) above); thus unless a child under 14 is charged with homicide or is jointly charged with someone older, this power is not exercisable against him and the most that can be ordered, however serious the offence, is a care order.

An order for prolonged detention is in any event only suitable if nothing else will do, but it seems increasingly popular for older juveniles convicted of very serious crimes: in one case, a sentence of 20 years detention upon a 16-year-old boy convicted of attempted murder was upheld (*R.* v. *Storey*, 1973). The Secretary of State chooses where the detainee may be held. Until he reaches 19, this may be in a youth treatment centre, or in a local authority or controlled community home (1969 Act, s. 30); thereafter he may go to borstal or prison, and in some cases there may have been no alternative from the beginning. The Secretary of State may release the detainee on licence at any time if this is recommended by the Parole Board (and if the detention is for life, after consultation with the Lord Chief Justice and if possible the trial judge) (Criminal Justice Act 1967, s. 61). This power led the court to suggest that however harsh such an order might seem, it should not be compared with a prison sentence of comparable length. Nevertheless, although the practice of considering release only once a third of the period had been served has been revised in the light of the very long periods now occasionally ordered (*Home Office letter*, 1974), a released offender remains subject to recall for the remainder of his sentence (1967 Act, ss. 61 and 62).

A juvenile found guilty of murder must be sentenced to be detained during Her Majesty's Pleasure (1933 Act, s. 53(1)). The effect is much the same as a sentence of life detention.

5 Child Abuse

The law has known for a long time that people are capable of treating children badly, although obviously its notions of what is bad for children have varied with those of society at large. Its first response was simply to punish the wrongdoer, and the special vulnerability of children made it necessary to devise special offences to protect them. Its second response was to devise means of removing them from the harmful environment. More recently, however, the deficiencies of both these methods have become apparent and more emphasis has been placed upon both prevention and rehabilitation. The selection of the most appropriate response in individual cases raises serious problems of principle and practice, but before attempting any discussion of these it is necessary to examine the legal details of each.

1. *Punishing the Abuser*

It is not possible to discuss all the offences with which people who maltreat children may be charged (see *Bevan*, 1973), but some account of the one most frequently used may be helpful. The offence of "cruelty to children," now contained in section 1 of the Children and Young Persons Act 1933, recognises that the ordinary offences of assault, wounding and the like are inadequate. Children have positive needs, both physical and psychological, and it is just as cruel to neglect to supply these as it is to "batter." In punishing neglect, therefore, the section imposes positive duties upon people caring for children which they do not normally have towards adults. The ingredients necessary for establishing the offence are as follows:

    (i)   The victim must be under the age of 16.

    (ii) The person charged must be 16 or over, and must in some way be responsible for the child by having "custody, charge or care" of him. The people presumed (under s. 17 of the Act) to have "custody" are both parents of a legitimate child, the mother of an illegitimate child, a legally appointed guardian, and anyone "legally liable to maintain" the child (this means someone such as a step-parent or putative father who has been ordered, or has entered into a legally binding contract, to pay maintenance). A person presumed to have custody under this section cannot abdicate his responsibilities by deserting the family, or even by agreeing with the mother that she should have custody; a court order depriving him of custody could take him out of the definition, but in most cases he would still be legally liable to maintain. A person to whom legal custody has been committed by a court presumably also has "custody" although the section does not mention this. The people presumed (again under s. 17) to have "charge" are those to whom charge of the child has been committed by any person who has custody, and the people presumed to have "care" are all those who have actual possession or control. Thus the father of an illegitimate child who is living with the family may have actual possession or control even though no affiliation order has been made.

(iii) The person charged must have assaulted, ill-treated, neglected, abandoned or exposed the child. These five words do not create water-tight compartments, however, and a particular case may well be described by more than one of them. "Assault" means either battery (the application of force) or assault (the threat of immediate battery) and the only problem it raises is that of drawing the line between lawful punishment and criminal assault (see page 13). "Ill-treat" could probably equally well describe all the other forms of behaviour, but it is vague enough to cover any sort of harmful conduct towards a child, including threats, abuse and similar "mental" cruelty. "Neglect" is omitting to take "such steps as a reasonable parent would take, such as are usually taken in the ordinary experience of mankind" (*R*. v. *Senior*, 1899). The standard is that of the reasonable parent, and so natural inadequacy or unusual religious views are no defence. There is no indication that it is limited to neglect to supply a child's physical wants, but a parent or other person legally liable to maintain a child is presumed to have neglected him in a manner likely to cause injury to health (see requirement (v) below) if he fails to provide adequate food, clothing, medical aid or lodging, or if being unable to do so, he has failed to seek the assistance of the state (s. 1(2)(*a*)). Failure to pay maintenance could also be neglect if the child was likely to suffer thereby. "Abandons" has a very limited meaning in this section, for it must involve the surrender of all care of the child without intending to resume it and, more importantly, without making alternative arrangements. "Exposes" is another vague portmanteaux term like "ill-treatment," but as it probably covers exposing the child to any unnecessary suffering or injury to health, it can (like neglect) cover sins of omission as well as commission.

(iv) Whatever form of behaviour is involved, it must be "wilful," but lawyers interpret this perhaps less narrowly than would a layman. "Wilfulness" does not mean "malice," so that it is no defence that a parent thought he was acting for the best, as in a case where a father deliberately refused to let his child receive medical treatment because of his peculiar religious views (*R.* v. *Senior*, 1899). It does not even mean that the defendant must have foreseen what the consequences of his behaviour would be, for a man of low intelligence who failed to call a doctor to his sick baby was convicted even though it was not proved that he foresaw the harm which resulted (*R.* v. *Lowe*, 1973, a decision which has quite frightening implications for every parent who has agonised over whether to call the doctor). All that "wilfulness" requires, therefore, is that the conduct itself, rather than the resulting harm, was deliberately intended.

(v) A much more important limitation on the offence is that the behaviour must always have been "in a manner likely to cause unnecessary suffering or injury to health." This is a necessary limitation in view of the scope of such terms as "neglect" or "expose," but in the past it has meant that some quite deliberate and reprehensible actions have escaped punishment : thus a man who abandoned children in a juvenile court while it was sitting was acquitted because in such circumstances substitute care would obviously be quickly arranged (*R.* v. *Whibley*, 1938). Nowadays a court might take a broader view of "unnecessary suffering or injury to health," for there is no reason why this should not cover mental, emotional or psychological injury or deprivation. It should also be noted that there is no need for the suffering or injury actually to materialise : it need only be "likely," and it is no defence that actual suffering or injury, or even the likelihood of them, was obviated by the action of another person (s. 1(3)(*a*), which makes the decision in *R.* v. *Whibley* even more surprising).

The offence can be tried either in the magistrates' court, where the maximum penalty is a £400 fine and/or six months' imprisonment or in the Crown Court, in which case the maximum term of imprisonment is two years. The penalties are higher if the person involved stood to gain by the child's death (see s. 1(4) and (5)).

The section is so broadly drafted that it can obviously cover almost any deficiency in child care. Indeed it leaves certain commonplace parental questions, such as when children can be left alone or when to call the doctor, undesirably vague. When and whether it (and indeed prosecution for any criminal offence) is a suitable means of protecting children from harm will be discussed in the concluding section.

2. *Care Proceedings*

Families, including the children in them, deserve some protection from arbitrary and officious interference from the state, however benevolent its intentions. If a family which is getting into difficulties is prepared to accept supervision voluntarily, or to allow children to be received into care under section 1 of the 1948 Act, all may be well and good; but if it is not, the authorities must take legal proceedings to give them the right to interfere (unless they already have it, for example where they have themselves boarded the child out in his present home). "Place of safety" proceedings of various sorts are an emergency means of removing children for a short time, but any long-term measures, whether of supervision or removal, normally require care proceedings under section 1 of the Children and Young Persons Act 1969 (although making the child a ward of court might be a possibility in a case where there were serious grounds for concern but not grounds for care proceedings). Care proceedings differ fundamentally from custody disputes between adults who are offering a child alternative homes. First, they are not technically disputes between adults at all, for it is the child who is brought before the court. Secondly, the court cannot simply decide what would be best for the child, for it must be satisfied that the defined grounds for intervention exist; some of these grounds cover matters which would not normally be understood under the term "child abuse," but it is simpler to include them in the discussion of the proceedings as a whole.

(i) *Who is involved?*

Care proceedings can only be brought by a constable (in effect any policeman), a local authority (save in education cases, a local social services authority), or an "authorised person" (only the NSPCC has been authorised) (s. 1(1)). The local authority for the area where the child lives or is found has a positive duty to make enquiries if it receives information suggesting that there are grounds for bringing proceedings, unless satisfied that enquiries are unnecessary (s. 2(1)). All applicants are of course dependent upon receiving information from the public, and provided that they can after investigation obtain enough evidence to prove the case, there should be no need to disclose the informant's name in the care proceedings themselves. Moreover, should the name become relevant in any other proceedings, the NSPCC and other potential applicants may still refuse to divulge it. This was decided in a preliminary dispute in a recent case where a child's mother was trying to get damages for nervous shock allegedly caused by the society's negligence in following up an allegation of abuse against her, in which the informant's name was obviously highly relevant (*D.* v. *NSPCC*, 1977). Whether such an action would succeed is quite another matter. In the case of the local authority, there is also a positive duty to bring proceedings if it thinks that the grounds exist, unless satisfied that this is neither in the child's nor the public interest (s. 2(2)); the court would thus be reluctant to blame the local authority unless it had acted quite unreasonably. Any applicant other than the local authority for the area where the child lives (or, if he does not

seem to live anywhere, where the facts arose) must first inform
that authority (s. 2(3)). There is no other legal provision about
consultation between the various bodies involved, but there is
administrative machinery, which will be described in the
section on "what to do?"

Care proceedings may be brought in respect of a "child"
(anyone under 14) or a "young person" (of 14 but under 17),
but unless it is necessary to distinguish between them, the word
"child" will be used for both. The child must physically be
"brought before the court"; the only exception is where he is
under five and either his parent or guardian is there or the
court is satisfied that the parent or guardian has been given
reasonable notice (s. 2(9)), but even then the court may insist
on the child's appearance. The child, unless he is conducting
his own case or the evidence relates to his own character or
conduct, may be asked to leave, in his own interests, while
certain evidence is being given (Magistrates' Courts (Children
and Young Persons) Rules 1970, r. 18(1)).

In many cases, the child's presence can be secured by a
simple summons, but if necessary a warrant can be obtained
from a magistrate (s. 2(4)). If, as is likely, a child arrested
under such a warrant cannot be brought to court immediately,
he may be taken to a "place of safety" and detained there for
up to 72 hours. If he cannot be brought before a full court
within that time, he must be brought before a single
magistrate, who may either make an interim order or release
him immediately (s. 2(5)). In many cases, however, the child
may already be subject to a place of safety order and so it will
be easy to secure his attendance.

As it is the child who is respondent to the application, it does
not matter whether or not the person with whom he is living
has parental rights over him; what matters is whether the
grounds can be proved in respect of him. However, other
people may well have a legitimate interest in the proceedings
and must be notified of them. Besides the appropriate local
authority (if it is not the applicant), the probation officer (if
the child is 13 or over), and (if the proceedings are for
discharge or variation of a supervision order) the child's
supervisor, these include the child's parent or guardian (if his
whereabouts are known to the applicant) and any foster parent

or other person with whom the child has had his home for not less than six weeks, ending not more than six months before the application (again if the applicant knows his whereabouts) (r. 14(3)).

The provision about foster parents is quite new. It was introduced because the case of Maria Colwell (*Report*, 1974) had raised some interesting problems about the parties to care proceedings. Maria had, of course, been removed from her mother in the then equivalent of care proceedings when she was still a baby, and the local authority had boarded her out with an uncle and aunt. After she had been with the uncle and aunt for some six years, her mother made an application for the care order to be discharged. The local authority decided not to oppose this application and it was granted. In the light of Maria's subsequent treatment and eventual death at the hands of her step-father, many were concerned that the people with whom she had spent so many apparently happy years had had no right at all to be heard in the proceedings to take her away from them. This provision will give anyone with whom the child has recently been living the right to argue against his removal, whether by the making of an original order or by the discharge of an existing one.

More importantly, perhaps, the case illustrated how easy it is to regard care proceedings as a battle between the authorities and the parents, in which the child's point of view may be overlooked. The law has tended to strengthen this impression. It is obviously right that a parent or guardian should be notified of the proceedings; that the court should be able to compel any parent or guardian to attend unless this would be unreasonable (Children and Young Persons Act 1933, s. 34); that the parent or guardian should be entitled to meet any allegations made against him in the proceedings (r. 14B); and that if an order is made, the parent or guardian should be able to ask for it to be varied or discharged (1969 Act, s. 70(2)). It is not so obviously right that the parent should be allowed to represent the child, yet the rules provide that the court must allow the parent to conduct the case on the child's behalf (r. 17). Until recently, the only exceptions were where the child or parent was legally represented, or where the parent himself had asked for the proceedings because the child was beyond his control, or where the child otherwise requested. In cases based on parental neglect or ill-treatment of young children, this seemed ludicrous; and even if the child was granted legal aid and a lawyer instructed, the lawyer might very well be confused about who his client was.

The case also demonstrated that the local authority social workers were in a similarly ambiguous position. They are representatives of their agency and the agency's function in care proceedings is to protect the child. But the whole form of the proceedings places the agency in opposition to both parents and child and then expects it to become a substitute parent. The individual worker may have to represent the authority as an advocate or give evidence against the parents, and will then have to carry out the court's order to supervise or remove the child. On top of this he may be expected to provide an impartial home surroundings report as agent for the court. In doing all these things he is bound to reflect both the decisions of his superiors and his own professional loyalties, which are equally ambiguous. The family-centred approach to casework (reflected in section 1 of the 1963 Act, as well as in the Seebohm reorganisation) means that the parent is often regarded as the "client" rather than the child. The worker can only help to keep the family viable and prevent abuse if he can form some relationship with the parents, and he may find it difficult to contemplate "betraying" his client by removing or keeping from her what may be all she has, her child.

As a result, the Children Act 1975 has added two new sections to the 1969 Act. When fully in force, they will provide that if there appears to be any conflict of interest between parent and child in care proceedings, or in proceedings for the discharge of orders made in care proceedings, or in appeals, the court can order that the parent is not to be treated as representing the child (s. 32A(1)). Where an application to discharge a care or supervision order made in a care proceedings case is not opposed, such an order will be mandatory unless the court is satisfied that it is not necessary to safeguard the child's interests (s. 32A(2)); because of the concern caused by the Maria Colwell case, this provision has been brought into force ahead of the full scheme. Once the court has made such an order, it must also appoint a guardian ad litem for the child, unless this seems unnecessary (s. 32B(1); see also rule 14A(1)). It is intended to set up 'panels of experienced social workers and probation officers who may be appointed guardians, but for the time being the courts will have to make arrangements to find a suitably qualified person who is independent of any authority which is a party to the proceedings (r. 14A(2)); suitable qualifications obviously include an ability to communicate with children, an appreciation of their needs, and some experience of care proceedings. The guardian will be expected to investigate all the circumstances, interview everyone he thinks appropriate, and ask to inspect any appropriate records (refusal of access to records would obviously be a matter of adverse report to the court). First and foremost, of course, he should try to discover the child's own point of view, and in the light of all his investigations decide whether it is in the child's interests for the application to succeed; unlike a lawyer, therefore, who is normally committed to representing his client's wishes (although he will advise on their implications), the guardian will be committed to his client's best interests, which may not be quite the same as his wishes: the guardian will however have no one else to whose interests he is committed. The guardian can then choose whether to apply for legal aid for the child and instruct a solicitor or, if not and unless the child objects, to conduct the case himself. He may also make a written report to the court, which will be covered by the same rules as home surroundings reports (these have been discussed in the previous chapter). Finally, at the end of the case, he should decide whether to appeal (r. 14A(6) and (7)).

The parent will still be able to meet any allegations against himself and to make representations to the court (r. 14B), but he will not be able to conduct the child's case (r. 17). He will also be able to apply for separate legal aid in order to enable him to take part (Children Act 1975, s. 65).

(ii) *Interim orders*

The proper court before which to bring the child is the juvenile court for the area where he lives. If he is brought before a different one, it may either dismiss the case or remit him to the proper one and either allow him to stay where he is or make an interim order in the meantime (s. 2(11)). Interim orders can also be made by a court or single justice after a child has been arrested pursuant to a warrant under section 2(4), by a court or single justice while a child is being detained in a place of safety under section 28 (see 3(i) below), and most commonly by a court before which a child has been brought in care proceedings but which is not yet in a position to decide what order, if any, ought to be made (s. 2(10)). The child must always be present at the making of an interim order, unless he is under five or prevented by illness or accident (s. 22(1); illness or accident are not excuses for absence from the care proceedings proper and thus may well be reasons for seeking an interim order). The court or justice always has the alternative of sending the child home, perhaps with a summons to appear later, perhaps for good; a full court also has the alternative of sending a young person who is too unruly to be committed to care to a remand centre (s. 22(5)). An interim order places the child in the care of the local authority for up to 28 days, but it may be discharged earlier or when it expires a fresh one can be made (what may happen while the child is in care under an interim order is discussed in Chapter 9).

(iii) *The grounds*

The applicant must prove, first, that one or more of seven "primary conditions" relating to the child is fulfilled, and, secondly, that the child is in need of care or control which he will not receive unless the court makes an order. As the proceedings are civil rather than criminal, the less stringent civil rules of evidence apply, so that both child and parents may be compelled to give evidence, and the burden of proof is probably on the "balance of probabilities" rather than "beyond reasonable doubt." The seven primary conditions are (s. 1(2)):

(*a*) "His proper development is being avoidably prevented or neglected, or his health is being avoidably impaired or neglected, or he is being ill-treated."

This seems to cover child abuse in its broadest sense, for it can refer to both physical and psychological development and health. It is wider than the criminal offence (see 1 above), and there is no need to prove deliberate intention or indeed who exactly was responsible for proven neglect or ill-treatment. It may be that care proceedings should be adjourned until the outcome of any prosecution is known, for the parent might feel aggrieved if a care order were made and he was later acquitted; but the acquittal may well not negative the existence of grounds for removing the child (indeed it would not even be admissible) and thus in some cases it may nevertheless be proper to proceed with care proceedings.

Despite its scope, there are some problems. Almost anything can prevent a child's proper development or impair his health, but the situation must be "avoidable" (this must mean objectively avoidable, for otherwise a parent who was doing her incompetent best would be totally invulnerable). Some problems are difficult for anyone to avoid. A subnormal mother caring in unsuitable accommodation for two tiny children with fragile bones may find it well-nigh impossible to avoid fractures, but given that a foster home would be virtually unobtainable, could a children's home do any better? Again, the condition is phrased in the present tense. If all that can be proved happened some time ago, is the child "being" ill-treated? And if nothing has yet happened, can nothing be done? The next two conditions are designed to provide a partial solution to the second question.

(*b*) It is probable that condition (*a*) *will* be satisfied "having regard to the fact that the court or another court has found that [it] is or was satisfied in the case of a child or young person who is or was a member of the household to which [this child] belongs."

Other children in households where there has already been abuse may thus be protected before anything has happened to them. This is so even though the first child has died, so that no care proceedings were ever taken in respect of him (*Surrey County Council* v. *S.*, 1974). There must however be a likelihood of risk to this child as well; some parents may make one the scapegoat, leaving the others in no danger.

(*bb*) It is probable that condition (*a*) will be satisfied "having regard to the fact that a person who has been convicted of an offence mentioned in Schedule 1 to the Act of 1933 is, or may become, a member of the same household as the child".

The offences listed include virtually all violent or sexual offences against children, including "cruelty to a child" (although there is a doubt about indecent assault). The person must actually have been convicted, but the other child may well have been quite outside this child's household. Risk to this child must still be shown.

(*c*) "He is exposed to moral danger."

Moral danger need not be limited to sexual danger, for it could surely cover danger from criminal associations or drug abuse, as well as the obvious cases of unlawful or promiscuous intercourse, homosexual practices, or incest (there is no need to show that offences are being committed). The condition has given rise to a fascinating case with much wider implications.

A 26-year-old Nigerian student came to this country with his 13-year-old Nigerian wife, to whom he was validly married under Nigerian muslem law. When they arrived, he was suffering from a venereal disease, but he had almost certainly had intercourse with his wife before she reached puberty and he intended to resume intercourse once he was cured. With this in mind he took her to be fitted with a contraceptive. The doctor thought that she was very young and informed the local authority, which brought care proceedings. They succeeded in the magistrates' court, but on appeal the High Court did not agree that marital relations between two people who were validly married according to the law of their own country could place the girl in moral danger (*Mohamed* v. *Knott*, 1969).

Moral danger is obviously a value judgment, and as such should surely take into account the customs and culture in which the people have been brought up. This is quite different from saying that people who commit criminal offences which are acceptable in their culture should be acquitted. Crime is a fact, whereas moral danger is a judgment (and the court thought that intercourse in this case could not be unlawful sexual intercourse with a girl under 16 because they were validly married).

(*d*) "He is beyond the control of his parent or guardian".

This is the successor to a long line of powers to deal with refractory children, who could originally be brought to court by their own parents. Nowadays this is impossible, but the parent may make a written request to the local authority for proceedings to be brought on this condition, and if the authority refuses or fails to do so within 28 days, the parent can apply to the juvenile court for an order directing them to do so; the child must not be present at this preliminary hearing (Children and Young Persons Act 1963, s. 3; incidentally, a recent radio programme suggested that a mother had been pressed to sign a form requesting care proceedings on this condition so that, in effect, the authority could obtain a care order by consent; one can understand the temptation to social workers faced with the problem of a boy going in and out of care under the Children Act 1948 and apparently having no grounds for a section 2 resolution, but it is to be hoped that this section would not be so abused).

The condition can of course be acted upon without parental pressure, and may sometimes be appropriate for children under 10 who are persistently committing crimes for which they cannot be prosecuted.

(*e*) He is of compulsory school-age and is not receiving efficient full-time education suitable to his age, ability and aptitude.

Proceedings under this condition must be brought by the local education authority (s. 2(8)). The condition is prima facie proved if a school attendance order has not been complied with, or if a registered pupil is not attending school regularly, or if someone habitually wanders from place to place taking the child with him, but the parent can still seek to prove that the child is nevertheless being properly educated (s. 2(8)).

The authority can also prosecute the parents (or those with actual custody) for failing to comply with a school attendance order or failing to secure the attendance of a registered pupil, but before doing so it has a duty to consider taking care proceedings (Education Act 1944, s. 40). The court trying the parents may also direct the authority to bring care proceedings. Removal of the child is no doubt usually a much more potent threat than prosecution.

The fact that a child is not attending school is of course highly relevant to proceedings brought on condition (*a*), for his proper development will almost certainly be prevented. There is nothing to prevent the evidence being put forward on that condition even though the education authority is not proceeding on this (s. 2(8)).

(*f*) "He is guilty of an offence, excluding homicide."

This was an integral part of the Act's scheme to prohibit or restrict the prosecution of some juvenile offenders so that they could only be brought to court, if at all, in care proceedings. Care proceedings of course require proof of the "care and control" test, which should limit court action to those cases where it is absolutely necessary. They also involve a more limited and less punitive range of possible orders than does prosecution and are thought to involve less stigma for the child. So that children should be no worse off because of this alternative, however, the Act provides that this condition cannot be found proved unless the court could have found the child guilty in criminal proceedings (s. 3(3)), which means that it cannot be used where the child is under 10 and that the "*doli incapax*" presumption, stricter criminal rules of evidence and burden of proof ("beyond reasonable doubt") all apply. There are also provisions to prevent the same offence being used twice in criminal proceedings or care proceedings (ss. 3(1) and (4)) and a separate right of appeal against a finding that this condition is proved, even though the court makes no order (s. 3(8)). The court can also order the payment of compensation, whether or not it makes any other order (s. 3(6)); and if the child is 14 or over, it may bind him over for up to a year to keep the peace or be of good behaviour instead of making an order under section 1(3) (s. 3(7)). Last proceedings on this condition may only be begun by the police or a local authority (s. 3(2)).

However, as the provisions prohibiting and restricting the prosecution of juveniles have not been brought into force, this condition remains largely a dead-letter. Juvenile crime has, of course, already been dealt with in the previous chapter.

Once one of the primary conditions has been proved, the court must still be persuaded that the child is in need of care or control which he will not receive unless the court makes an order. This is a separate and additional requirement, designed to limit compulsory intervention to cases where it is clearly the right solution for this particular child, and both courts and applicants should beware of assuming that it is automatically fulfilled once a primary condition has been shown. In *S.* v. *Bedfordshire County Council* (1977), a 12-year-old boy had been deliberately kept away from school by his parents since leaving his primary school because of their opposition to comprehensive education. Primary condition (*e*) was clearly satisfied and the juvenile court made a care order; the boy was placed in a children's home and sent to school. The Crown Court allowed his appeal, holding, first, that the care and control test had not been satisfied and secondly, that even if it had this would not have been an appropriate case for a care order. However, the local authority took the case further and succeeded in the Court of Appeal. The Crown Court had applied too narrow a test, suggesting that to be in need of care the boy had to be neglected in his day-to-day physical or emotional needs. The Act defines "care" to include "protection and guidance" (s. 70(1)), and deprivation of education, which is needed for a child's proper intellectual and even social development, can certainly come within the test, even if the home is otherwise extremely good. "Control" is defined to include discipline, but although that might often be needed in such cases, it was not in this. Despite the eventual outcome, however, the case shows clearly that the care and control test is not a formality.

Furthermore, it indicates that even when the grounds are proven the court has a discretion whether or not to make an order. The Crown Court was obviously worried about the damage involved in uprooting a happy and well-brought-up child from a good home and placing him in an institution with others from very different backgrounds. The Court of Appeal considered that this was outweighed by the need to secure a proper education, which in this case could be done in no other way. Where a baby with a loving mother has been subjected to minor violence by the father, the court's dilemma is even more obvious.

(iv) *The orders available*

Once the grounds have been proved, the court is specifically directed to consider the child's "general conduct, home surroundings, school record and medical history" (r. 20) before deciding what order, if any, ought to be made. If, as some thought in *S. v. Bedfordshire County Council* (above) the only order which would solve the problem will do the child more harm than good, then no order should be made. In most cases, however, the court will be faced with a choice of orders and will need some help in deciding which is best. Now would therefore seem the right time for it to consider the home surroundings report, although it will obviously be repeating much of the material relevant to proving the care or control test. The rules relating to these reports are the same in both care proceedings and criminal proceedings against juveniles and have already been discussed in the preceding chapter. The court may then choose between the following orders (s. 1(3)):

(*a*) An order requiring the child's parent or guardian to enter into a recognisance to take proper care of him and exercise proper control over him. A recognisance requires the parent to forfeit a specified sum, which cannot exceed £50, if he fails to take proper care or exercise proper control over the child for a specified period, which cannot exceed three years (s. 2(13)). The order can only be made if the parent consents (s. 1(5)(*a*)) and provides no more positive help for the child. Thus if proceedings are only brought or likely to succeed where they are necessary to secure the parents' co-operation, this order is only rarely likely to be effective.

(*b*) A supervision order. This order is one of the two principal protective measures available, yet with only minor variations, it is identical to the order which may be made in criminal proceedings against juvenile offenders. Most of the legal details have been discussed in the last chapter, but it is appropriate here to consider its effectiveness as a means of protecting children from abuse.

The child will normally remain where he is, although the court can require him to live with a named individual if that person agrees (s. 12(1)). This requirement is however more suitable for older juvenile offenders, for if a child needs to be removed from a home where he is at risk of abuse it will usually be better to make a care order, which will transfer full parental responsibility to the local authority. A supervision order merely places the child under the supervision of a local authority or, if he is 13 or over or if a probation officer is already working with another member of the family and the local authority asks that he should take this case too, of a probation officer (ss. 11 and 13(2)). This lasts for a specified period of up to three years, save that in care proceedings or on the discharge of a care order, a supervision order cannot last beyond the child's 18th birthday (s. 17). The supervisor's duty is to "advise, assist and befriend" the child (s. 14), but the order gives him remarkably little help in doing this, particularly if the parents remain unco-operative.

Thus although the order may contain the "prescribed provisions" for assisting the supervisor in carrying out his task (s. 18(2)(*b*)), only three have been prescribed (see Magistrates' Courts (Children and Young Persons) Rules 1970, Sched., form 44). These require the *child* to inform the supervisor at once of any change of address or employment, to keep in touch with the supervisor in accordance with his instructions including receiving visits at home if required, and (in care proceedings) to be medically examined in accordance with arrangements made by the supervisor. The position of the parents, who ought surely to be subject to some *express* obligations in these cases, is left totally unclear: presumably they cannot now object to the medical examination, but as occupiers of the child's home, can they refuse to let the supervisor in? If the supervisor becomes seriously concerned, his short-term solution is to seek a place of safety order or a warrant under section 40 of the 1933 Act (see 3 below), but failure to allow visiting of a supervised child is not automatically grounds for such a warrant as it is in the case of a private foster child. The only long-term solution is to apply for the supervision order to be discharged and replaced by a care order (s. 15(1)), which may well do the child more harm than good. The parents, on the other hand, acting on the child's behalf, can always ask for the supervision order to be completely discharged, although now if the supervisor does not oppose this the court will usually have to appoint a guardian ad litem for the child.

Furthermore, the order is quite unspecific about the supervisor's duties in such matters as regularity and frequency of visits, reporting back, and taking appropriate action should difficulties arise. This is in stark contrast to the Boarding-Out of Children Regulations (see Chapter 9), and some find it anomalous that the law provides so much protection for a child who has been boarded out with officially approved foster parents but so little for children who have been proved to be at some risk in their own homes (*Maria Colwell Inquiry Report*, 1974). Where the supervisor is a probation officer, some extra guidance is provided by the Probation Rules 1965, and no doubt in good local authorities the gap is filled by administrative directions. However, the Children Act 1975 (adding a new section 11A to the 1969 Act) allows the Secretary of State to make regulations with respect to the exercise by a local authority (not a probation officer) of its functions under a supervision order made in care proceedings (not in criminal proceedings) or on the discharge of a care order. No regulations have yet been made.

Finally, it should be noted that the court's power to sanction intermediate treatment or to order psychiatric treatment are the same as they are in criminal cases, where they are perhaps more likely to be used. Again, in care proceedings, the only sanction for lack of co-operation from either parents or child is a care order or compulsory admission to hospital.

(*c*) A care order. This places the child in the care of the local authority and thus obviously is the principal means of removing a child from a damaging home. It is also however the principal custodial treatment available for juvenile offenders, for the order has the same legal effect whether made in criminal or care proceedings. Furthermore, the responsibilities of the local authority while the child is in care are substantially the same as those towards children in care for any other reason, the principal difference being that he must remain there until he is 18 (or in some cases 19) unless the court subsequently decides to discharge the order. The legal details are thus dealt with in Chapter 9.

The most serious legal problem raised by care orders made in the context of child abuse is illustrated by the following comment:

"...when a child was taken into care the expectation was not that she would remain in care until the age of eighteen but that she would return to her own family when their circumstances had improved. It was put to us and we accept that there was a strong presumption that the magistrates would return a child to the parent once the parent's fitness was proved unless it could clearly be shown not to be in the best interests of the child" (*Maria Colwell Inquiry Report*, 1974).

In ordinary custody disputes between parents and non-parents (discussed in Chapter 10), the welfare of the child is now the first and paramount consideration and there is no presumption that the child should be returned when possible to his natural parents, although obviously their claims can be taken into account. It seems strange, therefore, that it should not prevail in disputes where the parents have already been shown to be inadequate. It is however difficult to argue that the "welfare principle" applies in care proceedings, partly because an order can only be made on certain defined grounds and partly because, once made, an order has the same effect as an order made in criminal proceedings; where the discharge of an order relating to a juvenile offender is in question, his welfare cannot always be the first and paramount consideration. The Children Act 1975 has attempted two solutions. A care order must not now be discharged if the child is under 18 and still in need of care or control, unless the court is satisfied that he will receive that care or control, whether through the making of a supervision order or in other ways (1969 Act, s. 21(2A)). Secondly, the provision of separate representation for the child, already in force where an application to discharge a care order is unopposed, may well result in a change of approach.

Once a care order has been made, there is no reason why the child should not be boarded-out with a view to adoption (or, eventually presumably, to custodianship). The order will prevent the parents removing the child if an application is made, and although it does not remove the need for the parents' agreement to adoption, the circumstances in which it was made may well supply grounds for dispensing with that agreement. Where a child has been seriously abused, it seems strange that a completely fresh start, and on terms which are known to be more likely to succeed than is long-term fostering, has rarely been attempted. Perhaps attitudes, both of social workers and courts, are now becoming more flexible (see *Kellmer Pringle*, 1972).

(*d*) A hospital order. This authorises the child's removal to and detention and treatment in a hospital, initially for a year but thereafter renewable virtually indefinitely by the hospital authorities. The patient can however be discharged at any time by the hospital and once he reaches 16 can apply periodically to an independent Mental Health Review Tribunal. The court has no further control over the matter.

The order can only be made if the requirements of section 60 of the Mental Health Act 1959 are met (1969 Act, s. 1(5)(*b*)). These include written or oral evidence from two doctors, one an approved specialist in mental disorder, that the child is suffering from mental illness, psychopathic disorder, subnormality or severe subnormality, and that his condition is of a nature or degree warranting his detention in hospital for treatment. The court must then, in all the circumstances, consider this the most suitable method of dealing with the case. A hospital order may be combined with a care order (1969 Act, s. 1(4)), although otherwise orders made in care proceedings cannot be combined. The object of this is no doubt to ensure that if the child is discharged from hospital the authority will remain responsible for his welfare, but the same result could be achieved by a care order, for the local authority could then arrange admission to hospital. A hospital order, however, may last for ever, while a care order is bound to end some time.

(*e*) A guardianship order. This places the child under the guardianship either of the local authority or of an individual approved by the authority. The guardian has the same powers over the patient's person as has the father of a child under 14 (see Chapter 1). The grounds are the same as for hospital orders, save that the child's condition must warrant guardianship rather than hospital treatment. Thus it is usually used for subnormal patients, whose condition cannot be cured by treatment but who require help and support if they are to live in the community. It is however hardly ever used, perhaps because the same result can be achieved by a care order or a supervision order, but it has the advantage that it can last into the child's adult life and that its renewal and discharge are taken out of the court's hands.

(v) *Appeals*

It is often thought that care proceedings are quasi-criminal indictments of the parents, and some of the rules already mentioned contribute to this impression. Juvenile courts are, after all, primarily designed for the trial and treatment of juvenile offenders (see Chapter 4). Furthermore, appeals are heard by the Crown Court, which is primarily a court for the trial of serious adult crime. Perhaps more seriously, it is only possible to appeal against the *making* of an order in care proceedings; the child can do so (s. 2(12)) and so can the local authority if it considers that it was not the right authority to be named because the child lives somewhere else (s. 21(5)); there is no right to appeal against the *refusal* of an order. Again, it is only possible to appeal against the dismissal of an application to discharge a care or supervision order or against certain variations of such orders (ss. 16(5) and 21(4)); it is not possible to appeal against the granting of such a discharge. This has caused serious problems in at least one reported case, although it may sometimes be possible to retain the child on a place of safety order or by making him a ward of court (*Re D.*, 1977). On a pure point of law, however, either side may appeal from juvenile court or Crown Court to the High Court.

3. *"Place of Safety" Powers*

In many cases the authorities may not yet be in a position to decide whether care proceedings can or should be brought, but may need to take emergency action to remove a child or to prevent his removal from hospital. There are several possibilities:

(i) *Section 28(1) of the Children and Young Persons Act 1969*

Any person (such as a hospital or local authority social worker) may apply under this subsection to a single magistrate, at any time and in any place. The applicant does not have to *prove* anything — he must simply satisfy the magistrate that *he* has *reasonable cause to believe* that any of primary conditions (*a*) to (*e*) (see 2(iii) above) is (or in the case of condition (*b*) would be found by an appropriate court to be) satisfied in respect of the child or young person in question (an alternative ground relates to child entertainers about to be taken abroad without a licence). The magistrate can then authorise the applicant to take the child to a place of safety, where he may be detained for 28 days or a shorter specified period. A place of safety is a community home which is either provided or controlled by a local authority, or any police station, or any hospital or surgery, or any other suitable place the occupier of which is willing temporarily to receive the child (Children and Young Persons Act, 1933, s. 107(1)). There is no need to tell the parents beforehand, but the detainer must, as soon as practicable afterwards, explain the reasons to the child and take such steps as are practicable to explain matters to his parent or guardian (1969 Act, s. 28(3)).

There is no right of appeal against the order (except by way of application to the High Court on a point of law), nor is there any power to renew it. But an application for an interim order may be made either to a court or to a justice before it expires (but if a single justice makes an interim order it can only last for 28 days from when the child was first detained) (s. 28(6)). The court or justice could however direct the child's immediate release, even though the place of safety order had not yet expired. It has thus been held that a *parent* may apply for an interim order under this subsection, even though he hopes that the application will fail and the child be sent home (*R*. v. *Lincoln* (*Kesteven*) *County Justice, ex. p. M.*, 1976).

That case raised fundamental questions about the use of place of safety orders. Three years earlier, care proceedings founded on conditions (*a*) and (*c*) had been taken in respect of a young girl, and a care order made. The father then applied for it to be discharged. After a lengthy hearing before a full court, he succeeded and a supervision order was substituted. The social workers were most concerned, but had no right of appeal. One of them therefore applied only three days later for a place of safety order under this subsection and succeeded. It is hardly surprising that the father felt aggrieved, but he again had no right of appeal. He therefore applied to the High

Court to quash the order on the ground that it was an abuse of the process of the court. This however the High Court refused to do, for the procedure was designed to allow emergency action where the social worker honestly and reasonably believed that the child was in danger, and there was no doubt that he did (the court did however allow the father to proceed with his application for an interim order, but the report naturally does not reveal whether he succeeded in securing the child's release).

It may seem surprising and disturbing that an emergency procedure with so few safeguards can thus be used to counteract a carefully argued decision of the full court, but this case was unusual. The full court had refused to hear evidence that the father had committed incest with two other daughters living at home, apparently on the ground that treatment of other children could only be relevant to primary condition (*b*). The High Court held that they should not have excluded this evidence, for it was clearly relevant to the case. The magistrate who made the place of safety order had of course heard the whole story. If the evidence had indeed been inadmissible the decision could have been different, and in most cases a social worker would find it hard to persuade a magistrate to differ from the full court on identical evidence. The real mischief, of course, lies in the deficiencies in the appeal system in care proceedings.

(ii) *Section 28(2) of the 1969 Act*

This allows a police officer to detain a child or young person if he has reasonable cause to believe that any of primary conditions (*a*) to (*d*) is (or in the case of condition (*b*) would be found by an appropriate court to be) satisfied. There is no need for any order; but after the child's detention, the case must be referred to a senior police officer, who after enquiries may either release the child or arrange for him to be detained in a place of safety (s. 28(4)). The detention cannot last longer than 8 days (s. 28(5)) and the child, and if practicable his parent or guardian, must be told of the reasons for it (s. 28(3)) and of a special right to apply immediately to a magistrate for release (s. 28(4) and (5)). If the child has to be detained longer before care proceedings can be started, an interim order (s. 28(6)) will be necessary.

(iii) *Section 40 of the Children and Young Persons Act 1933*

Sometimes a social worker or police officer may suspect abuse but be unable to gain entry to find the child. Under this section any person who is acting in the child's interests may apply to a single justice at any time or place. The applicant must show reasonable grounds to suspect that a child or young person has been or is being assaulted, ill-treated or neglected in a manner likely to cause unnecessary suffering or injury to health, or that any of the offences listed in Schedule 1 to the Act (which includes virtually every sexual or violent offence against a child as well as cruelty and neglect) has been or is being committed in respect of him. The justice may then issue a warrant empowering a *police officer* to enter specified premises, by force if need be, to search for the child, and if the suspicions are justified, to remove him to a place of safety (s. 40(1) and (3)); he may also be authorised to arrest any offenders at the same time (s. 40(2)). The applicant is allowed to go too, unless directed otherwise by the justice, who may also direct that a doctor may accompany them (s. 40(4)).

The child can be kept in the place of safety for any specified period up to 28 days (Children and Young Persons Act, 1963, s. 23(1)); thereafter he must be released or received into care under section 1 of the Children Act 1948 (if the grounds exist), or brought before a juvenile court, which can then make an interim order or release him (s. 23(5)). Unlike cases under section 28 however, this section makes it clear that the *local authority* must bring him to court (he need not be physically present if he is under five or prevented by illness or accident, s. 23(4)); hence the occupier of the place of safety, if not the local authority, must tell the authority of his reception as soon as possible (s. 23(3)).

Various things are automatically *presumed* to be reasonable cause for the suspicions required to get a warrant. These include refusal to allow the local authority to visit a privately-fostered child, or to inspect a private foster home, under the Children Act 1958; equivalent refusals in the case of children protected under the Adoption Act 1958 and refusal to allow the DHSS to inspect community homes, voluntary homes, places where children in care are accommodated, places where children are boarded-out by voluntary organisations, or places where private foster children or protected children are accommodated (Children and Young Persons Act 1969, s. 58). The presumption does *not* however apply to refusal to allow visiting or removal by the local authority or voluntary organisation of a child boarded out by them, or to refusal to allow visiting of a child under a supervision order, although obviously a warrant may be obtainable if reasonable suspicion can be shown. Removal is of course only possible if the suspicions prove well-founded after entry has been gained.

(iv) *Section 7 of the Children Act 1958*

This contains an independent and wider power to seek removal of a private foster child from unsuitable surroundings and take him to a place of safety. It has already been discussed in Chapter 2.

(v) *Section 43 of the Adoption Act 1958*

This contains an independent power to seek removal of a child who is a "protected" child under the Adoption Act 1958. It is in almost identical terms to the power under the Children Act 1958.

It should not be forgotten that social workers have no general power to enter other people's property without their consent. They must have a specific power which applies to the particular case (for example, a foster child or protected child); otherwise they may need a warrant under section 40 above so that a policeman can force his way in.

4. *What to Do?*

Despite the diversity of legal remedies available, child abuse presents extraordinary problems to the practitioner, not least because so many different professionals with varying outlooks may be involved. An example may serve to highlight some of these.

A two-month-old baby is brought to the casualty department by his 17-year-old mother and 19-year-old father, who
are not married to one another because of her parents'
opposition. The baby has bruises and minor scratches on his
face, and his mother says that she noticed them when she got
home from shopping having left the baby with his father. The
father says that the baby must have pulled himself up on a
rattle stretched across his cot and hurt himself then. The
bruises however seem more consistent with a blow to the face
with the open hand. The baby is well nourished and normally
developed, and the mother seems to look after him very well
while he is in hospital. The father is of low intelligence,
emotionally unstable, with a minor criminal record for
dishonesty, and is currently on probation. He has not worked
for some time and they live on supplementary benefit in a
one-roomed flat. The mother does not know what to think
about the incident and is pulled by conflicting loyalties to the
father, baby and her parents.

The first step recommended in all cases of reasonable
suspicion of non-accidental injury (*DHSS circular*, 1974) is to
admit the child to hospital. Here this is no problem if the
mother agrees, for the father will have no right to remove the
baby. If any difficulty is anticipated, a place of safety order
under section 28(1) should be easy to obtain. Where the
suspicions are less firm than here, any professional concerned
is advised to discuss the case with a senior colleague, to decide
whether the risk of *not* arranging hospital admission can be
taken and whether in any event a case conference should be
called. The next step is to call a case conference. This should
include the people with statutory responsibilities for the child,
those concerned with services likely to be relevant, and those
with helpful information about the child and his family. In
this case it is likely to involve the responsible hospital doctor,
the hospital social worker, a senior social worker from the local
authority, an area social worker with knowledge of the family,
the father's probation officer, the health visitor, the G.P., the
NSPCC if they were involved (in some places case conferences
are arranged through the NSPCC), and anyone else who may
be able to help (if this were a school-child, the teachers and
education welfare officer would also be invited). In many

cases the police will also send a representative.

The object of getting these people together is to pool information and ideas, to make sure nothing is overlooked or dismissed, to encourage collective decisions and to discourage inconsistent and ill-planned unilateral action. But what is such a case conference to do?

In the first place, as here, there is often considerable doubt about whether non-accidental injury can be proved. Babies cannot, and older children often will not, say what has happened to them. Unless the parents admit it, expert evidence will often be necessary, along with photographs and other circumstantial material. It is perhaps unfortunate that legal advisers seem rarely to be called in at the beginning, for doctors and social workers are naturally reluctant to proceed unless they are fairly sure of success: not only is hostile cross-examination to be feared, but much worse are the consequences for their relationship with clients and their chances of helping in the future should legal proceedings fail. All too often, the readier the parents are to admit it, the readier is case conference to take legal action, which is surely not an acceptable deciding factor.

But when should legal action be taken? Prosecution is a matter for the police, and doctors and social workers are often reluctant to involve the police, because they see prosecution as an inappropriate and inefficient response. The criminal law is aimed at deterring the potential offender in advance, deterring the actual offender from doing it again, and marking the extent of society's disapproval. Those involved with child abuse tend to be very conscious of the many and intolerable stresses which so often lie behind it (*Renvoize*, 1974; *Carter*, 1974). These not only make nonsense of any theory of deterrence based on an expectation of rational behaviour in a crisis, but also supply strong moral mitigation against retribution. However, it is surely necessary to retain the notion that child abuse is a crime (and it is usually several crimes), not only to deter the more rational but also to make it clear that society does not regard it as acceptable behaviour. And if it is a crime, it is often difficult to justify treating it any differently from many other offences where deterrence may be just as unrealistic and mitigation just as obvious.

The justification for a humane and discriminating prosecution policy may however be found in the interests of the child himself. He will not be helped if parents are deterred from confessing their difficulties by a fear of punishment, nor if that punishment destroys the hope of rehabilitating a *viable* family unit. The police and the courts are coming to realise this, and the police have a justifiable grievance if they are not allowed to contribute towards the decision-making process.

The question of care proceedings is even more difficult. To take this baby away is the only sure means of preventing the injury happening again, for the mother cannot be forced to leave the father. Yet this will be to deprive him of the care of a good and loving mother, and no social worker can guarantee that the substitute care provided will be anything like as good. If, as happened with Maria Colwell, that care is good but the mother later asks for her child back, the social workers are not only faced with the problem of knowing what the court's attitude towards discharging the order will be, but also with knowing when to prefer substitute care to that of the natural parents. This is one of the most hotly debated subjects in the whole of social work, both theoretically and in individual cases (see *Howells*, 1974). Even if it is accepted that good substitute parenting is better than bad natural parenting, how can one distinguish the completely unsatisfactory home from the one which could function quite well with better housing, better day-care facilities and adequate casework support? The general public is only too ready to criticise social workers, rarely understanding the extent of their difficulties and sometimes even forgetting that it is after all the child abusers who must bear the primary responsibility. On the other hand, social workers themselves may sometimes be unreasonably optimistic about the practical possibilities of prevention and rehabilitation, and they are not helped by the ambiguous position in which the law places them.

Part III
Anomalous Families

6 Unmarried Parents

The institution of marriage may well have been devised in early societies in order to recognise and establish the relationship between a father and his children (*Mair*, 1971). A man may derive spiritual, emotional and material advantages from having children, but whereas motherhood may easily be proved, fatherhood may not. A formal ceremony between man and woman, after which it is assumed that any children she may have are his, is the simplest method of establishing a link. Whatever the origin of the institution, however, it seems virtually inevitable that any legal system which recognises and promotes marriage must make some distinction between children who are born within it and those who are born outside it. It seems equally inevitable that that distinction will centre round the relationship between father and child. However, a system which must *differentiate* between legitimate and illegitimate need not necessarily *discriminate* against the latter, and English law is gradually coming to appreciate this. For many of the children, the legal disadvantages of illegitimacy will pale into insignificance beside the economic and social disadvantages of being brought up in a one-parent family; but the idea of positive legal discrimination in their favour in order to compensate for these has not yet taken shape.

1. *Legitimacy and Illegitimacy*

In 1973, some 8.6 per cent of live births were registered as illegitimate. The proportion has been rising steadily since the mid-50s, although there has been a levelling-off since 1967, when it reached 8.4 per cent. Society's tolerance both of extra-marital sexual relationships and of illegitimacy itself has increased considerably, and with the rise of marriage breakdown, so has the proportion of women "at risk". Knowledge and practice of contraception is by no means as widespread as might be expected (*Bones*, 1973), and there are still psychological barriers for many unmarried women, for some will be reluctant to admit that it might be necessary and others may subconsciously be seeking pregnancy (*Pochin*, 1969). The levelling-off may however be attributable in part to the Abortion Act 1967, although as many as 40-45 per cent of abortions are carried out upon married women. It remains to be seen what effect the recently-established free family planning service will have.

But which children does the law label "illegitimate"? The answer is rather more complicated than might be thought, for it depends upon whom the law will label "legitimate."

(i) *Legitimacy at common law*

A child is legitimate if his mother and father were married to one another either at the time of his conception *or* at the time of his birth. Thus in 1973 there were roughly twice as many extra-marital conceptions as there were illegitimate births. However, while the proportion of extra-marital conceptions has itself been rising steadily, the proportion of those where the parents decide to marry before the birth has been falling equally steadily. The great increase in illegitimacy during the War may have been caused, at least in part, by the parents' being unable to marry in time or at all, but no such external cause now operates. It must be that fewer couples are seeing the hasty marriage as the best solution.

By "mother" and "father," the law here means the woman and man biologically responsible for the child's conception and birth. Thus a child born as a result of artificial insemination from a donor other than the mother's husband is technically illegitimate, and unless they adopt the child, the husband will only have the limited status of a step-father, however much he wanted the event to take place. In this particular case, legislation to depart from the principle of genetic relationship might be desirable, for in practice the presumption of legitimacy must mean that it is departed from in many less deserving cases.

(ii) *The presumption of legitimacy*

The simple rules above are considerably modified in practice because the law *presumes* that certain children are legitimate unless the contrary is proved. Thus every child born to a married woman is assumed to be her husband's child. This applies even though the child must have been conceived before the marriage, or where the marriage has ended by death or divorce within the normal period of gestation before the birth. Thus the presumptions can conflict if a woman who was widowed or divorced less than nine months before the birth has remarried while pregnant; a court would probably choose the most likely father (*Re Overbury*, 1955), but some might suggest that the law should still presume that she did *not* commit adultery? The presumption does not arise if at the time of conception the husband and wife were living apart under a court order which officially released them from their duty to live together; but the only such orders, apart of course from divorce after which they are no longer husband and wife anyway, are a decree of judicial separation and a magistrates' court order containing a "non-cohabitation clause"; mothers who are informally separated may therefore find that the court applies the presumption when they try to have their illegitimate children adopted without telling the absent husband.

The presumption has always been rebuttable, but the common law required very strong proof to rebut it, for the courts shrank from exposing both the child and his mother to the severe legal and social disabilities of illegitimacy and adultery. Thus they reached some extraordinarily artificial decisions, for even in 1949 the Court of Appeal refused to find a wife guilty of adultery although her child had been born 349 days after her husband had left on military service (*Hadlum* v. *Hadlum*). Nowadays, however, the consequences of illegitimacy and adultery are much less severe, and it may be in no one's interests to foist a spurious child upon an unwilling and incredulous husband. Thus the Family Law Reform Act 1969 now provides that the presumption may be rebutted by evidence which shows that it is "more probable than not" that the child is illegitimate (s. 26).

There are two types of rebutting evidence. One seeks to show that the husband and wife did not or could not have intercourse at the relevant time (although this presents the courts with much difficulty about identifying the relevant time). The other seeks to show that even if they may have had intercourse, the child was not the product of that intercourse. The usual way of doing this is now by blood tests, for not only are they very reliable for certain purposes, but the court now has power to direct the parties to co-operate. The whole subject of blood tests will be considered under affiliation proceedings (see 3(i) below), but it should be noted that anyone who is seeking relief from a court relying on the presumption of legitimacy may be denied that relief if he refuses to undergo a blood test, even though there is no evidence to rebut the presumption. The courts may also be prepared to admit other evidence of physical characteristics, notably of course of race, but they do not have power to *order* such "anthropological" tests.

Even though the presumption may now more easily be rebutted in court proceedings, it still applies to the great majority of children born to married women, and must result in many children who are biologically illegitimate being treated as legally legitimate. Apart from humanity, the reason is severely practical and already stated: maternity and marriage are easy to prove, whereas paternity is not.

(iii) *Defective marriages*

Logically, if the parents' marriage is invalid, the children should be illegitimate, but statute has been kinder. Some defects (principally inability or wilful refusal to consummate a marriage) merely render a marriage voidable, so that it remains valid unless and until one of the parties obtains a decree annulling it. Nowadays the children of such a marriage remain legitimate despite the decree (Matrimonial Causes Act 1973, s. 16, also Sched. 1, para. 12). Other defects, however (principally that one party was already married or was under 16) render a marriage void, so that it may be disregarded without any court proceedings. Logically, of course, any children should be illegitimate, but since 1959 any such child (whether born before or after that date) has been regarded as legitimate, provided that at the time of the act of intercourse leading to his conception, or at the marriage if it was later, *either* or both of the parents *reasonably* believed that the marriage was valid (Legitimacy Act 1976, s. 1; the father must have been domiciled in England at the date of birth). There will obviously be problems for a child who is trying to establish his legitimacy on the basis of what his parents thought before he was born, particularly as this may well be for succession purposes after the parent in question has died. Nor is it yet decided whether a genuine mistake about the *law* can be "reasonable." Luckily, the section will be less important now that the succession rights of illegitimate children have been improved (see 4 below), and for succession purposes it only applies to dispositions of property taking place after 1959. One very odd feature, however, is that it *can* apply to successions to peerages and other titles, whereas legitimation cannot.

(iv) *Legitimation*

The common law insisted that the marriage must take place before the birth; hence the need to get out the shot-gun. However, since 1926 a child has been regarded as legitimated if his parents marry after his birth, and since 1959 this has been so even though his parents could not have married when he was born because one was at the time validly married to someone else (such cases were originally excepted because it was thought that to allow them would encourage adultery). The parents should then re-register the birth as though the child had been born legitimate, and unless the husband was originally registered as the father or there has been an affiliation order or declaration of legitimacy, he should be there at re-registration to confirm his paternity (see Legitimacy Act 1976, ss. 2, 3 and 9). If an illegitimate child has been adopted by his mother or father alone, he can still be legitimated and they may apply for the adoption order to be revoked.

Legitimation does not allow succession to titles and its effects upon other succession and property rights are complicated. For dispositions after the end of 1969, illegitimate children have much-improved rights; but once legitimated, a child will have the more extensive succession rights of a legitimate child; however, for dispositions before January 1, 1976, these improved rights only apply if the legitimation took place *before* the disposition; for later dispositions it does not matter when the legitimation took place, except that if the recipient's date of birth is important, he is taken to have been born on the date of the legitimation, unless he was already entitled to the property as an illegitimate child (Legitimacy Act 1976, ss. 5, 6, 10(1) and Sched. 1).

Thus a legitimated child is almost, but not quite, in the position of one whose parents married before he was born. It is not possible to estimate the proportion of illegitimate children who are subsequently legitimated, for although the National Child Development Study found that by the age of seven as many as 27 per cent. of their illegitimate children were still living with *both* natural parents (*Crellin, Kellmer Pringle and West*, 1971), most will probably have been living in stable extra-marital unions. Indeed, one of the principal reasons advanced for allowing an "innocent" spouse to be divorced against her will after five years of separation was the supposed existence of many children who might then be legitimated (*Law Commission*, 1966). There seems however to have been no dramatic increase in legitimations since this was introduced.

2. *The Illegitimate Child and his Parents*

The legitimate child benefits both directly and indirectly from his parents' marriage. From the moment of his birth, the identity of his father is known and he can enjoy an automatic legal relationship, involving both rights and responsibilities, with both his parents. If the relationship between his parents breaks down, his welfare must be specifically considered if they are to get a divorce, and financial provision can be ordered both for him and for the parent who is looking after him. The illegitimate child has to prove who his father is, has no automatic relationship with him, and cannot benefit from any procedures regulating his parents' legal relationship, for they have none. Indeed, the common law originally went further and held that a child born outside the legally approved family unit was "nobody's child" and thus scarcely enjoyed a legal relationship with his mother. However, case law gradually accorded her similar rights of custody and upbringing to those of the father of a legitimate child; this is now confirmed by statute, which provides that unless and until a court order or resolution deprives her, the mother has the parental rights and duties exclusively (Children Act 1975, s. 85(7)). This section will therefore deal with the consequences of that approach for the upbringing of the child, including the registration of his birth, his custody, reception into care, and possible adoption, while later sections will deal with the family's financial problems and with the child's property and succession rights.

(i) *Registering the birth*

Naming the father on the registration of the child's birth has no effect as such upon their legal relationship, but it is most valuable evidence of paternity for purposes such as affiliation or succession. It is all the more valuable because a child cannot go to court and seek a binding declaration of his paternity (whereas it is possible to obtain a conclusive declaration of *legitimacy*), nor has the father any other means of publicly acknowledging his child, as many might wish to do. The only other possibility is a finding in affiliation proceedings and these have many limitations (see 3(i) below).

It is only possible to register or re-register the birth so as to show the father's name in three circumstances: (i) at the joint request of mother and father; (ii) at the request of the mother, if she declares that he is the father and produces a statutory declaration from him that this is so; or (iii) (when section 93 of the Children Act 1975 is in force) at the request of the mother, on production of an affiliation order naming him (and, if the child is over 16, the child's written consent) (Births and Deaths Registration Act 1953, s.10). Thus the mother cannot register the father's name without his co-operation or an affiliation order, but equally the father cannot do so without her co-operation.

A person registering a birth has to state the surname by which it is intended that the child should be known. The choice is for the mother, for she has parental rights. She will usually choose her own, but there is nothing to prevent her using the father's or indeed any name she wishes. Nor is there anything to prevent her or the child changing it later. Although a statutory declaration or deed poll is useful evidence of this, it is not essential. In English law you can call yourself what you like.

(ii) *Custody and related matters*

The National Child Development Study (of all children born in one week in 1958) found that only 23 per cent. of the illegitimate children were placed with strangers for adoption. The great majority remained with their mothers, and by the age of seven, no less than 27 per cent. were still living with *both* natural parents (*Crellin, Kellmer Pringle and West*, 1971); this lends support to earlier findings (reported by *Wimperis*, 1960), that as many as a third of illegitimate children were born to relatively stable extra-marital unions. Nevertheless, whatever the family situation, the mother is the one with the right to take her baby home from hospital, to decide what education and religious upbringing he should have, to decide what medical treatment he should be given, whether he should go abroad, and later on whether he can marry before the age of 18; she alone can appoint a guardian for him in her will. The father, even if he is living with them, has no automatic rights in these matters, although as a person with actual custody he may incur criminal liability for neglect or ill-treatment, or for failing to educate the child properly.

Until 1959, the only thing that a father could do to try and obtain some voice in his child's upbringing was to make him a ward of court. This cumbersome and expensive procedure is of course open to anyone who is genuinely concerned about a child's welfare, although the courts may have been prepared to give the natural father's wishes some special consideration (see *Re Aster*, 1955). The Legitimacy Act 1959 made a significant step forward by allowing the father of an illegitimate child to apply as an ordinary parent for custody or access under what is now the Guardianship of Minors Act 1971 (ss. 9 and 14). The courts' procedure and powers have already been discussed in Chapter 3.

Important though this development was, it should not be over-estimated. The father still has no rights unless and until the court decides to give him some (and if the mother has already placed the child for adoption, this may be too late). If he is unsuccessful in his application, the fact that he was interested enough to make it has no effect on his relationship with the child. In particular, the court has no power under the Guardianship of Minors Act to order him to make payments either to the mother or to the child; the mother must still bring affiliation proceedings.

In deciding the case, the welfare of the child is the first and paramount consideration, but it may be that the mother's wishes are still entitled to more weight than the father's as a secondary consideration. Where the mother is out of the picture, however, the courts may take the benefits of blood relationship into account in deciding what is best for the child (see *Re C.(M.A.)*, discussed under (iv) below). Nevertheless there is an impression that the father of an illegitimate child has an uphill struggle, even if he is only asking for access, which would be granted almost automatically to the father of a legitimate child (see *Barber*, 1975). If this impression is accurate, and this is hard to tell, not only does it reflect a stereotype of the putative father as a man with little or no concern for the offspring of a casual relationship, despite all the evidence that this is often far from true (see for example, *Wimperis*, 1960, *Pochin*, 1969, *Barber*, 1975); it is also likely to reinforce it.

A custody order will give the father several additional rights. He (and not the mother) will be able to decide whether the child can marry before 18. He (as well as the mother) will be able to appoint a guardian to act in the event of his death. Its effects on children in care and upon adoption are particularly important and are discussed below.

(iii) *Children in care*

Many mothers who decide to keep their children have a great deal of difficulty in doing so. The National Child Development Study found that by the age of seven one in nine of their illegitimate children who had stayed with their mothers had had to go into care at some time, compared with one in 50 of the whole cohort (*Crellin, Kellmer Pringle and West*, 1971).

Here again, unless there is a custody order in favour of the father, the mother is the sole "parent" for the purposes of the Children Act 1948 (s. 59(1)). The father has no right to remove the child whom she has placed in care, although he is included in the definition of "relative," so that the authority could allow him to take the child (either under section 1(3) or under section 13(2)) if it wished. If however he obtains a custody order, he becomes the "parent" to the exclusion of the mother (s.6(2)), and he would have the right to remove the child unless a section 2 resolution could be passed on his account.

In *R.* v. *Oxford Justices, ex p. H.* (1975) the mother had placed the child in care and a section 2 resolution had been passed on account of her mental illness. It was held that this did not affect the father's right to apply to a court for custody, and that the magistrates should at least hear his application and decide what would be best for the child. In the earlier case of *Re K.* (1972), however, the High Court upheld the magistrates' refusal to make an *access* order in the father's favour, in similar circumstances: not because they had no power to hear the application, but because if the child was to remain in care it was no doubt right to leave such matters to the discretion of the authority in which parental rights were vested by statute (see further in Chapter 9 on the relationship between local authorities and the courts).

(iv) *Adoption*

Adoption as a whole is discussed in Chapter 11, but the position of the putative father is particularly relevant here. In adoption, the child's welfare is the first but not the paramount consideration, for the parents' agreement to the loss of all relationship with the child is necessary unless it can be dispensed with on one of the specified grounds. The general principle however is that the father of an illegitimate child is *not* a "parent" and so his agreement is not needed (*Re M.*, 1955). To this there is now one exception, for his agreement, in addition to that of the mother, is needed if he has obtained a custody order (Children Act 1975, Sched. 3, para. 39(d)).

The present rules also provide that if he is liable by virtue of an affiliation order or even a private agreement to contribute to the maintenance of the child, he must be made a respondent to the application so that his views can be heard (Adoption (County Court) Rules 1976, r. 4(2)(e)). Furthermore, if the guardian ad litem in the course of his enquiries hears of anyone claiming to be the father who wishes to be heard he must immediately inform the court (Sched. 2, para. 10), which can then decide whether he ought to be made a respondent (r. 4(3). The guardian however does not have to take positive steps to seek the father out.

A right to be heard is not the same as a right to refuse consent; it will be little use unless the father has a positive alternative to offer the court. Thus some fathers opposing adoption apply for custody or make the child a ward of court. If this is done the courts have said that both applications should be heard together, so that a proper choice of alternatives can be made. There is no problem about this in the High Court or county court, but as adoptions are still heard by magistrates in the juvenile court, while custody is heard in the domestic court, such cases may have to be transferred to the High Court.

The problem arises in three quite different contexts. If the mother has decided to place the baby with strangers for adoption at an early age, the father may have difficulty in preventing her. Once placement has happened, the court's choice will be between prospective adopters, who are no doubt suitable in every way and have been caring for the child from an early age, and the putative father, who is related to the child by blood but has had no opportunity of forming an emotional relationship with him, and is unlikely to have either such a good home or such a good mother-substitute to offer. Thus in most cases the child's welfare will demand that he is adopted and the father is virtually powerless to prevent it (see *Re Adoption Application 41/61*, 1963, and *Re O.*, 1965).

However, in one highly unusual and controversial case (*Re C. (M.A.)*, 1966) with just those facts, the father was successful. He had hoped to marry the mother but she had changed her mind and excluded him from all arrangements for the child. He was now reconciled with his wife, who made an excellent impression on the judge, and they could offer a good home. The judge took account of the risks of moving a toddler from the only home he had ever known, but he also took account of the psychological help which knowledge of a blood relationship can give to the formation of attachments. Thus, despite criticism that it gave undue weight to the "blood-tie," the case may have been an important step in the recognition of the relationship between father and illegitimate child.

A similar trend appears in the very different case of an adoption application by the mother and the step-father she has now married. To become the legitimate child of two parents still offers a child solid advantages of which the courts are well aware (*F. v. S.*, 1973). If the putative father corresponds to stereotype and is out of the picture, there can be no doubt of this. In some cases, however, his relationship with the mother was as stable as many marriages, and his relationship with the child is still as good as any other father's. He may not want or be able to offer an alternative home, but his objections to the total severance of ties could be as valid as those of a "legitimate" father (and the courts are increasingly reluctant to allow step-parent adoptions of legitimate children). Nevertheless, in 1968 one father's objections were seen as frivolous compared with the advantages of wiping out the "stigma of bastardy" and enabling the child to become "so far as possible" a respectable member of society (*Re E.(P.)*). Nowadays, the courts have modified both their language and their attitude. In two cases, albeit as an exceptional measure, they have made access by the putative father a condition of granting the adoption (*Re J.*, 1973; *Re S.*, 1976); and when custodianship is introduced, the courts will be specifically encouraged to consider it as an alternative to adoptions by step-parents, even though the child may thus remain illegitimate; this would seem a less artificial solution than an adoption with an access condition for those cases where there are grounds for preserving the links with the natural father.

Different again is adoption by the mother on her own. Such adoptions give the child slightly better succession rights from the mother's family, although they will deprive the child of any succession rights from the father. They are also the only means whereby an illegitimate child born to an English mother abroad can obtain United Kingdom citizenship; citizenship is normally acquired either by being born here, or by descent from a United Kingdom father; it cannot be acquired by descent from a United Kingdom mother, but it can be acquired by being adopted here by a United Kingdom adopter. Apart from this, however, the merits of such sole adoptions are highly questionable; the mother can no longer obtain or retain the benefit of an affiliation order, and so the child is deprived of all relationship with his father for no particular purpose. Thus the courts are now prohibited from granting an adoption on the sole application of the child's mother or father, unless the other natural "parent" is dead or cannot be found or there is some other special reason to exclude him (Children Act 1975, s. 11(3)); although the word "parent" does not normally include the putative father of an illegitimate child, this provision was clearly designed with him in mind and it is to be hoped that the courts will so construe it.

3. *Money*

Of all the problems facing the mother who decides to bring up her baby on her own, money is probably the most serious. All one-parent families are likely to be materially less well-off than their two-parent counterparts, but mothers of illegitimate children are the least well-off of this already disadvantaged group (*Finer Report*, 1974; *Ferri*, 1976). Unlike divorced and separated mothers, they cannot turn to the father for support for themselves as well as the child. Unlike widows, they cannot claim a pension from the state or their husband's employers. Yet they are more likely than either to be left unsupported at the very time when they are unable to support themselves because the baby is so young.

The law does less than it could to help. The *only* ways in which a father can be made to maintain his illegitimate child are by agreement or by affiliation proceedings, which compare very unfavourably with the procedures for obtaining financial provision for children of broken marriages (and these incidentally include illegitimate "children of the family," so that it may be easier to obtain more substantial provision from

the child's step-father than from his natural father).
Affiliation proceedings, maintenance agreements and state
benefits will be considered in turn.

(i) *Affiliation proceedings*

These are descended from procedures designed to enable
the poor law authorities to recoup their expenditure on
illegitimate children (as indeed they still are), and were only
extended to the mother by the Poor Law Amendment Act
1844. Their ancestry is still clearly apparent.

(a) The court

Proceedings can only be brought in the magistrates' court,
which is principally concerned with petty crime, rather than in
the High Court or the county court which are generally
regarded as more satisfactory family tribunals. They are
"domestic" proceedings and thus are heard in private with
limitations on press reporting (which is extremely rare), but
appeals lie to the predominantly criminal Crown Court,
whereas other domestic appeals go to the Family Division of
the High Court.

(b) The applicant

In most cases, proceedings must be brought by the mother
and she is often reluctant to do so. She may be deterred by
embarrassment at what can still be an unpleasant and even
humiliating experience, or by a desire to save the father from
similar embarrassment, or by a wish to have nothing more to
do with him, or by the difficulties of proof, or by the
knowledge that if she is on supplementary benefit the order
will be of no personal benefit to them even if it is paid. Still less
will she wish to apply if someone else is looking after the child.
Thus it is hardly surprising that only a small proportion of
mothers who keep their babies do apply.

Furthermore, the mother can only apply if she is a "single
woman" at the time of the application (Affiliation Proceedings
Act 1957, s. 1) or was one at the time of the birth (Legitimacy
Act 1959, s. 4). "Single woman" covers not only the

unmarried, widowed or divorced woman, but also the married woman who is separated from her husband and has lost her *common law* right to be maintained by him (as she almost invariably will have done, having committed adultery to have the child) (*Whitton* v. *Garner*, 1965). There seems no good reason why an illegitimate child should ever be deprived of the chance of his father's support, whatever his mother's marital status.

If the mother does not herself obtain an order, the Supplementary Benefits Commission may bring proceedings if it has paid benefit for the support of the child (Supplementary Benefits Act 1976, s. 19). Similarly, a local authority may bring proceedings if the child is in voluntary or compulsory care (Children Act 1948, s. 26) or provided with Part III accommodation (National Assistance Act 1948, s. 44). In each case, it does not matter whether the mother is a "single woman," or even that she herself has tried to get an order and failed. Apart from these provisions, anyone else who is looking after the child cannot apply for an order and thus must rely on the mother to do so. However, when the custodianship procedure is in force, a custodian who is not married to the child's mother will be able to apply for an order provided that the mother has not already obtained one (Children Act 1975, s. 45). This will of course depend upon a custodianship order's having been made, and this itself will take time, but it will not matter whether the mother is a "single woman."

If, however, the mother has obtained an order, it is possible for it to be varied to make the money payable to some other person or authority (see (e) below).

(c) Time limits

Not only will the child usually be dependent on his mother's willingness to apply; he must also rely on her to do it in time, which is normally either before the birth or within three years of it. However, if the defendant made payments in cash or kind for the child within three years of the birth, she may apply at any time, and if he ceased to live in England within three years of the birth she may apply within 12 months of his return (1957 Act, s. 2, as amended by the Affiliation

Proceedings (Amendment) Act 1972, s. 2). There seems little
excuse for these rigid rules, especially when blood tests have at
least a 72 per cent. chance of excluding someone wrongly
accused of fatherhood. Furthermore, the other applicants may
be able to succeed even though the mother would be out of
time. The SBC can apply within three years of paying benefit,
the local authority within three years of the child going into
care, and the custodian within three years of the custodianship
order. In each case the child could be well over three, although
it may be that an order must be obtained before he is 13 (see
(e) below).

(d) Proof

The law is not prepared to accept a woman's word as to who
is the father of her child; if she gives evidence in support of any
application, her evidence must be corroborated, not in full but
at least in some "material particular" (Affiliation Proceedings
Act 1957, s.4). The case law on corroboration is extensive, but
it usually takes one of three forms.

The father may have admitted his paternity, either in court
or to some third party. A social worker to whom such an
admission has been made may be called upon to give evidence,
unless the admission was specifically made in the course of
negotiations towards a settlement of the mother's claim. The
worker may therefore feel obliged to tread warily and warn the
alleged father of the possible consequences of telling her
anything (see *Pochin*, 1969). An admission can be express, for
example by allowing himself to be registered as the father, or
by implication from conduct, such as paying money (in
Graham v. *Tupper*, 1965, it was held, just, to be corroboration
that, when asked by a friend how the mother was, the
defendant replied that she had not yet "got rid of it"). An
admission that he has had intercourse with the mother at all
may be sufficient to corroborate her evidence in some
"material particular" (*Simpson* v. *Collinson*, 1964).

Alternatively there may be circumstantial evidence that they
had intercourse at the relevant time. Evidence of opportunity
to do so is not enough, for it must be shown that they were
likely to take advantage of such an opportunity; some

opportunities are more likely to be taken advantage of than others.

Last, there may be blood tests. Indeed the defendant who strenuously denies his paternity is just as likely to want a blood test as is the woman who is seeking for corroboration. Blood test evidence depends upon the fact that certain characteristics in blood are transmitted from one generation to another by well-established principles; it is thus possible to say that a particular man *could not* have had a child with this child's sort of blood by a woman with the complainant's sort of blood. The discovery of more and more genetically transmitted blood characteristics (apart from the well-known blood groups) has meant that the chances of *excluding* a particular man may be as high as 72 per cent. (see *Dodd*, 1969). A blood test cannot yet positively establish that a particular man is the father, but it can help to do so, either by excluding other possible candidates, or by showing that only a small proportion of men, of whom the defendant is one, could be the father.

It is always possible for the parties and the person with parental rights over the child to agree that blood tests should be taken, but the Family Law Reform Act 1969 now provides that the court can *direct* this to be done. This applies not only in affiliation cases but in *any* civil case in which paternity of a child falls to be determined (divorce and matrimonial proceedings alleging adultery are the most obvious examples, but it may also be relevant in a succession case provided that it is not necessary to test the deceased's blood). Blood samples may be directed to be taken from the child, his mother, and any party to the proceedings who is alleged to be the father, but not from anyone else (s.20(1)). The court simply directs; the person concerned, or if he is a child under 16 the person who has care and control of him, may object (s.21). If someone does object, however, the court may draw such inferences from this as seem proper (s.23), and no doubt they will be unfavourable. The tests are carried out by independent analysts under regulations made by the Secretary of State (s.22), but the costs are payable by the parties (or the legal aid fund).

The court has a discretion as to whether to direct a blood test. In an affiliation case there can be no reason to refuse a direction, but in other cases where the result may be to "bastardise" a child presumed to be legitimate, doubts have been expressed as to whether this is in his best interests. The view of the House of Lords before the Act was that in general it was better that the truth be known: he will scarcely be helped if his mother's husband insists on repudiating him and the opportunity of establishing his true parentage is lost (see *S.* v. *S.*, 1972).

Finally, however, corroboration is only necessary if the mother herself gives evidence, although if she does not, some other means of proving paternity will be needed. Since 1972, she is no longer required to give evidence, and although this change was designed for cases where she had died before the hearing, it will also help other applicants who are unable to secure her co-operation. If she herself is applying, but refuses to give evidence, the court would no doubt draw the obvious conclusion.

(e) The order

The court can only order the father to pay the expenses incidental to the child's birth, the funeral expenses of a child who has died, and a weekly sum for the child's maintenance and education (1957 Act, s. 4(2)). It has recently been held that the baby's layette is included in the expenses incidental to his birth, but apart from this there is no power to order a lump sum or other capital provision, such as housing, for the child. Yet many mothers might welcome this rather than periodical payments, which are notoriously difficult to enforce; and apart from the soluble problem that affiliation proceedings can only take place in the magistrates' courts, there seems no good reason why the courts' powers should not be as extensive as those to award financial provision on divorce.

In one respect, however, the illegitimate child is always likely to be at a disadvantage, for apart from the vague reference to the expenses incidental to the birth, there is no power to award maintenance for the mother herself. Since 1968, there has been no upper limit on the weekly amount which magistrates may order for the child, and it could be that they are entitled to take into account the mother's increased expenses and loss of earnings, but there is no indication that they do so. Most orders are extremely low, apparently lower than those for legitimate children (*McGregor, Blom-Cooper and Gibson*, 1970); no doubt defendants are usually both younger and poorer, and all are aware that the order will usually benefit the Supplementary Benefits Commission rather than mother or child.

Payments need not be made after the child reaches 13 unless the court directs that they should continue (1957 Act, s. 6); this is almost invariably done, but the provision may indicate that an order cannot be made for the first time after the child has reached 13. The order normally ceases at the age of 16, but may be continued for periods of two years at a time, up to the age of 21, if the child is or will be engaged in a course of education or training (s. 7(2)).

Once an order has been made, it may be varied not only in amount but also so that payment can be made to a different recipient: to the SBC if benefit is later paid (but the diversion procedure is more common, see below); to the local authority if the child goes into care; to the mother if she goes off benefit or the child leaves care; or to some other person who is looking after the child (even though the last could not have applied in the first place).

Enforcement may be by attachment of earnings or even committal to prison, but the evidence suggests that many affiliation orders are not paid and no enforcement measures are taken (*McGregor, Blom-Cooper and Gibson*, 1970). It is rarely worth it.

Apart from the many technical defects mentioned already, affiliation orders have one other major fault. They may establish paternity, and the finding is then conclusive for the purpose of any other civil proceedings unless the contrary can be proved (Civil Evidence Act 1968, s.12). But they do not establish any other legal relationship between father and child, apart from the obligation to pay money. They cannot grant him access or any other rights, apart from the right to be heard in adoption proceedings. Not surprisingly, therefore, the parties may regard them more as a punishment than any genuine attempt to "affiliate" him to his child.

(ii) *Agreements*

The mother and father can enter into an agreement for the child's maintenance and this will be enforced by the courts (*Ward* v. *Byham*, 1956). Provided that the terms are clear, there is no particular formality required, although it is obviously sensible to have a properly drawn-up document. Even if the mother agrees not to do so, the agreement does not prevent her later bringing affiliation proceedings (*Follit* v. *Koetzow*, 1860), although this might be a breach of contract.

There are obvious advantages in a private arrangement, and it may well make provision which could not be made by court order. In one case a man who bought a house for the accommodation of the mother of their twin illegitimate daughters was held to have granted her a contractual licence to remain until they had finished school. She obtained £2,000 damages for breach of contract when he evicted her (*Tanner* v. *Tanner*, 1975; but contrast *Horrocks* v. *Forray*, 1976).

(iii) *State benefits*

A working woman who has paid sufficient contributions will be entitled to maternity grant (£25) and a maternity allowance for 18 weeks. From April 1977, a working woman may also be entitled to maternity pay from her employers (who can reclaim it from the maternity pay fund); this will be 9/10ths of her usual wages less any maternity allowance, for 6 weeks, (Employment Protection Act 1975). That Act will also entitle her to return to her job provided that she gives notice beforehand and does so within 29 weeks of the birth. If she does return and the pay is low, she may be entitled to Family Income Supplement (whereas a married woman who is sole bread-winner is not). Last, she is entitled to child benefit (Child Benefit Act 1975).

If the mother is not working she is extremely likely to have to rely on supplementary benefit. This is totally means-tested; any child benefit will be deducted, as will any earnings above £6.00, and any payments made by the father unless she has assigned the benefit of an affiliation order to the Supplementary Benefits Commission. This diversion procedure means that any money paid by the father to the court is paid directly

to the Commission and she gets the same amount of benefit
whether or not he has paid. The Commission prefer this
course to the alternative of obtaining or varying an order for
themselves. Supplementary benefit is of course lost if the
mother lives with another man "as his wife"; the problem is
whether this phrase merely means a sexual relationship, so that
benefit is lost whether or not he is supporting the woman and
her child, or whether some such support must be shown. The
law is ambiguous but the Commission appear to concentrate
more on the sexual relationship (*Lister*, 1973). Benefit is not
payable to someone under 16, unless an exceptional case can
be made, and so the very young mother must be dependent
upon her family.

The limitations of supplementary benefit and court orders
have led the Finer Committee (1974) and others to suggest a
Guaranteed Maintenance Allowance for all one-parent
families. This would give them an income comparable to that
of widows at present, but in the present economic climate will
not be introduced.

4. *Succession*

It is quite extraordinary that having denied the relationship
between father and child while the former was alive, the law is
now prepared to recognise it when he dies. There are three
separate issues:

(i) *Construction of wills and settlements*

It was always possible to leave property to a named
illegitimate child, but now a general gift to "children" or
"issue" is presumed to *include* the illegitimate unless the
contrary is stated (Family Law Reform Act 1969, s.15,
reversing the previous rule). No doubt solicitors preparing wills
now tactfully draw to their clients' attention the advisability of
excluding them.

(ii) *Intestacy*

Before January 1, 1970, an illegitimate child could not
claim anything if his father or his father's relatives died

without leaving a will, and he could only claim from his mother if she had no legitimate children (thus she was often advised to adopt him if she got married). Now, an illegitimate child is entitled to participate in the intestacy of *either* parent, equally with any legitimate children (Family Law Reform Act 1969, s.14(1)). The parents are also entitled to participate in his (s.14(2)); this seems particularly unfair when the mother who has struggled to bring up the child alone is later deprived of half his property, if he dies without leaving a widow, children or a will.

The illegitimate child is still not in the same position as a legitimate; he cannot participate in the intestacy of his grandparents or collateral relatives such as brothers and sisters, and nor can they in his.

(iii) *Family provision*

The statutes which enabled dependants of a deceased person to apply to the court if they were deprived of reasonable provision either by a will or the rules of intestacy originally excluded illegitimate children. This was changed by the Family Law Reform Act 1969 (s.18) and far more comprehensive powers have now been introduced in the Inheritance (Provision for Family and Dependants) Act 1975 (discussed in the next chapter).

For all these purposes, the relationship must of course be proved, and this may present serious difficulties unless there has been a court order, maintenance agreement or the father appears on the child's birth certificate.

5. *Commentary*

Obviously, in the absence of a marriage between the child's mother and father, there has to be some special provision for establishing any relationship between the child and his father. The defect of English law is first that it is difficult to establish such a relationship as a fact, and secondly that once established that fact has only limited legal consequences.

Thus if the father freely admits his paternity, the only way he can officially acknowledge it is through the child's birth certificate, with the mother's co-operation (although a statutory declaration might be admissible in evidence in a later dispute). If he does not admit it, neither the child nor his mother can go to court for an official and binding declaration of paternity while the facts are still fresh in everyone's minds, whereas it is possible to obtain a declaration of legitimacy. The only method of proving paternity which will be accepted for other purposes unless the contrary is proved, is affiliation, and the manifold disadvantages of this have already been discussed.

Even if paternity is clearly established, the father's relationship is limited to paying money for the child and providing for him, either intentionally or by accident, on death. If the father wishes to take any part in the child's upbringing, he must bring separate proceedings for custody, which may very well not be appropriate. And if he does that, he cannot at the same time be ordered to pay maintenance.

All this would be perfectly understandable if all putative fathers corresponded to stereotype, although it would only serve to reinforce that stereotype rather than to encourage the pattern to change. The evidence however suggests that many fathers are either living with the mother or at least interested in the welfare of mother and child. The evidence also suggests that illegitimate children as a group are seriously disadvantaged when compared with their peers even in other one-parent families. The law could make a greater contribution towards changing this.

7 Guardians

The death of one or both parents is obviously a tragedy for a child, but it is a tragedy with far fewer unfavourable consequences for him than almost any other discussed in this book. There are almost always material disadvantages associated with growing up in a one-parent family, but the financial and housing situation of the bereaved is markedly better than that of others (*Finer Committee*, 1974; *Ferri*, 1976). Nor do children who have lost a parent show a significantly increased risk of delinquency (*Rutter*, 1971), or educational problems (*Ferri*, 1976), or even long-term emotional disturbance (*Rutter*, 1971; *Ferri*, 1976) although some have found a link between bereavement in adolescence and later depressive illness. Bereavement is of course quite a different experience from other types of separation or loss. It is rarely accompanied by prolonged hostilities and bitterness between the parents, or by legal disputes about the children's future. It attracts only sympathy and compassion from society and none of the condemnation still attached to marital breakdown and illegitimacy.

1. *Caring for the Orphaned Child*

If a parent dies, the law rarely has to arbitrate a dispute between warring claimants for the child's custody. It does, however, have to regulate what will happen to him, or more specifically to the parental rights and duties over him. This is normally determined by the law of guardianship. Some statutes give a specially extended definition to the term "guardian" (as in, for example, the Children and Young Persons Act 1933, s.107(1), or the Education Act 1944, s.114(1), but *legal* guardianship is a relationship with a child which entitles the guardian to exercise parental rights over him; it is quite different from "custody", which is a selected bundle of those rights and may be conferred by guardianship or court order.

For practical purposes, there are three types of guardian. *Natural* guardians are the child's own parents. The rule that the father of legitimate children is their sole guardian while he is alive has never been expressly abolished, but this no longer matters as mother and father now have equal rights and authority. The mother of course has sole rights over an illegitimate child unless the father obtains a custody order. *Testamentary* guardians are those appointed by the parents to take their place in the event of death. *Court-appointed* guardians are those appointed by the courts under a variety of powers arising on the death of either or both parties. (It should perhaps also be remembered that the High Court is technically the guardian of a child who is made a ward of court, but this is usually not connected with the parents' death and is dealt with elsewhere.)

Generally speaking an appointed guardian enjoys the same rights over both the child and his property (Guardianship Act 1973, s.7) as does a natural parent. His consent is necessary both to marriage and to adoption. He is however under an obligation to respect the parents' wishes about the education and religion of the child, unless these are overridden by the welfare principle. He is presumed to have custody of the child for the purposes of criminal liability for neglect or ill-treatment. He cannot however be ordered by any court to pay maintenance to anyone else for the child. He will incur criminal liability if he fails to educate the child properly. He is also subject to some independent control, for the High Court (but only the High Court) has power, in the interests of the child's welfare, to remove a non-natural guardian, and, if it wishes, to appoint someone else to take his place (Guardianship of Minors Act 1971, s.6). An unrelated guardian who is looking after the child is not however subject to the legal controls over private foster parents. Society appears more prepared to trust the parents' choice after their death than when they are alive.

What then is the guardianship position if one or both parents die?

(i) *If one parent dies*

Nowadays the surviving parent will normally be sole guardian (Guardianship of Minors Act 1971, s.3(1) and (2)), but there are several exceptions.

(*a*) The dead parent may have executed a deed or will appointing someone to be guardian after his death (Guardianship of Minors Act 1971, s.4(1) or (2)). No doubt all sensible people should do this, but many have an almost superstitious reluctance to make a will and many wrongly think of it as an expensive step which is only necessary for the rich. Such a guardian will act jointly with the surviving parent unless the latter objects (s.4(3)), in which case the guardian will be excluded unless he makes an application to the court (which may be the High Court, the local county court, or unless the child is over 16, the local magistrates' court, see s.15). He may also apply if he thinks the surviving parent is unfit to have custody of the child. The court can then choose between leaving the surviving parent as sole guardian, or ordering them to act jointly, or even excluding the surviving parent (s.4(4)).

If they act jointly, each may exercise his powers without consulting the other, provided that the other has not "signified disapproval" (Children Act 1975, s. 85(3)). If they disagree, either may apply to a court, which can make whatever order it decides proper (Guardianship of Minors Act 1971, s.7; a magistrates' court cannot make any order relating to the child's property, s.15). The court can also make a custody order, grant access to the surviving parent (but not apparently to the guardian, which is a pity), and order the surviving parent (but again not the guardian) to pay maintenance for the child (s.11). If the surviving parent is excluded from guardianship the court can still make any custody order it thinks fit, grant access to the surviving parent and order him to pay maintenance for the child (s.10).

(*b*) If no guardian has been appointed by the dead parent, or if he appointed someone who has died or refused to act, a court has power to appoint a guardian to act jointly with the survivor (s.3(1) and (2)). If it does so, the position will be the same as where a testamentary guardian acts jointly with the survivor (see above), but there is no corresponding power to exclude the surviving parent.

This is a rather strange power. No reference is made to who may apply and it is not easy to imagine in what circumstances the court would think it appropriate to make an appointment where one parent was still alive. Presumably a concerned relative might apply with a view to asking for custody of the child (under s. 11). This would rarely be in the child's best interests (see *Re H.*, 1959), but it is a possible course where the parents were divorced or separated and the one with custody dies without appointing a guardian.

(c) The above rules normally still apply even though the parents were divorced or separated before the death and even though it is the parent awarded custody who dies. The surviving parent will still be sole guardian, unless the deceased had appointed a testamentary guardian, or the court makes an appointment (under s. 3), or, but this is extremely rare, the court which granted a decree of divorce or judicial separation made an order under section 42(3) of the Matrimonial Causes Act 1973 that the surviving parent was unfit to have custody of the children. The effect of this is to deprive him of his automatic right to custody and guardianship if the other parent dies (s.42(4)).

The problems that this situation can cause are amply illustrated by the case of *Re F.* (1976). After a stormy marriage, including some violence by the father which was witnessed by the little girl, the parents separated when their daughter was 3½. The mother insisted that the father should leave when she discovered his affair with another woman. Some months later the father returned, forced his wife and child out of the house and installed the other woman. The wife went for some time to her parents and later got a flat near them. She was awarded custody at the divorce. The father had a child by the other woman and later married her. He sent presents and some money for his elder child but saw little of her, principally because of the hostility of the mother and grandmother. The mother became ill and the grandmother and aunts looked after the child while she was in hospital. When the child was 7¾, her mother died. Eleven days later the father came and took her away to live with him and his new family.

This he had every right to do. The grandmother might have

been able to apply to be appointed guardian under section 3, but she chose the more obvious course of making the child a ward of court. By the time the case was heard, a year later, the little girl was well settled with her new family and the Court of Appeal decided that she should remain there. In that case, where the choice was between elderly grandparents, who though very close to the child were extremely hostile to her one surviving parent, and her father, who was now settled with a new young family and prepared to recognise and respect the child's fondness for her grandparents, the outcome may have been the best in the long run. In cases where the child is well settled with a step-parent and his family when the death occurs, it might be disastrous. The moral is obviously to plan ahead; the parent with custody can apply for the order to be varied giving joint custody to herself and the step-parent and complete matters by appointing the step-parent guardian in her will.

(*d*) The above rules only apply to legitimate children. If the mother of an illegitimate child dies, the father is not entitled to act as guardian unless he obtains or has already obtained a custody order. The court will be able to appoint a guardian under section 5 (see below) as there is no parent, no guardian, and no one else having parental rights. If the child is or goes into care the local authority will be able to pass a section 2 resolution on account of the mother's death, although the father could still make an application for custody. The father's death will normally be quite irrelevant, for he has no power to appoint a testamentary guardian unless he has obtained a custody order which is still in force immediately before his death (s.14(3)).

(ii) *If both parents are dead*

For legitimate children, there are three possibilities:

(*a*) If both parents have appointed guardians, they will act jointly (s.4(5)). The rule that each may exercise his powers unilaterally unless the other has signified disapproval (Children Act 1975, s.85(3)), still applies, although it is curious that appointed guardians should be able to make decisions about, say, their ward's property, without reference to one another. If

the guardians disagree, they may apply to the court
(Guardianship of Minors Act 1971, s.7), but there is no express
power to make custody orders (see *Re N*. on page 163);
presumably the court could decide where the child should live,
but in some cases it might be desirable to make him a ward of
court.

(*b*) If only one parent has appointed a guardian, he will
have sole responsibility. There is no power in a court to
appoint someone to act with him (although of course the High
Court could replace him), unless the parent who failed to
make an appointment died first and the court has already
appointed someone under section 3. That guardian would
continue to act after the survivor's death, either alone or
jointly with someone appointed by the survivor (s.4(6)).

(*c*) If neither parent has appointed a guardian and there is
no other person with parental rights over the child, any person
can apply to a court to be appointed guardian (s.5(1)). This
can be done even though the local authority has parental
rights by virtue of a section 2 resolution (s.5(2)), which will
come to an end if a guardian is appointed (Children Act 1948,
s.2(8) as substituted by s.57 of the Children Act 1975).

One of the grounds for reception into care under section 1 of
the Children Act 1948 is that the child has neither parent nor
guardian, and a section 2 resolution vesting parental rights in
the local authority can also be passed (provided, once the
procedure is in force, that there is no custodian); it will also be
rather easier to make a custodianship application once both
parents are dead, for the shorter qualifying periods will apply
without the need for parental consent; it would however be
simpler to apply to be appointed guardian.

No doubt a great many orphaned children are cared for by
relations without any formal appointment as guardians. As
people with actual custody or charge, they may incur criminal
liability for neglect or ill-treatment or for failure to educate
the child properly. They would not however have any parental
rights or authority, for example over such matters as marriage,
and this could well be to the child's disadvantage. Non-related
people who undertake the care of orphaned children without
being appointed guardian are subject to the legal controls over
foster parents whereas guardians and relatives are not.

2. *Money*

The reason why widows' families tend to be better off than other one-parent families lies mainly in the operation of social security benefits, but private pensions and inheritance also play a part.

(i) *Succession*

A parent who loses a partner through death can normally expect that whatever capital assets they had, including the house, will remain intact, whereas after divorce or separation those assets will usually have to be shared in some way between two households. This advantage may be counter-balanced by the loss of the deceased's earnings, but pensions may sometimes compensate for this and periodical payments on divorce or separation are notoriously unreliable.

If a parent dies without leaving a will, the surviving spouse is entitled to personal chattels and the first £25,000 of the estate absolutely, and also to a life interest in half any remainder. The other half is held on trust for the children until they reach 18 or are married, when they become entitled to the principal. The income can be used for maintenance or education before then. The children will also succeed to the surviving spouse's life interest in the same way. If there is no surviving spouse, the whole estate is held on trust for the children (the position is of course quite different if there are no children but that is not relevant here) (Administration of Estates Act 1925, ss.46 and 47). "Children" now includes the illegitimate.

If the couple owned their home as "joint tenants," the dead partner's half automatically goes to the survivor. If they owned it as "tenants in common," or the dead parent was the sole owner, the survivor is entitled to ask for it to be transferred as part of the £25,000; or if it is worth more, she may pay the difference (if she has it) (Intestators' Estates Act 1952). If the house was rented under a tenancy protected by the Rent Acts, the survivor will normally be entitled to succeed to the tenancy whether the landlord likes it or not (Rent Act 1968, s. 3 and Sched. 1). These provisions only apply if the survivor was living there at the death, but in many cases they will mean that the family does not run the risk of losing its home.

If the deceased parent did make a will, it will normally have been with the object of making proper provision for his family. Sometimes, however, a will or the rules of intestacy can produce unjust results. A man may have left a substantial legacy to a charity or to his mistress, perhaps intending to disinherit his family or perhaps not realising how small his estate would be; or the rules of intestacy may mean that a wife, who left her husband to cope with the family many years ago but from whom he never obtained a divorce or a decree of judicial separation (which prevents the rules operating), can come and claim the majority of the estate from the children; or again an illegitimate child who is now self-supporting may come and claim a share from legitimate children who are still dependent upon the deceased, or vice versa.

If for any reason the will or the rules seem unjust, a variety of people may now apply to the courts for reasonable financial provision from the estate. These include the surviving spouse, any former spouse of the deceased who has not remarried (unless at the divorce they agreed that she should not be able to do so because the divorce settled the property distribution), any legitimate or illegitimate child of the deceased of whatever age, any other child who was treated as a child of the family in relation to any marriage to which the deceased was a party (that is, any child, apart from one officially boarded out with them, who was treated by both spouses as a member of their family, whatever his parentage), and any other person who was being maintained by the deceased immediately before his death (which could include the mother of his illegitimate child). The court can then award periodical payments, or lump sums, or order that property be transferred to or settled upon them, or that property be bought out of the estate and transferred to or settled upon them. In doing so it will take into account the needs and resources of all the claimants and any beneficiaries under the will, and many other factors such as the manner of the children's education or the conduct of the claimants towards the deceased. Provision for the surviving spouse should be full financial provision, at least as good as she might expect on divorce (and as the other principal claimant to the family's assets is now dead it will usually be better). Provision for other claimants is only to be what is reasonable for their maintenance, so that children who are past dependency may not benefit (Inheritance (Provision for Family and Dependants) Act 1975).

(ii) *Social security and other benefits*

Provided that he has paid the appropriate contributions, a woman who has lost her husband may be entitled to one of three widow's benefits. Widow's allowance is available (in the absence of any retirement pension) to any widow to tide her over the first 26 weeks after her husband's death (Social Security Act 1975, s.24). Thereafter, as long as she has with her, or is maintaining, a child of the family under the age of 19, she will be entitled to widowed mother's allowance (s.25). Even if there are no children or after the children grow up, a woman is entitled to widow's pension if she was between 40 and 65 when her husband died or she ceased to be entitled to widowed mother's allowance (s.26). Once she reaches 65, she can claim a retirement pension.

These benefits may not be enough on their own to enable her to manage without supplementary benefit, for they do not include a variable amount for housing costs, but they have the great advantage that they are not means-tested. She can claim even though she has a private pension from her husband's employers and even though she has a full-time job. A divorced, separated or unmarried mother has any maintenance payments and earnings above £6 deducted from her supplementary benefit and cannot claim at all if she has a full-time job. The widow will have to pay tax once her income reaches the threshhold, which is often a sore point, but she should perhaps be glad that she is allowed to have such an income. Widow's benefit is however lost if she remarries or cohabits.

A divorced woman whose former husband dies cannot claim widow's benefit. She is not a widow (this is a major reason for a woman to oppose divorce). If however her former husband satisfied the contribution conditions and she has with her or is maintaining a child of the family for whom her former husband was paying maintenance before his death, she can claim the child's special allowance (s.31). This is meant to compensate her for the loss of those maintenance payments (although his estate may be able to do that) and so it is somewhat surprising that it is lost if she cohabits, for the child's maintenance would not have been.

A widower is not entitled to any of these benefits, although he may receive a private pension from his wife's employment. He is however more likely still to be at work and can at least set-off a higher allowance against income for tax purposes, to take account of the single parent's higher expenses.

Someone who is caring for or maintaining an orphaned child who is not his own may be able to claim guardian's allowance, for which there are no contribution conditions. He is entitled if either (a) both parents are dead (but in the case of an illegitimate child only the mother need be dead unless the father's paternity has been established) or (b) only one parent is dead, but all reasonable efforts have failed to trace the whereabouts of the other or the other is in prison (s.38). Although this is called a guardian's allowance, there is no need for the claimant to be appointed legal guardian. Child benefit is not payable in addition to guardian's allowance, which is of course higher.

None of this adds up to riches or happiness for the orphaned child, but the very existence of these benefits is a fair indication of society's attitude to bereavement compared with the other causes of family breakdown.

8 Step-parents

Step-parenthood is obviously quite common. The National Child Development Study sample (of all children born in one week in 1958) contained, on follow-up at the age of 7, 7 per cent. who had lost one or both parents, and by the age of 11 the proportion had risen to 11.4 per cent. (*Ferri*, 1976). But at each follow-up about one in three of sole parents had married again (or in a few cases were cohabiting). However, remarriage was much more common among lone fathers, who seem to attract almost universal sympathy (*Marsden*, 1969). It was least common amongst widows, as might be expected, for although many divorced women may be reluctant to repeat what has been an unhappy experience, in some divorce cases a parent-substitute has already appeared on the scene. A high proportion of mothers who keep their illegitimate children but who do not live with the natural father, seem to provide them with a step-father quite soon (*Crellin, Kellmer Pringle and West*, 1971).

1. *The Legal Status of Step-parents*

Whatever the cause for the break-up or non-existence of the natural family, the basic proposition remains the same: marriage to the remaining parent (still less cohabitation) gives the step-parent no automatic parental rights over the children. The problems this is likely to cause do, however, differ somewhat according to whether the natural parent was widowed, divorced or never married to the children's father. These problems will be examined first, while in the next section we shall look at the various ways in which they can be solved. Last, we shall look at what can happen if the marriage between a natural parent and a step-parent breaks down, for at that point the law is prepared to recognise the relationship.

While parent and step-parent are together, the fact that the latter has no parental rights over the children may not matter very much. He will have the same responsibilities towards them as anyone with actual custody. The most serious irritant is likely to be the children's surname. If the natural parent has sole parental rights (either because the children are illegitimate or her husband died without appointing a guardian), there is nothing to prevent her changing the surname to that of the step-father if she so wishes. If however she simply has custody after a divorce, she cannot change the surname without her former husband's consent (*Y.* v. *Y.*, 1973; *Re T.*, 1963).

If the step-parent dies, he may of course make a will benefiting his step-children, but if he fails to do so they will not have any right to participate in his intestacy. If the children feel unjustly treated, they can now make an application for reasonable financial provision from his estate, for they will have been treated by the deceased as members of his family (Inheritance (Provision for Family and Dependants) Act 1975, s.1(1)(*d*)). The court's powers are now extensive (they were explained in the last chapter), but they can only be used for the purpose of making reasonable provision for the children's maintenance, and so may not benefit a step-child who has become self-supporting. In these cases the court also has to take into account the extent to which the step-father assumed financial responsibility for the children and the liability of anyone else (such as a divorced or putative father) to contribute to their maintenance. These powers are therefore not the same as automatic inheritance rights.

If the natural parent herself dies, the step-parent's position can be very difficult unless steps are taken to provide for it in advance. If she was divorced from the natural father, the natural father will usually be the only person with parental rights and will be able to come and take the children away if he wishes (see *Re F.*, on page 155). Even if the child was illegitimate or the natural father is dead, the step-father will still have no parental rights. The case of *Re N.* (1974) concerned two little girls born in 1962 and 1965. Their father died shortly after the birth of the younger, and their mother remarried in 1966. She died in 1970. Shortly before this, the maternal grandmother moved in with the family and she had since looked after them with the step-father. They began to disagree about the girls' upbringing and in 1973 each applied to the magistrates to be appointed guardian. The magistrates held that they had no power to make an appointment (under section 5(1) of the Guardianship of Minors Act 1971), because the step-father was a person having parental rights. The High Court held however, that they did have power to do so because step-parenthood as such conferred *no* parental rights. The court also pointed out that even if the magistrates went ahead and appointed either (or even both) of them guardian, there might still be difficulties because there is no power to make custody orders in that situation. That difficulty would still have applied even if the mother had appointed him guardian in her will, but he would at least have been the one with the right to determine the child's upbringing.

2. *Acquiring some Status*

Most of the above problems can be solved by the parties making appropriate wills, but some cannot. Step-parents however often want more. They, and the natural parents they marry, frequently wish for some legal recognition and security for their new family. This is a natural desire, although if it stems from a wish to exclude the other natural parent altogether, or from some insecurity in the emotional relationship between step-parent and children, it is question-able how far the law should go towards satisfying it. There are several alternatives.

(i) *Adoption*

Adoption is naturally a popular solution to the problem, for it solves all the new family's legal difficulties once and for all. In 1971, nearly half the adoption orders made in England and Wales were in favour of a natural parent and step-parent, and more than half of those related to legitimate children (*Stockdale Report*, 1972).

There is usually no legal obstacle to adoption by the step-parents of illegitimate children, for the father's consent is not needed (cases where the putative father and a step-mother are applying to adopt are extremely rare, but then of course the mother's agreement would be necessary unless it could be dispensed with). The courts are generally sympathetic to the adoption of illegitimate children, although, as seen in Chapter 6, they have recently been prepared to give more weight to the putative father's objections. There is equally no legal obstacle to the adoption of legitimate children where the other parent has died (without appointing a guardian). The advantages are more questionable, for there are not the disabilities of illegitimacy to be removed, the adoption may confuse and even distress an older child, and it will deprive him of all succession rights from his natural father's family.

Therefore, when the new custodianship procedure is introduced and a step-parent applies to adopt, either alone or jointly with the natural parent he has married, the court will have a duty to treat the application as one for custodianship if it is satisfied that the adoption would not be any better for the child (Children Act 1975 s. 37(1); this will not apply to the step-parents of children involved in divorce for they are similarly catered for in other ways). Any necessary agreements to the adoption will have to be given or dispensed with, but as already seen this will not usually be a problem. Where such a direction is given, it will not matter that the qualifying periods of care before custodianship have not been fulfilled.

The most serious problems, however, arise with adoption applications after the natural parents have been divorced. Often the desire to adopt is strongest here, for it will enable the children's name to be changed and will exclude forever the troublesome natural father. But his agreement will be necessary unless it can be dispensed with, and even if he is only too willing to give it (because he will then be absolved from all financial responsibility) the adoption still has disadvantages for the children.

The courts are extremely reluctant in these circumstances to dispense with the natural father's consent. In *Re D.* (1973) the father left home and, apart from Christmas, Easter and birthday presents and some clothes, made no provision for his wife or children. He saw them a few times after the parting but lost touch completely when the mother remarried and moved away. When he traced them again, he objected strongly to the use of the step-father's surname and to the adoption, but the mother asked for his consent to be dispensed with on the ground that he had persistently failed, without reasonable cause, to discharge his parental obligations. The court refused to do so. The failure must be so grave that the child would derive no advantage from maintaining contact with his natural parent.

A similar attitude was displayed in *Re B.* (1975), where the court refused to hold that a father who had seen little of his son since the parting was withholding his consent unreasonably. The question was whether his desire to remain the child's father was both honest and reasonable, and it was. (These cases make an interesting comparison with those about the fathers of illegitimate children discussed in Chapter 6, for those fathers had shown much more concern for their children but the adoptions were granted.) The court was prepared to hold the father unreasonable where he was a practising homosexual and the child a boy aged nine (*Re D.*, 1977), but this was obviously an unusual case.

Indeed, in *Re B.* the court itself questioned the whole benefit of such adoptions. Even where the father is prepared to disappear completely from the scene, the severance of natural relationships, and their replacement by artificial ones, can damage the child both legally and emotionally (see *Stockdale Report*, 1972), whereas most of the alleged advantages of adoption can be achieved in other ways. The Children Act 1975 thus reflects the views both of the Stockdale Committee and the High Court. It now provides that, even where the other natural parent consents, the court shall *not* grant an adoption order to a parent and step-parent (s.10(3)), or to a step-parent alone (s. 11(4)), if it thinks that the matter would be better dealt with by a custody order in the divorce proceedings. *Re B.* (above) also made it clear that *magistrates'* courts should not make adoption orders which are inconsistent with custody and access orders made at the divorce without referring the matter to the divorce court.

(ii) *Custody*

If the natural parents are divorced, therefore, there is an obvious and officially encouraged alternative to adoption. The step-parent can apply to the divorce court for the original custody order to be varied, or for a custody order to be made at all, giving joint custody to his spouse and himself (Matrimonial Causes Act 1973, s.42(1) (6) and (7)). This will give the step-parent custody rights which will stand even though his spouse dies; but it will not deprive the other parent of access to his children or of the possibility of seeking a variation of the order at a later date. The children's surname will remain the same unless the natural father agrees to a change, but any succession problem can be solved by making a will.

Where the child is illegitimate or the first marriage was broken by death, the step-parent will soon be able to apply for custodianship (custodianship will not be available to the step-parent of children involved in divorce, unless the parent other than the one he married has since died or disappeared, for only then is he unable to apply in the divorce proceedings: Children Act 1975, s.33(5) and (8)). If the step-parent first applied to adopt and the court directed that he be treated as having applied for custodianship (s.37), no qualifying period will be necessary, although it will almost invariably have elapsed. Otherwise, the child must have had his home with the step-parent for the three months preceding the making of the custodianship application (s.33(3)(*a*)(ii)). He will also need the consent of a person having legal custody of the child (s.33(3)(*a*) (i)), but this will be supplied by the parent to whom he is married. If that parent has also died or disappeared, there will in most cases be no one else with legal custody, and so the shorter qualifying period will still apply (see s.33(6)). If by any chance someone else does have legal custody and will not consent, the step-parent would have to have looked after the child for a total of three years including the three months before the application (s.33(3)(*c*)); but it is hard to imagine a case in which that would be so.

The procedure and effects of custodianship are discussed in Chapter 10. In cases such as these the effect is much the same as a custody order in divorce, and it does include the right to

decide whether the child can marry before the age of 18
(Marriage Act 1949, s.3 as amended).

3. *The Break-down of the New Family*

Where the marriage between a step-parent and a natural
parent is broken by the death of either, there will be no legal
proceedings relating to the marriage itself, and the position
with regard to the children will largely depend on what steps
have been taken (by court orders or by wills) to provide for it in
advance. If nothing has been done, the step-parent can still
apply to be made guardian, or for custodianship, or even for
adoption.

Where their marriage breaks down for other reasons,
however, there are much more likely to be legal proceedings,
and the law has taken advantage of this opportunity to
recognise the factual relationship between a step-parent and
step-children (this is typical of a general tendency for advances
in child law to develop out of mechanisms for regulating the
parents' marriage).

Thus in matrimonial proceedings before magistrates' courts,
the court can make custody, access and maintenance orders
about any "child of the family." The definition includes,
besides children of the marriage, a child of either party to it
who has been *accepted* as one of the family by the *other*
(Matrimonial Proceedings (Magistrates' Courts) Act 1960,
s.16(1); this definition was inadvertently repealed in the
Children Act 1975, but the courts will probably construe the
phrase in the same way).

In proceedings for nullity, judicial separation or divorce, the
court can make similar orders, again about any "child of the
family," but the definition is rather different. Besides children
of the marriage, it includes any child (apart from one boarded
out by a local authority or voluntary organisation) who has
been *treated* by *both* parties as a member of their family
(Matrimonial Causes Act 1973, s. 52(1). The differences are
that it is not limited to step-children although it includes
them; the criterion is not acceptance by the step-parent but
the way in which each parent has behaved towards them; and
whereas a man cannot "accept" a child whom he wrongly

believes to be his, he can "treat" such a child as one of the family.

These provisions mean that on the break-up of the marriage, the step-father (or indeed step-mother) can be ordered to pay maintenance for his step-children. The divorce court is however specifically instructed to take into account the extent to which he assumed any responsibility for the child's maintenance and if so, the extent, basis and length of this, whether he did so knowing that the child was not his, and the liability of any other person to maintain the child (Matrimonial Causes Act 1973, s.25(3)). On the other hand, these provisions also mean that the step-parent can apply for either custody of or access to his step-children; if that is granted, not only will he have obligations — he will also have some rights.

9 Local Authorities

On March 31, 1975 there were 99,120 children in the care of local authorities in England and Wales. Most of the reasons for their being there have already been mentioned in the context of the various legal crises of childhood, but the subject is so important that it clearly must be dealt with as a whole, even if this involves some repetition. There are three legal questions. How do children come into care? How does the local authority look after them while they are there? And how do they leave? However, the first and the last are inextricably linked, for the reason for the child's coming into care determines the nature and extent of the local authority's rights as against the parents, which in turn determines the legal circumstances in which the child may leave care. While the child is in care, however, he may be looked after in the same ways no matter what the reason for his being there. The simplest division of the subject therefore seems to be into two : entering and leaving care, and care in care. A final section will consider the relationship between the powers of local authorities and the jurisdiction of the courts.

1. *Entering and Leaving Care*

(i) *Section 1 of the Children Act 1948*

This section is the foundation of the modern child care system, for the majority of children come into care under it. Its purpose is to empower and oblige local authorities to provide substitute care for children whose parents are unable to look after them, thus reducing the demand for less satisfactory private arrangements. The service is however expensive and so can only be made available to those in genuine need, as defined by the section and interpreted in individual cases by the authority. The defined criteria have already been discussed in Chapter 2 and need not be repeated here.

The cardinal feature of the section is that it does *not* empower local authorities to remove children against their parents' wishes. Although sometimes parents may be advised to consider reception into care as a means of relieving stress which might result in child abuse and compulsory removal, or of avoiding the need for a child in trouble to appear in court, the parents must always be willing for the child to go into care. The section expressly states that the receiving authority does not thereby acquire any right to keep the child should a parent or guardian wish to take over his care (s. 1(3)). "Parent" or "guardian" refers to any person with a legal right to the child, normally either parent of a legitimate child, the mother of an illegitimate child, or a legally appointed guardian; but if a court has awarded custody to any person (for example, husband or wife in a matrimonial dispute, or the father of an illegitimate child, or, when the procedure is in force, a custodian) that person is "parent or guardian" to the exclusion of anyone else (s. 6(2)). This can cause problems where the parent with custody has placed the child in care and the other parent wishes to remove him. The local authority may either regard that parent as a "relative or friend" and allow the child out of care, but this has its own problems (see below), or refuse on the ground that the other has custody. The solution will then depend on the courts' willingness to vary a custody order while a child is in care, which is part of a much larger problem of the inter-relationship between courts and local authorities (discussed at 3 below).

The fundamental principle was enacted partly so that parents could feel confident that in using the service they did not run more risk of losing their children than they would if they made private arrangements. It also reflected society's increasing awareness of the dangers of separating children from their parents. Hence, but quite independently of the proposition that the receiving authority does not thereby acquire any right to keep the child, the section also aims to rehabilitate the family if at all possible. Thus authorities have a positive duty to try and secure that the care of a child received under the section is taken over by a parent, guardian, relative or friend (s. 1(3) again, but the two parts are quite separate). However, this is not an absolute duty which must be observed in every case; it only arises where it is consistent with the child's welfare. The two parts of the subsection have undoubtedly raised some tricky legal and practical problems.

If a relative or friend wishes to take the child and the local authority considers this against his best interests, there is no problem about refusing, because (unless he obtains a custody order) the relative or friend has no legal right to claim the child. If the authority thinks that it would benefit the child, however, should it allow him out of care without the parent's consent? The section seems to suggest that it should, although it insists that the relative or friend should if possible be of the same religion as the child or give an undertaking to bring him up in it; yet the authority has no parental rights over the child and the person with those rights has deliberately entrusted responsibility to the authority. Might he not feel aggrieved if the authority abdicated that responsibility without consulting him? Luckily, the authority could instead board the child out with the relative or friend, or even allow him to have temporary charge. It would thus retain overall control, and this would surely be more consistent in most cases with both the child's welfare and the parent's rights.

If on the other hand it is a parent or guardian who wishes to take the child, the problem is reversed. There is no difficulty at all if the authority considers this in the child's best interests, as it usually will. But it is increasingly being realised that rehabilitation of the natural family is not always in the best interests of a child who has been separated from it, perhaps because relationships within it were so negative that separation was in fact beneficial rather than detrimental, or because the separation happened at such an age or so long ago that new relationships have been established which it would be more damaging to break. The authority, however, has no parental rights. What then is it to do if it concludes that return to the parent or guardian is not in the child's best interests?

In a few cases, it could do nothing, for the parents are not always able to enforce their claims. In one significant but exceptional case, a local authority had taken a 14-year-old girl into care and boarded her out. Two years later her father asked for her return. The authority tried unsuccessfully to persuade her to do so. An instruction to the foster parents that she should be returned similarly produced no result. The father then tried to get her back by making her a ward of court (she was by then too old for habeas corpus to succeed against her will) but not surprisingly the judge refused to intervene. The father's last step was to sue the local authority, asking for a mandatory injunction (that is, a positive order) that they should remove the child and return her to him. This the court emphatically refused (*Krishnan* v. *Sutton London Borough Council*, 1970).

The case was exceptional, partly because the court could scarcely be expected to order the local authority to remove an unwilling girl from unwilling foster parents and return her to a father who had been unable to succeed against the foster parents directly, but also because of the girl's age. It is significant, however, for a clear statement that the duty to return the child is *not* an absolute one and need not be observed in every case. It is one thing to say that local authorities do not acquire any rights simply because they receive a child under section 1 (recently re-emphasised in *Bawden* v. *Bawden* (1975) disapproving some extraordinary remarks in *Halvorsen* v. *Hertfordshire County Council*, see page 175); it is quite another thing to say that they can always be *forced* to return the child.

However, law-abiding local authorities cannot be expected to make a practice of refusing to return children to the people who have a legally enforceable right to their possession. They must look for ways of counteracting that right. One solution is to make the child a ward of court and ask the court to decide what would be best for him. The procedure has been described in Chapter 3, and was in fact used by the local authority in the famous case which firmly established that the child's welfare took precedence over parental claims (*J.* v. *C.*, 1970); but it is expensive and time-consuming and neither the courts nor local authorities would care to see it used often. Another solution, once Part II of the Children Act 1975 is in force, will be to advise the foster parents of a child who has been boarded out to make a custodianship application, but unless parental consent has been obtained, this will only be possible if the child has had his home with them for a total of three years. The most obvious solution is of course to pass a "section 2 resolution" (see below), but this can only be done if the defined grounds exist and may be challenged by the parent in court. Care proceedings are not designed for this situation, but it is just possible that primary conditions (b), (bb), (c) or (d) might be proved even though the child was still in care. Finally, if the parent can be prevented from taking the child away, an adoption application may be considered.

Thus some possibilities exist, and the Children Act 1975 has taken an important step by giving local authorities who have had a child in their care for six months a breathing-space of 28 days in which to consider them. Section 56 makes it a criminal offence to help or persuade a child who has been in care under section 1 for six months to run away, or to take such a child away without lawful authority, or to harbour or conceal him or prevent his return, unless of course the local authority consents. And this applies equally to the parent or guardian unless he has given the authority 28 days' notice of his intention. The period of six months was selected because of evidence that after that time the chances of the child returning home diminish rapidly (*Rowe and Lambert*, 1973). Some would say that it is too short to avoid the danger of loss of parental confidence in the service, although of course unless the authority can either persuade the parents to change their minds or itself take action during the 28 days the parents will still have the right to take the child after that. Others would say that six months is too long, at least for a very young child, and that any arbitrary time limit will encourage parents to remove their children too hastily to avoid running the risk. The section therefore gives the Secretary of State power, with parliamentary approval, to prescribe different periods for both the six months and the 28 days, and no doubt he will wait to see how it works out in practice.

(ii) *Resolutions under section 2 of the Children Act 1948*

Even in 1948 it was accepted that there should be some exceptions to the cardinal principle of section 1. Thus in certain quite narrowly-defined circumstances, a local authority which had received a child into care under section 1 was empowered to pass a resolution which would vest parental rights in the authority and enable it to resist the parents' claims for the child's return. The procedure is unique in that it is the only way in which a person may be deprived of parental rights without the order of a court, but an aggrieved parent has the opportunity of challenging the resolution in the juvenile court.

Resolutions can only be passed in respect of children who are already in care under section 1. Thus they are not a means of removing children from undesirable homes. There has also been some doubt about whether they may be passed if the parent has requested the child's return; once the child has been in care for six months, section 56 of the Children Act 1975 (see above) must remove this doubt; before then, it depends upon whether a child remains "in care" until actually handed over, or whether despite his physical presence, he is no longer "in care" because the authority then has no right to keep him; this was the practical problem in the extraordinary case of *Halvorsen* v. *Hertfordshire County Council* (1974), where the mother was challenging the validity of a resolution passed after she asked for the child back. Unfortunately, the court seems to have thought that the mother had no right to reclaim the child, which must be wrong, whereas it could simply have decided that "in care" means physically in care. The point must surely still be regarded as undecided.

The grounds are set out in section 2 of the 1948 Act as substituted by section 57 of the Children Act 1975:

(*a*) That his parents are dead and he has no guardian or (when Part II of the Children Act 1975 is in force) custodian. "Parent" and "guardian" have the same meaning as they have in section 1. Indeed, the Director of Social Services could instead apply to a court to be made guardian of an orphaned child, but as a child whose parents are dead may readily be taken into care under section 1 (if he is not already there), a section 2 resolution is a simpler way of achieving the same object, which is to make someone responsible for the child's long-term future.

(*b*) That *a* parent, guardian or (when in force) custodian of his:

(*i*) Has abandoned him. If a parent's whereabouts have

remained unknown for 12 months after the child has come into care, the parent is "deemed" to have abandoned him (it is otherwise extremely difficult to prove that a parent has abandoned the child in such a way as to commit a criminal offence).

Or (ii) Suffers from some *permanent* disability rendering him *incapable* of caring for the child.

Or (iii) While not falling within (ii), suffers from mental disorder within the meaning of the Mental Health Act 1959 which renders him *unfit* to have the care of the child. Mental disorder (which in effect covers any mental abnormality which a doctor considers a disorder rather than an advantage) need not be permanent, and "unfit" is a broader term than "incapable."

Or (iv) Is of such habits or mode of life as to be unfit to have the care of the child. There must obviously be an element of permanence or at least persistence here, but the wording is broad enough to include alcoholism, promiscuity, criminality, vagrancy and a great many other things besides.

Or (v) Has so consistently failed without reasonable cause to discharge the obligations of a parent as to be unfit to have the care of the child. This is similar to the ground for dispensing with parental consent to adoption and a court's interpretation of the "obligations of parenthood" would no doubt be the same.

The 1975 Act introduced two further grounds:

(*c*) That a resolution under ground (*b*) is in force in relation to one parent of the child, who is, or is likely to become, a member of the household comprising the child and his other parent. This was to meet the problem that resolutions under ground (*b*) only transfer to the authority the parental rights of the unfit parent, so that if the other parent had parental rights (or could obtain them by court order) he could still assert them even though he might be living with the unfit parent. This ground enables the authority to ensure that the child will never live with the unfit parent, even though no criticism can be made of the other.

Or (*d*) That throughout the three years preceding the passing of the resolution the child has been in the care of a local authority under section 1, or partly in the care of a local authority and partly in the care of a voluntary organisation. This was to meet the criticism that, unless the child was orphaned, resolutions could only be passed on the ground of fairly narrowly defined parental unfitness. Yet no matter how faultless the parent, there may come a point when the child has been in care for so long that removal would repeat and redouble the dangers of the initial separation (see *Goldstein, Freud and Solnit*, 1973). The period is the same as that which qualifies foster parents to apply for custodianship without parental consent, and is equally open to the criticism that for some children it is far too long, or alternatively that it may provoke parents to remove their children just in time. The Secretary of State again has power, with parliamentary approval, to prescribe a different period.

Unless each person deprived of parental rights by a resolution has consented to it in writing, the local authority must immediately, if it knows where he is, give him written notice of it, telling him of his right to object. If he then, within a month of receiving this notice, serves a written counter-notice objecting to the resolution, the resolution will automatically lapse 14 days later, unless within that time the local authority refers the case to the juvenile court (the procedure and effects are all set out in the substituted section 2).

It is then for the juvenile court to decide whether the resolution should lapse, and to prevent this the local authority must prove the existence of the grounds, both at the time of the resolution and of the hearing. Under the 1975 Act, it must also prove that the resolution is in the interests of the child. This is a welcome safeguard whatever the ground, but is particularly important in the context of the two new grounds introduced by the Act.

The effect of a resolution is to vest parental rights and duties in the local authority, but if it is passed only on account of one parent (as in ground (*b*)) and he had parental rights jointly with another person, the authority will also hold parental rights jointly with that other person. (It might then have to consider the advisability of passing another resolution, on ground (*c*), on account of the other person.) "Parental rights and duties" means all rights and duties with respect to both the child and his property (see Chapter 1), and this goes further than the "legal custody" which may be granted to a custodian. It does not however include the right to decide whether the child can be adopted, which remains with the natural parent. Nor does the resolution allow the authority to change the child's religion. The parent is still under a duty to maintain the child and to keep in touch with the authority and of course the resolution may later be rescinded. It is not therefore as final as adoption.

Resolutions normally continue in force until the child is 18. They automatically cease to have effect if the child is adopted (or, when the procedure is in force, "freed" for adoption), or if a guardian of the child is appointed under section 5 of the Guardianship of Minors Act. The local authority can rescind the resolution at any time if this would be for the child's benefit (Children Act 1948, s. 4(2)). In addition, a parent or guardian who has been deprived of parental rights by the resolution, and who is unable to persuade the authority to rescind it, can apply to the juvenile court for it to be determined. He must then prove either that there was no ground for making it or that it should now be ended in the child's own interests, no easy task (Children Act 1948, s. 4(3)).

The Children Act 1975 (s. 58), provides for an appeal by either side from any decision of a juvenile court in respect of a section 2 resolution. Eventually it will also provide, where the court thinks it necessary, for the child to be made a separate party to proceedings in either court and to be represented by a guardian ad litem.

The object of section 2 resolutions is surely not merely to provide against the possibility that a parent may seek to remove a child against the authority's advice. It has the more positive aim of providing a substitute legal parent (albeit an institutional one) for a child whose parents are dead, or unfit, or, under the new Act, have been separated from him for a long time. Custodianship, when in force, will have a similar object, with the advantage that the substitute parent is someone who is actually looking after the child. Authorities who are planning the long-term future of such children will no doubt wish to consider the relative merits of passing a resolution or advising the foster parents to apply for custodianship where this is possible. Indeed, even if a resolution is already in force, it seems that there will be nothing to prevent the foster parents' applying; the effect of any custodianship order made may well not be to deprive the authority of all its parental rights, but only of the right to legal custody for the time being. The authority may however wish to consider rescinding the resolution as its objects will largely have been achieved.

(iii) *Care orders under the Children and Young Persons Act 1969*

A care order differs fundamentally from reception into care under the 1948 Act, for its principal purpose is to remove a child from home whether he or his parents like it or not. This is thought a serious interference with both the liberty of the child and the ordinary rights of parenthood, and thus can only be done by order of a court. The great majority of care orders is made under the Children and Young Persons Act 1969, which provides for the same type of order to be used in two quite different situations. In care proceedings under section 1 of that Act, the order is seen as the best way of protecting a child who, for one of seven defined reasons, has been shown to be in need of care or control which he will not receive unless the court makes an order; care proceedings have been discussed in the chapter on Child Abuse and the grounds need not be repeated here. In criminal proceedings, the order is seen as the most appropriate method of dealing with a juvenile who has been found guilty of an offence which in the case of an adult would be punishable by imprisonment (s. 7(7)(*a*)). The court's purpose may have been principally to reform and rehabilitate the offender, or to protect society from his depredations for a time, or to mark the extent of society's disapproval of his conduct, or more probably a mixture of all three; apart from detention centres and borstal, a care order is the court's only means of removing an offender from home. As the order is made in so many different circumstances, it is scarcely surprising that difficulties have arisen.

The main difficulty is that, whatever the reason for which it was made, the order has the same legal effect. The local authority must receive the child into its care and keep him there as long as the order is in force "notwithstanding any claim by his parent or guardian" (s. 24(1)); but while he is in care, the authority has much the same powers over and responsibilities towards him as it has with any of the other children in its care. Not only is there nothing to distinguish the different types of care order children; there are only one or two legal rules which distinguish care order children from all the rest.

The most important is that, as well as having to keep the child in care despite parental claims, the authority has all the "powers and duties" which a parent would have over the child were it not for the order (s. 24(2)). It is not entirely clear how these differ, if at all, from the parental "rights and duties" which are vested in a local authority by virtue of a section 2 resolution. They certainly do not include the right to change the child's religion (s. 24(3)), and thus it could be argued that they do not include the power to sanction medical treatment which that religion would forbid; on the other hand, there seems nothing to prevent the authority bringing the child up in no religion at all (unless atheism or agnosticism are themselves religions?), in which case the treatment might be sanctioned; luckily there are other solutions to this particular problem (discussed in Chapter 1). Nor do they include the right to agree to the child's adoption; this remains with the natural parents, but the care order may enable a suitable placement to be made and there may well be grounds for dispensing with the natural parents' agreement in some cases. It is not clear whether these powers include the right to decide whether the child may marry before 18, or any right to control his property as opposed to his person.

Secondly, it is expressly stated that the authority has the right to restrict the liberty of a care order child (s. 24(2)), whereas it is extremely doubtful whether a parent has the right to do this, at least once the child has reached the "age of discretion" (apparently 14 for boys and 16 for girls). This right is obviously necessary for some of the criminal offenders, but it is not restricted to them, nor are the powers to recapture absconders (see 2(iv) below).

Thirdly, the local authority must appoint an independent person as a "visitor" for certain children subject to care orders.

These are children aged five or over, who are accommodated in community homes or other establishments which they have not been allowed to leave during the past three months for the purpose of ordinary attendance at school or work, and who either have not lived with, visited or been visited by a parent or guardian during the past year, or have had only infrequent contact with them (s. 24(5)). The visitor's function is to visit, advise and befriend the child, and he is entitled to apply on the child's behalf for discharge of the care order. The visitor may resign or the authority may end his appointment, but if the circumstances are the same, the authority must appoint a replacement (s. 24(6)). These provisions reflect an obvious ambivalence in the local authority's relationship with the children in its care under the 1969 Act. One the one hand, the authority may be trying to do its best for the child (subject to the need to respect the public interest); but on the other, it may be doing so in circumstances and in a way which possibly the child and probably his parents do not want; it is thus part friend and part foe.

The final difference between care order children and other children in care is that in certain circumstances the authority (again presumably as foe to one child but friend to the others) may apply to the court for a child of 15 or over who is disrupting life in a community home to be transferred to borstal (see the discussion of borstal training in Chapter 4).

A care order prima facie lasts until the child reaches 18, unless the child was already 16 when it was made, in which case it lasts until he reaches 19 (s. 20(4)). If the order would normally expire at 18, it is possible for the authority to apply to have it extended until 19, but only if the child is in a community home or a home provided by the Secretary of State and because of his mental condition or behaviour it is in his or the public interest that he should remain there (s. 21(1)).

A care order may be discharged by the juvenile court at any time (s. 21(2)). Either the local authority or the child, or the child's parent or guardian (s. 70(2)) or visitor (s. 24(5)) acting on his behalf, may apply. If the application is unsuccessful, however, no one may apply again within the next three months unless the court gives its consent (s. 21(3)). If the application is successful and the child is still under 18, the court may if it wishes make a supervision order to replace the care order. The discharge of care orders raises problems which are perhaps the most serious disadvantage of using the same order to deal with both juvenile offenders and children at risk of abuse. Some young offenders undoubtedly felt aggrieved when the determinate "stretch" of three years in an approved school was replaced by an indeterminate care order which might or might not mean that they were kept in secure accommodation. For them, the right to apply for discharge at three-monthly intervals was surely an important safeguard, yet their welfare could not be made the first and paramount consideration in such applications, for considerations such as the protection of the public might be equally important. Where, on the other hand, the child has had to be removed from an unsatisfactory home, there are surely strong grounds for suggesting that his welfare should be the first and paramount consideration in any application from (in effect) his parents for his return. This is after all the criterion adopted in ordinary custody disputes between non-parents and natural parents who may be much less open to criticism (see the case of *J.* v. *C.*, 1970, on page 217). It would however be difficult to lay down a different criterion for discharging orders made in criminal or care proceedings, because juvenile offenders may be dealt with under either. Following the Children Act 1975, three changes have made some attempt to solve the problem. The right of foster parents to be heard and the right of the child to separate representation apply only to orders made in care proceedings. The new criterion for discharging orders (s. 21(2A) of the 1969 Act) applies to both criminal and care proceedings: the court must not discharge a care order relating to a child under 18 who "appears to be in need of care or control" unless it is satisfied that, whether through the making of a supervision order or otherwise, he will receive that care or control. Whether this will remove any presumption that an abused child should eventually be returned, and encourage more forward planning, remains to be seen.

Among such forward plans might be adoption, as already seen, and an adoption order automatically brings a care order to an end. When Part II of the 1975 Act is in force, an application by foster parents for custodianship might be encouraged; the effect of such an order on a care order remains obscure.

(iv) *Interim care orders and remands to care*

These are both temporary measures for taking or keeping a child away from home while a case is waiting to be disposed of. Interim care orders are made pending or in the course of care proceedings (see Chapter 5), while children who have been charged with or convicted of criminal offences and are remanded or committed for trial or sentence otherwise than on bail must normally be committed to the care of the local authority (see Chapter 4). In each case someone who is too unruly to go into care may be committed to a remand centre if one is available, or, if he is an alleged offender, to prison; this power only applies to boys aged 14 or over and girls aged 15 or over.

If the child is committed to care, the powers and duties of the local authority are the same as in an ordinary care order (s. 24(1) and (2)); but an interim order only lasts for 28 days or a shorter specified period, and in the case of an order made by a single magistrate this is calculated from the day when the child was first detained (s. 20(1)); and a remand or committal lasts until the date fixed for the child's next court appearance. In the first case, the local authority must bring the child back to court when the order expires, unless the court makes an exception because the child is under five or because of illness or accident (s. 22(2)); and in the second, the authority must allow the child to be taken back to court (s. 24(4)). In each case, if the authority finds a young person unruly it can go back to court and ask for him to be sent instead to a remand centre or, for an offender, prison; the same age limits apply (ss. 22(5) and 23(3)). In a criminal case, the child can apply for bail at his next court appearance or appeal to a judge. In an interim care order, either the child or the local authority may apply for its discharge under section 21(2), but if this is refused no one can apply again unless the court consents (s. 21(3)(*a*)); the child can also apply to a High Court judge for its discharge, but if this is refused the local authority cannot exercise its power to allow someone else to take over charge and control of him unless the High Court consents (s. 22(4)).

When the child appears in court again, and the case is still not disposed of, the court may make a further interim order (s. 22(3)) or again remand him to the care of the local authority. Too much delay before a case can be proved ought however to be regarded with suspicion; that is the purpose of only allowing orders or remands of limited duration.

(v) *Committal to care in other cases*

Courts hearing a variety of cases in which the future of children is in issue may decide that there are exceptional circumstances making it undesirable for the child to be entrusted to any individual and may thus commit him to the care of the local authority. As has already been seen in Chapter 3 this may be done in divorce, nullity or judicial separation proceedings, in matrimonial proceedings before magistrates' courts, in custody proceedings under the Guardianship of Minors Act 1971, and where proceedings are taken to make a child a ward of court. The power has recently been extended to cases where an adoption application has been refused and when Part II of the Children Act 1975 is in force, it will be possible on an application to make or to revoke a custodianship order.

These orders have a totally different effect from that of care orders made under the 1969 Act. The authority has the duty to receive the child into its care as if under section 1 of the 1948 Act, but it has both the right and the duty to keep him there despite his parents' claims. It does not, however, acquire any parental rights and duties over and above those that it always has where children are received into care, and it may sometimes be subject to the directions of the court.

(vi) *Miscellaneous situations*

There are a few other situations in which a local authority may actually be looking after someone who is not technically in its care. These include children accommodated by the local authority in pursuance of "place of safety" orders; mentally disordered children who may be accommodated in community homes even though they cannot be received into care under the

1948 Act (Mental Health Act 1959, s. 9); and people over compulsory school age but under the age of 21 who may be accommodated in community homes which cater for children over compulsory school age and are convenient for the place where the person works or is being educated (Children Act 1948, s. 19). As these people are not "in care," most of what follows does not apply to them.

2. *Care in Care*

Whatever the legal route along which the child arrived in care, the law relating to his treatment while there is essentially the same, and is largely governed by Part II of the Children Act 1948. The general duty of local authorities to all these children is laid down in section 12(1) (as substituted by s. 59 of the Children Act 1975):

"In reaching any decision relating to a child in their care, a local authority shall give first consideration to the need to safeguard and promote the welfare of the child throughout his childhood, and shall so far as practicable ascertain the wishes and feelings of the child regarding the decision and give due consideration to them, having regard to his age and understanding."

While this duty is clearly most relevant to placement and other decisions relating to the child's stay in care, the section was redrafted with positive planning for the child's long-term future in mind. It is thus also aimed at decisions on whether he should be allowed to leave care, for as has been seen, there is now much more which can be done to avoid this if it is indeed contrary to his best interests. There is also an increasingly flexible attitude towards the aims of the child-care service, although this is still a matter of considerable debate. The need to consult the child is quite new, although it surely reflects good practice.

This general duty is modified in two respects, principally to take account of the increasing numbers of children who arrive in care because of criminal offences, but they apply to all children in care. First, section 12 (1A) allows the local authority to exercise its powers in a manner which may not be consistent with its duty to the child, if this seems to be necessary for the purpose of protecting members of the public. Secondly, if the Secretary of State considers it necessary, for the same purpose, to give directions to a local authority about how it should deal with a particular child in its care, the local authority must comply with them, even if they conflict with the general duty (Children and Young Persons Act 1969, s. 27(3)).

Section 12(2) of the 1948 Act reminds local authorities that in providing for children in care they must make such use of the facilities and services available for children in the care of their own parents as appears reasonable in each case. Children in care have been deprived of so much that it is particularly important that they should not be deprived of services which children at home may take for granted, be they schools, play-groups, youth clubs, hospitals, clinics, the youth employment service, or whatever.

(i) *Placement*

The advantages of local authority care, at least in an ideal world, are that it has a wide range of child-care facilities open to it and expert staff to select the placement which is most appropriate for each individual child, to handle it with sensitivity to the needs and feelings of all involved, and to make constructive long-term plans based on regular reviews. The placement alternatives legally available are set out in section 13 of the Children Act 1948 (as substituted by section 49 of the Children and Young Persons Act 1969) and each must be considered in turn.

(a) Boarding-out

Before the 1969 Act, local authorities had a positive duty to board out all children in their care, unless this was impracticable or undesirable. This legal preference for foster-care was removed partly because research had indicated that the initial enthusiasm for it was not always born out by results, particularly as so many long-term placements broke down (*Dinnage and Kellmer Pringle*, 1967), and partly because it was not appropriate to many of the juvenile offenders now coming into care. Approximately 40 per cent. of the children in care are now boarded out (*DHSS*, 1975), but it remains the single most popular choice. It is subject to the detailed provisions in the Boarding-Out of Children Regulations 1955 (made under section 14 of the 1948 Act), which make an interesting comparison both with the law relating to private fostering (discussed in Chapter 2) and with supervision orders over children living at home (discussed in Chapter 4). The Regulations apply whenever a child is boarded-out, by a local authority in whose care he is or by a voluntary organisation, with foster parents "to live in their dwelling as a member of their family," unless this is merely for a holiday of not more than 21 days or the child has been placed with a view to adoption (reg. 1).

Short and long-term fostering. The Regulations distinguish in various ways between short-term placements for less than eight weeks (reg. 24) and long-term placements for more than eight weeks (reg. 16). If a placement which was originally expected to be short continues beyond eight weeks, the long-term regulations come into force, so that anything required by them which has not in fact already been done must be done immediately, unless the extension is not expected to last more than four weeks, in which case the long-term regulations do not apply unless and until it goes on longer than that (reg. 30).

Selection of foster parents. Children may only be boarded-out with married couples, or with women, or with their grandfathers, uncles or elder brothers, but this does not prevent a foster child remaining where he is if a foster parent dies or a foster mother leaves (reg. 2). More importantly a child cannot be boarded-out unless a social worker has first visited the foster parents and their home and reported in writing that they will be suitable to the child's needs. In short-term placements this is all that is required (reg. 25), and indeed need not be repeated if a child receiving full-time education has already been boarded-out there within the past four months, for example, during holidays from boarding school (reg. 29). In long-term placements, however, the social worker must be personally acquainted with the child and his needs or at least fully informed of them, and must report that the foster home is likely to suit those particular needs. He must also report specifically upon the foster parents' reputation and religion and their suitability in age, character, temperament and health to have the charge of the child, upon whether any member of the household is suffering from a physical or mental illness which might adversely affect the child, or has been convicted of an offence making it undesirable for the child to associate with him, and upon the number, sex and approximate age of the people in the household. The authority has a positive duty not to board-out the child unless his history and the reports indicate that boarding-out in that household would be in his best interests (reg. 17). All this should involve both the careful selection of foster parents in the first place and equally careful matching of individual children and families, very different from the situation where parents are forced into the private market.

Medical examination. Except in an emergency, a child must not be boarded-out unless he has been medically examined within the three months beforehand, and the doctor has made a written report on his physical health and mental condition (reg. 6). Thereafter children under two must be examined within a month of placement and at least every six months, and children over two must be examined within a month if they were not examined beforehand and at least every year (reg. 7). In addition, adequate arrangements must be made for medical and dental attention as required (reg. 8). Regulations 6 and 7 do not however apply to short-term placements of school-children who have already been boarded-out with the same foster parents within the past four months (reg. 29).

Religion. Long-term foster parents must if possible be of the same religion as the child and must in any event give an undertaking to bring him up in, and encourage him to practise, his own religion (reg. 19 and Sched.). Short-term foster parents must either give the same undertaking or be notified by letter of the child's religion and the obligations they would have had under the undertaking (reg. 27); again, this need not be repeated if they have already had the same school-child within the past four months (reg. 29).

The foster parents' undertaking. The authority must ensure that long-term foster parents sign the statutory undertaking (reg. 20), unless the child is over compulsory school-age when first boarded-out with them, in which case they need only sign such parts of the undertaking as seem appropriate (reg. 23(2)). Short-term foster parents taking a child who is not over compulsory school-age must either sign the undertaking or be informed by letter of the obligations contained in it (reg. 27); again, this need not be repeated if they have already had the same school-child within the past four months (reg. 29). The undertaking itself (Schedule) is quite extraordinary. Apart from religious upbringing it covers obvious things such as looking after the child's health, consulting a doctor whenever he is ill, allowing him to be medically examined when the authority requires it, permitting anyone authorised by the Secretary of State or the authority to see the child and visit the house at any time, and notifying changes of address in advance. But it also contains two provisions which some think are mutually contradictory: to care for the child and bring him up as they would a child of their own and to allow him to be removed from their home whenever the authority requests it. This illustrates the difficulty and ambivalence of the foster parents' task, as well as a potentially yawning gap between the popular and professional views of long-term fostering. Its implications, and in particular the extent to which the authority may enforce it or the foster parents seek to counteract it, are discussed under "Removal" below and in the next chapter. Incidentally, the undertaking contains nothing about education, but as persons with actual custody of the child, the foster parents have the same duties as parents in this respect.

Visits. In long-term placements of children who are not over compulsory school-age, a social worker must see the child and visit the home within a month of the placement, and thereafter as often as the child's welfare requires, but not less than once every six weeks for children under five and once every two months for children over five; if the child has been in the foster parents' household for more than two years, however, he need only be visited every three months (reg. 21(*a*) and (*b*)).

Children who cease to be of compulsory school-age while
boarded-out must be visited within three months of this and
thereafter every three months; children who are first
boarded-out over that age must be visited within a month and
thereafter every three months (reg. 23(3)(*a*) and (*b*)). In
addition, a social worker must always visit within a month of
the foster parents' moving house (reg. 21(*c*) and 23(3)(*c*)) and
immediately if there is any complaint by or concerning the
child, unless action on it seems unnecessary (reg. 21(*d*) and
23(3)(*d*)). In short-term placements of children who are not
over school-age, a social worker must see the child and visit the
house within two weeks and thereafter every four weeks (reg.
28(1)). If the child is over school-age, a social worker must see
him (but not necessarily the home) within a month (reg.
28(2)). If a school-child has already been boarded-out with the
same foster parents within the last four months, he and the
home need only be visited within a month of the new
boarding-out (reg. 29(*a*)). In all cases, a social worker must
visit immediately if there is any complaint by or concerning the
child, unless action on it seems unnecessary (regs. 28(1)(*c*)
(2)(*b*) and 29(*b*)).

Every time a social worker sees a child who is boarded-
out, he must, after considering the welfare, health, conduct
and progress of the child, make a written report, and every
time he visits the foster home he must make a written report
about its condition (reg. 9). There is, after all, no obligation
for the same worker to visit each time, although if possible this
is obviously good practice.

Boarding-out in another area. Children must not be
boarded-out outside England and Wales unless special
circumstances make this desirable (reg. 3), but they may be
sent to foster parents who live in the area of another authority.
In long-term cases, the care authority must (unless it is urgent
or another child has been boarded-out by it in the same
household within the past three months) first ask the area
authority to report within 14 days if anything is known which
might make the proposed placement detrimental to the child
(reg. 17(*c*)). In all cases, the care authority must give
particulars of the placement to the area authority (regs. 18 and

26), and inform the area authority when and why the placement ceases and whether it is intended to board out another child in that household (reg. 12(1)). In turn, the area authority must tell the care authority if it learns of any ground for thinking that the placement may no longer be in the child's best interests (reg. 12(2)). The care authority may if it wishes arrange for the area authority to perform any or all of its supervisory duties in relation to any or all of its children boarded-out in that area and of course to report back as arranged (reg. 13). Last, if the supervising officer, whichever authority he is from, removes a child because he seems to be at risk, the other authority must be informed (reg. 5(2)).

Boarding-out by a voluntary organisation. The above regulations apply just as much to children boarded-out by voluntary organisations as they apply to children boarded-out by local authorities. The relationship between the organisation and the local authority for the area is the same as that between a care authority and an area authority described above. However, the area authority does have the additional responsibility of ensuring that the organisation is in a position to carry out the supervisory duties properly, and if it is not, the authority must take them over. It can only do this with the organisation's consent or after a month's notice during which the organisation can appeal to the Secretary of State. The authority can always allow the organisation to take over again, and after a year the organisation can appeal to the Secretary of State to be allowed to do so (reg. 14). It is also possible for a voluntary organisation to board-out a child in its charge who is in fact in the care of a local authority (reg. 15). The care authority must be told of the placement and why it ends; and if the area authority takes over the supervisory duties (under regulation 14), the care authority must be told and the regulations will for the time being apply as if the care authority had done the boarding-out.

Records and registers. Authorities must keep up-to-date case records of all children boarded-out by them, whether in their own area or elsewhere, or for whom they are performing the supervisory duties (reg. 10(1)); voluntary organisations must keep similar records for all children they board out (reg. 10(2)). These records are confidential, for it has been held that the authority cannot be compelled to produce them to the court in wardship proceedings (*Re D.*, 1970), although it is obviously contemplated that the authority should be encouraged to disclose them to the guardian ad litem of a child involved in care proceedings. They must be kept for at least three years after the child reaches 18 (or dies younger) and be open to inspection on behalf of the Secretary of State (reg. 10(3)). Local authorities must also keep registers of all the children boarded-out in their area, whether or not they are performing the supervisory duties (reg. 11(1)). These must contain the name, sex, date of birth and religion of each child, the name, religion and address of the foster parents, the name of the boarding-out authority or organisation (and in cases under regulation 15, the name of the care authority), the dates of beginning and ending, the reason for ending, and a note of any arrangements for the area authority to perform the supervisory duties (reg. 11(2) and (3)). Registers must be kept for at least five years after the child has or would have reached 18 and be open to inspection on behalf of the Secretary of State.

Removal. An authority or organisation must not allow a child in its care to remain boarded-out with any foster parents if it appears that this is no longer in his best interests (reg. 4). Furthermore, if the supervising social worker considers that the conditions endanger the child's health, safety or morals, he may remove the child immediately (reg. 5(1)). If the foster parents are, for good or bad reasons, unco-operative, the authority may seek to enforce the undertaking by bringing habeas corpus proceedings (see *Re A.B.*, 1954); this applies even where the local authority has no parental rights, for it has a better right to possession than have the foster parents; if the authority has parental rights, however, there are simpler means of recovering children which are discussed in the section on absconding (see 2(iv) below). If there are serious grounds for concern about the child, a search warrant could always be obtained under section 40 of the Children and Young Persons Act 1933 (see Chapter 5), although refusal to allow the visiting or removal of a boarded-out child is not automatically grounds for suspicion under that section, as it is in the case of private foster children.

Foster parents who feel that removal is not in the child's best interests may attempt to forestall it by making the child a ward of court, or, when the procedure is in force, by applying for custodianship, or by applying for adoption, or even, in some cases, by doing nothing. These are fully discussed in the next two chapters.

(b) Community homes

The Children and Young Persons Act 1969 required the setting up of children's regional planning committees (s. 35), with the duty of preparing comprehensive plans for providing a suitable variety of homes to meet the needs of the children in care in the region (s. 36) and submitting these to the Secretary of State for his approval (s. 37). The only stipulation was that the plans should include facilities for observation and assessment (s. 36(4)(*b*)). Otherwise the idea was that the authorities and organisations in the area should get together to avoid duplication and achieve maximum variety and flexibility. All the homes, whether residential nurseries, ordinary children's homes, or homes which approximate to the old remand homes or approved schools, are called "community homes."

Some community homes are provided by the local authorities in the region, which have a duty to provide, manage, equip and maintain any home which the regional plan expects them to provide (s. 38). Others are provided by voluntary organisations, but under instruments of management (ordered by the Secretary of State in accordance with the regional plan, ss. 39 and 40) which provide for one of the local authorities in the region to participate in running them. These are of two types. In "controlled" community homes, the local authority is responsible for managing, equipping and maintaining the home, and anything done by the managing body is done as agent for the authority. The employment of staff is a matter for the local authority, but it may be allowed to make arrangements with the voluntary organisation for people not employed by the authority to undertake duties there (s. 41). In "assisted" community homes, the voluntary organisation remains responsible for management, equipment and maintenance and the managers are agents of the organisation, which is also responsible for employment. The local authority may be represented on the managing body, and also (unless it or the instrument of management exempts certain types of employees) it must be consulted about both the engagement and summary dismissal of employees and can after consultation require the organisation to dismiss an employee (s. 42). Controlled and assisted community homes are exempted from the provisions about registration, regulation and notification of particulars relating to other voluntary homes (see below) (s. 44).

All community homes are subject to the Community Homes Regulations 1972 (made by the Secretary of State under section 43). These cover such matters as medical care, fire precautions, religious observance, and discipline. There are also detailed provisions about authorising the use of secure accommodation and for ensuring that if secure accommodation is available it is not refused to a child for whom it is necessary (regs. 11 and 12). Community homes are subject to inspection on behalf of the Secretary of State (ss. 58 and 59). Obstruction is not only a criminal offence but also automatically grounds for a warrant to search for children under section 40 of the Children and Young Persons Act 1933 (see Chapter 5).

(c) Homes provided by the Secretary of State

The Secretary of State has power to provide homes for children in care who are in need of particular facilities and services which are unlikely to be readily available in community homes (Children and Young Persons Act 1969, s. 64). These are to be known as Youth Treatment Centres (*DHSS*, 1971) and are designed for particularly disturbed adolescents, usually those who have committed serious criminal offences, but at present only one is in operation.

(d) Voluntary homes

Some homes provided by voluntary organisations are community homes, but local authorities may also accommodate children in other voluntary homes, provided that the managers agree. A voluntary home is defined as any home or institution for the boarding, care and maintenance of poor children supported wholly or partly by voluntary contributions or by endowments, apart from mental nursing homes, residential homes for the mentally disordered, and schools (Children and Young Persons Act 1933, s. 92 and Children Act 1948, s. 27). The person carrying on such a home must register it with the Secretary of State (s. 29 and see Voluntary Homes (Registration) Regulations 1948) and also notify him annually of the prescribed particulars relating to the home (1933 Act, s. 93 and 1948 Act, s. 32 and see Voluntary Homes (Return of Particulars) Regulations 1949 and 1955). The homes are subject to the Administration of Children's Homes Regulations 1951 (made by the Secretary of State under s. 31 of the 1948 Act) which are similar in content to the Community Homes Regulations apart from those concerning secure accommodation. The Secretary of State may, after notice, cancel the registration of any home which is not conducted in accordance with his regulations (or directions made under them) or is otherwise unsatisfactory (s. 29(4)). There is a right of appeal to an appeal tribunal against the refusal or cancellation of registration (s. 30), but even if the time for this has not expired, or an appeal is pending, the Secretary of State can require the local authority for the area of any home which is unregistered or which he proposes to remove from the register, to remove all or any of the children from it. The children must then be received into the local authority's care (if they are not so already) even though the grounds under section 1 of the 1948 Act may not exist (s. 29(6)).

(e) Other arrangements

Section 13 also contains a compendious power for the local authority to make such other arrangements for the child's accommodation and maintenance as seem appropriate to it. Obvious examples are hostel accommodation for older children who are working, or residential schools, or hospitals for the mentally ill or mentally handicapped, or, regrettably, bed and breakfast accommodation where nothing else is available.

(f) "Home on trial"

The local authority may allow a child in care, either for a fixed period or until it decides otherwise, to be under the "charge and control" of a parent, guardian, relative or friend (s. 13(2)). This power now applies to any child in care, whether or not the authority has parental rights, and this could lead to confusion.

For example, if a local authority allows a child who is only in care under section 1 of the 1948 Act to go home to the person with parental rights, is it sending him out of care altogether or simply sending him home on trial? If it decides to do the latter, what is the position if the parents refuse to send him back? It appears that there is nothing the authority can do unless it can pass a section 2 resolution (and see page 175 for the problems of doing so once the parents have asked for the child back). Again, if a local authority allows a child to go to a relative or friend, is it boarding him out, or sending him there on trial under this section, or allowing him to go out of care altogether (under s. 1(3), see 1(ii) above for the problems of doing this if the parents do not agree)?

The power is of course most important if the child is subject to a section 2 resolution or a care order, for then it is a criminal offence to refuse to return him (Children and Young Persons Act 1963, s. 49; Children and Young Persons Act 1969, s. 32(3)). There are also means of recovering children who are subject to care orders or section 2 resolutions (see (iv) below). The power of course enables such children to go home on holiday, or with a view to seeing whether the resolution should be rescinded or application made for the care order to be discharged. Sometimes, however, care order children have had to be sent home because no suitable placement could yet be found. If they then repeated the offences which had led to the original order, the magistrates felt understandably aggrieved. To some extent this was the result of the transitional period following the 1969 Act, when approved schools could refuse to take individual children even though they had room. Now that community homes should not refuse if they have room, the problem is more likely to be shortage of space than unduly soft-hearted social workers, and the Secretary of State's new power to make grants specifically for secure accommodation (Children Act 1975, s. 71) may be some help.

(ii) *Review*

The amended section 12 indicates that greater emphasis should now be placed on long-term planning for the future of children in care (and see also *DHSS*, 1976), for there seems to be an alarming number of cases where the situation has been allowed to drift on for years with only a vague hope of rehabilitation within the family (*Rowe and Lambert*, 1973). Long-term foster placements must be reviewed within three months and thereafter at least every six months (Boarding-Out of Children Regulations 1955, reg. 22). The regulation requires the review to be made, so far as practicable, by people who do not normally act as visitors, but modern practice would encourage case conferences in which the social worker, foster parents, parents and the child himself were involved, as well as senior staff (*DHSS*, 1976). In addition, the local authority has at present a duty to review the case of each child in its care every six months, and if he is subject to a care order to consider whether to apply for its discharge (Children and Young Persons Act 1969, s. 27(4)). This duty was thought to be inadequate and imprecise, and the Children Act 1975 will amend it so as to require authorities to conduct reviews in accordance with regulations to be made by the Secretary of State; these will cover the manner and frequency of review, and the considerations to be taken into account, and it will be most interesting to see what emerges.

(iii) *Parents*

The parents' legal rights in relation to children in care differ according to the route along which the child arrived there and thus have already been discussed. They do not however include a right to be consulted about the child's placement, or even a right to visit him there. Both are at the local authority's discretion, although community homes and voluntary homes must provide adequate facilities for visiting (Community Homes Regulations 1972, reg. 10, Administration of Children's Homes Regulations 1951, reg. 14), and local authorities are allowed to pay the expenses of parents (and others) who would not otherwise be able to visit without undue hardship (Children Act 1948, s. 22). The High Court and divorce courts have power to give directions to local authorities to whose care they have committed children, and this could include directions about visiting (*Re Y.*, 1976). Whatever the legal situation, however, good practice surely dictates that the parents should be involved as much as possible in decisions relating to their children and every effort made to preserve their relationship with the child unless this is harmful (which is not the same as temporarily distressing) to him.

Parents do however have obligations. First, they must keep the authority informed of their whereabouts and can be prosecuted for failing to do so (Children Act 1948, s. 10; Children and Young Persons Act 1969, s. 24(8); this does not apply to remands, interim care orders, or care orders made in matrimonial and similar proceedings).

Secondly, they may have to contribute towards the cost of the child's stay in care. Where a child under 16 is in care under the Children Act 1948 or under a care order other than an interim order made under the 1969 Act, his father and his mother, or if he is illegitimate, his mother, have a duty to contribute (Children and Young Persons Act 1933, s. 86; Children Act 1948, ss. 23 and 24), except in respect of any period in which the child is allowed home on trial (1969 Act, s. 62(2)) or after the local authority has received notice of intention to apply to adopt (Adoption Act 1958, s. 36(2)). Once the child reaches 16, he is liable to contribute for himself if he is in paid full-time work (1948 Act, s. 24(3)).

Normally, of course, contributions will be a matter for agreement between the contributory and the local authority (1969 Act, s. 62(3)). Indeed, the authority cannot go to court for a contribution order unless it has first proposed an amount and either they have failed to agree within a month or there has been default in the agreed amount (1969 Act, s. 62(5)).

The amount proposed must not be more than the authority would be prepared to pay if the child were boarded-out, whether in fact he is or not (1969 Act, s. 62(4)). If the authority does go to the magistrates' court for a contribution order (1933 Act, s. 87), the court cannot order a larger sum than that proposed by the authority (1969 Act, s. 62(6)), and if later proceedings are taken to vary this, the authority must make a similar proposal and again the court cannot exceed it (1969 Act, s. 62(7)).

If a child in care is illegitimate, the authority can either apply for an existing affiliation order against the putative father to be varied in its favour, or if there is none, for an affiliation order in its own right (see Chapter 6). If a child is committed to care in the course of matrimonial or similar proceedings, the court itself can order maintenance to be paid for the child (see Chapter 3).

(iv) *Absconding*

Not all children in care are prisoners. If a child who is only in care under section 1 of the 1948 Act runs or is taken away there is little the authority can do to recover him unless it is prepared to make him a ward of court or take care proceedings; but once he has been in care for six months, anyone, including a parent, who helps him may be guilty of a criminal offence (see 1(i) above).

If a section 2 resolution is in force, the same offences may be committed by anyone who helps the child run away, or takes him away, or prevents his returning (1948 Act, s. 3(8)) and there is an additional offence of failing to return him when asked from a period of home trial (1963 Act, s. 49). There is now also a specific means of recovering the actual child (although habeas corpus may also be effective), for the Children Act 1975 gives magistrates power to order someone believed to have the child to produce him in court, and to issue warrants authorising social workers to search for him and take him back (s. 67).

Children who are remanded or committed to care under the 1969 Act can always be arrested without warrant by a police officer if they absent themselves from wherever the authority requires them to live (s. 32(1)). Habeas corpus would also be possible, but magistrates already have power to order someone believed to be able to do so to produce the child in court (s. 32 (2)), and the Children Act 1975 has also given them power to issue search warrants to police officers, who may then of course arrest the child (s. 68(5)). It is of course a criminal offence to harbour or assist such an absconder (1969 Act, s. 32(3)).

(v) *After-care*

Discharged care orders may of course be replaced with supervision orders if the child is still under 18 and these provide compulsory after-care for up to three years or until the child reaches 18. Otherwise, local authorities' statutory after-care responsibilities are limited to children who leave care in late adolescence (apart of course from continued preventive work under section 1 of the 1963 Act). Thus authorities have a duty to advise and befriend children in their area who leave the care of a local authority or voluntary organisation when they are over the compulsory school age (Children Act 1948, s. 34). This duty only lasts until the child is 18, however, and so must be intended to provide some protection for children who are taken from care when they are old enough to work. If a child leaves care over the age of 17, authorities have power, if he requests it, to visit, advise and befriend him up to the age of 21, and in exceptional cases can give him financial assistance (Children and Young Persons Act 1963, s. 58). This is more obviously aimed at the child who leaves care at or near the legal limit and who may well have little or no contact with his family or other helpful adults. Local authorities have more general powers to make contributions towards the maintenance of people who remained in care until after the compulsory school-age, or to pay educational grants to people who left care when they were 17 or over (1948 Act, s. 20), presumably because many such children will not be able to expect any help from their parents.

3. *Local Authorities and the Courts*

To what extent should the courts exercise their many powers to make orders relating to children (set out in Chapter 3) while those children are in care? The answer seems to depend on the type of power involved and the circumstances in which the court is being asked to exercise it.

If the court is being asked to exercise its ancient and extremely broad jurisdiction to make a child a ward of court, it is clear that the local authority's statutory responsibilities do not oust the court's powers altogether (see *Re M.*, 1961); but the court is anxious not to use them to interfere in any way which will detract from the powers which Parliament has given to the authority. There can be no question of detracting from Parliament's intentions if the authority is acting in breach or disregard of its statutory responsibilities (for example, where it had got thoroughly confused and so misled the mother that she lost her right to object to a section 2 resolution, *Re L. (A.C.)*, 1971); or if the local authority has itself made the child a ward of court in order to resolve competing claims (as happened in *J. v. C.*, 1970); or if the court's powers can be of some assistance to the authority (as was suggested in *Re B.*, 1975). In such cases there is no reason why the court should not intervene.

If, however, foster parents are seeking to prevent the removal of a child by making him a ward of court, the court will not normally wish to interfere with the decision of a local authority which has parental rights by virtue of a section 2 resolution (*Re M.*, 1961) or a care order (*Re T. (A.J.J.)*, 1970), for Parliament must have intended to leave the matter to the social workers. If such a child is only in care under section 1 of the 1948 Act, the court would probably not interfere if the authority were simply changing the child's placement, for here again the whole object of the legislation is to leave matters to the experts; but where the parent has asked for the child's return and the authority is acting in response to that, the court would usually be prepared to hear the case, for it is essentially a dispute between parent and foster parent in which the authority, even now, has little discretion (*Re S.*, 1965).

Where the court is being asked to exercise some power conferred upon it by statute, it is much more difficult to deduce what Parliament may have intended. If the child is in any event to remain in care, it is not surprising that the courts have been reluctant to grant applications for access (see *Re K.*,

1972) save in those cases where they have specific power to give directions to the authority (see *Re Y.*, 1976), because this is a direct interference in the authority's day-to-day responsibility for the child (although it does seem an amazing gap that the 1948 Act has so little to say about access).

There are other situations, however, in which the courts should be prepared to make or vary orders even though a child is in care. If, for example, a husband and wife are separated or divorced, and the parent granted custody has since placed the children in care, surely the other parent should not be prevented from asking the court to vary the order so that he may look after his children? Or if the mother of an illegitimate child has placed the child in care, surely the father should be able to apply for custody if he wishes to look after his child? The court in such cases must always treat the welfare of the child as the first and paramount consideration, and if it considers that he would be better remaining in care, it can always commit him to care or perhaps make a "split" order granting custody to the parent but care and control to the authority for the time being.

The courts are indeed prepared to make orders in such cases, even if the rights of the other parent have become vested in the authority by virtue of a section 2 resolution. Thus the High Court held that the magistrates *should* have heard a custody application from the father of an illegitimate child, even though the mother's rights had been transferred to the authority because of her mental illness (*R.* v. *Oxford Justices, ex p. H.*, 1975); the Court of Appeal upheld a county court judge's decision to make an interim adoption order (which is in effect a custody order) even though the mother's rights had been transferred to the authority, which objected to the order (*S.* v. *Huddersfield Borough Council*, 1975); and the divorce courts will certainly make custody orders about children who are in care (*Bawden* v. *Bawden*, 1975). In view of the restricted definition given to "parent" in the Children Act (see 1(i) above), these cases are surely right, for otherwise the court would not be able to correct a decision to award custody to a parent who was unable to cope and the parent who might be able to cope would have no right to remove his child from care. However, the local authority ought clearly to be given a hearing in such cases, as there might be very good reasons why the child should not be removed. (This should not be a problem, at least in the higher courts, but there may be technical difficulties if the authority is not a party to the proceedings and wishes to appeal, see *Bawden* v. *Bawden*, 1975.)

If a care order has been made, the conflict is more between different jurisdictions of the courts than between the courts and local authorities. The sensible solution would be for the same court to be able to grant or vary a custody order and to discharge a care order, but unfortunately the two proceedings take place in different courts, and there have been some contradictory decisions about the proper sequence of events (compare *H.* v. *H.*, 1973, with *Re P.*, 1967).

The matter is further complicated because it is quite clear that the new custodianship jurisdiction is intended to apply to children in care no matter what the route along which they arrived there. Foster parents and relatives should surely not be in any better position to apply for custody than a natural parent who happened to be deprived of it at the time when the child was placed in care but who can now offer a home.

10 Relatives and Foster Parents

"Fostering" is a convenient term where a child is being looked after by someone other than his natural parents but has not been legally adopted. This obviously includes a wide variety of arrangements, with relatives or with non-relatives, for short or long periods, with or without the intervention of a child-care agency. In some, the term "foster parent" would be inappropriate and so the more neutral term "care-giver" will be used. Each situation, however, presents the law with essentially the same two problems. To what extent can and should it impose some control on the making and conduct of such arrangements? And to what extent should it give the care-givers any security in their relationship with the child?

1. *Control*

Control in this context normally means the opportunity or obligation of social workers to monitor or choose the people offering substitute care, to supervise the arrangements once made and to intervene to protect the interests of the children involved. The legal details have already been described in the chapters on Substitute Care and Local Authorities, but it may be helpful to summarise the conclusions here. First, the law's policy is to refrain from interference in arrangements made in the parents' own home, save by way of criminal sanctions for neglect and procedures for removing children who are in danger of abuse. Society still respects the integrity of the family unit and some would say that the security and welfare of children are not promoted by allowing too much scope for officious intervention (*Goldstein, Freud and Solnit*, 1973). Official help and support is another matter (as is demonstrated by section 1 of the Children and Young Persons Act 1963).

It is once the child steps outside his parents' home that

positive controls begin to operate, but even here there are two notable exceptions. If a private arrangement is made with a child's close relatives, neither the requirements of private fostering nor the sanctions against unregistered child-minding apply. Presumably this reflects an assumption that children are less at risk in their extended family; certainly familiarity may lessen the trauma of separation. In some cases, of course, children being cared for by relatives are formally in the care of a local authority, either because the authority has deliberately arranged this or because they have approached the authority with a view to obtaining the financial assistance of the boarding-out allowance. In such cases the relatives are subject to exactly the same controls as any other local authority foster parent, and indeed there may be situations of intense family rivalry where the authority deems it best to remove the child. The other exception is when children are being cared for by legally-appointed guardians after their parents' death. Even if they are unrelated, there is no provision for social work control, although the High Court has some power to intervene. Parents have thus an unfettered right to choose an unrelated care-giver who will have virtually full parental rights after their death, yet if they arrange for non-relatives to look after the child during their life-time, statutory controls will operate.

However, as has been seen, the nature and effectiveness of those controls differs very substantially according to whether the parents have delegated responsibility to a local authority or voluntary organisation (or in some cases been obliged to surrender the child to the local authority) or have made their own arrangements. In the former, legal responsibility lies primarily with the agency, which can automatically choose, arrange and monitor each individual placement, as well as planning for when and how it should end. In the latter, control in effect depends upon the initiative of the care-giver in notifying or registering with the local authority, which has only limited powers to prohibit placement or to refuse registration, and on the readiness of the local authority to deploy scarce social work resources in supervising or inspecting arrangements for which it was not primarily responsible. Save in the few cases where the authority can take steps to remove the child, the placement's ending is entirely a matter for parents

and care-givers. Thus while there is general agreement that
separation of children from their parents involves, if not actual
danger, grave stresses and strains from which both the children
and the adults involved require the protection of sensitive and
skilled social work involvement, the chances of their receiving
this differ radically according to the type of arrangement
made.

2. *Security*

One of the principal justifications for social work involvement
in arrangements for the care of children away from home is the
extreme difficulty of the care-giver's task. She must be able to
supply both the physical and psychological needs of a child
who has experienced the stress either of separation from his
most-loved adult or of previous negative relationships with the
adults around him. Furthermore, she must usually do this not
as a total substitute for the absent parents but as someone who
shares the responsibility with both the agency (if any) and the
parents. And, save in cases where the placement actually
breaks down, it is the agency or the parents who decide if and
when the child should leave.

Looking after someone else's child thus involves heavy
responsibilities without any automatic legal security. If the
child is privately placed either with relatives or with foster
parents, the natural parents retain the right to remove the
child at will (although they may not always be able to enforce
that right, see below). This is so whatever they may have
agreed with the care-givers, for it is not possible to surrender or
transfer parental rights by agreement (Children Act 1975, s.
85(2), enacting the previous common law). If the child has
been boarded-out by a local authority or voluntary organisation the foster parents must undertake to return the child when
asked by the agency (although again this may not always be
enforceable, see below). The agency may of course be asking
for the child because it has itself decided to end the placement;
or because it has no legal right to refuse the parents' request
for the child's return — this is a matter for the agency to
decide and so foster parents should not return the child to the
parents on their own initiative; or because although the agency

had parental rights, a court has decided to return them to the parents — but at least people who have been looking after a child for six weeks will now have a right to be heard on an application for the discharge of a care order made in care proceedings.

Whatever the circumstances requiring the child's return, it obviously needs sensitive handling. A skilled social work agency should at least have prepared its foster parents for this, have made some attempt to maintain contact between natural parents and their children, and even have tried to counsel the parents against asking for the child's return if it is not in his best interests. However, although in practice the position of local authority foster parents may be better, at present their legal position is rather weaker than that of other care-givers, for they will usually find it more difficult to persuade the courts to intervene on their behalf (see below). Furthermore, although the modern professional texts on fostering emphasise the need to select and to educate foster parents who can accept this fundamental insecurity (for example, *Trasler*, 1960; *George*, 1970), recent research has indicated just how difficult this is (*Adamson*, 1973). It is scarcely surprising that the popular view, at least of long-term fostering, not only fails to appreciate the legal complexities but has also expressed considerable scepticism about the professional approach.

The problem is one of aims. In the days when children came into public care because they had been orphaned, abandoned, or removed from extremely unsatisfactory homes, it was easier to see foster care as a "fresh start." When the service was extended to children from perfectly adequate homes whose need for substitute care arose from illness or other misfortunes and was often purely temporary, the emphasis was bound to change. The parents had to feel that they did not run the risk of losing their children forever if they used the service. Moreover, this coincided with a growing understanding of the dangers of separating children from their most-loved parent-figures, and of the confusion and self-doubt experienced by many children who are brought up away from their natural parents (see *Bowlby*, 1951). Thus the aim became to rehabilitate and reunite the natural family if at all possible, and this was later reinforced by the aim of preventing the separation in the first place (Children and Young Persons Act 1963, s. 1). However, there will always be some cases in which this is neither a realistic nor a beneficial aim. The natural parents may never have demonstrated the unquestioning commitment or established the warm relationships which are normally the great strengths of the natural family and which enable it to survive many temporary separation experiences. Or, whatever the original situation, the separation may have been so long or so complete that relationships of equal warmth and commitment have now been established in the substitute family, and it must be asked whether the dangers of disrupting this are not greater than any risks to the child's self-image in adolescence (see *Goldstein, Freud and Solnit*, 1973). It is striking that the most recent authoritative guide to fostering practice (*DHSS*, 1976) places great emphasis on the need for flexibility in suiting both short and long-term plans to the changing situation and needs of each individual child.

It is against this background that the legal position of all types of care-giver must be seen. They start from a position of total insecurity. In this there are two chinks, for if the child has been involved in care proceedings they will often have a right to be heard in those proceedings, and in certain circumstances a parent or agency may find it difficult to enforce the right to possession, so that the foster parent may achieve something by doing nothing. However, the best way of counteracting a claim for possession is to take proceedings designed to give the care-giver a better right. At present this can only be done by attempting to make the child a ward of court or by applying to adopt, but when Part II of the Children Act 1975 is in force, an application for custodianship may be possible. Adoption will be discussed in the next chapter, where it will be seen that certain developments, making it harder to remove a child while an application is pending and easier to dispense with the natural parents' agreement, may improve the foster parents' chances of success. The legal niceties of doing nothing, wardship proceedings, and the new custodianship procedure will be discussed below, and a final section in this chapter will examine the attitude so far adopted by the courts to disputes between natural parents and non-parents; it is considerably more flexible than might be supposed.

(i) *Doing nothing*

This will only succeed if the parents or agency are unable to enforce their claim to possession, assuming of course that they have not simply arrived and removed the child. A parent's claim to possession will rarely be enforced against an older child (see Chapter 1, and also the case of *Krishnan* v. *Sutton London Borough Council*, 1970, on p. 173), or if it is not in the child's best interests. A local authority with parental rights under a section 2 resolution or care order may be able to use its powers to recover absconders, but apart from that an agency will be in no better position than a parent. It is still safer in most cases to take action to forestall their claims.

(ii) *Making the child a ward of court*

Any of the parties involved, whether relatives, foster parents, the agency or the child's own parents, can seek to resolve the problem by making the child a ward of court. The procedure has already been described (in Chapter 3). The court may of course decide that the child should go to the parents or agency, but if he remains subject to the court's guardianship, the court can decide how, where and by whom he shall be cared for.

However, if the child is in the care of the local authority, the position is complicated by the court's reluctance to interfere in the authority's statutory responsibilities (this has been discussed in the last chapter). From the point of view of the foster parent who is trying to prevent removal of the child, this means that the court will not allow wardship to challenge the merits of a decision of a local authority which has parental rights by virtue of a section 2 resolution or a care order. If the authority does not have parental rights, the court will probably not interfere if the authority is simply changing the child's placement, but it will hear a case once the parent has asked for the child's return, for as the authority has very little discretion, the dispute is much the same as one between parents and private foster parents. The court will however intervene if the local authority is acting in breach or disregard of its statutory responsibilities or if it has been asked to do so by the authority. The principal case relating to disputes between parents and foster parents (*J. v. C.*, 1970, discussed at 3(i) below) related to a child in care under section 1 of the 1948 Act who had been made a ward of court by the local authority.

Thus despite its very broad scope, wardship is not an ideal method of granting some security to a deserving care-giver. Even if the case is one in which the court is prepared to intervene, proceedings must take place in the Family Division of the High Court. This is often geographically inconvenient, although the High Court does sit outside London. The procedure is careful, but somewhat complicated and often regrettably slow. Legal representation is virtually essential and the child will often be separately represented by the Official Solicitor. Unless legal aid is available the expense to all will be considerable. Last, if the care-givers are to succeed the child must remain a ward of court, and thus any alteration in the status quo or major decision relating to his future must be referred to the court at further expense. The remedy is thus in practice limited to a small number of comparatively well-off or unusually determined litigants and indeed the court would be quite unable to cope with large numbers. Its existence and scope does however put the new custodianship jurisdiction into some perspective.

(iii) *Applying for custodianship*

Until Part II of the Children Act 1975 is in force, wardship, with all its limitations, remains virtually the only way short of adoption of establishing a claim to someone else's child. (It is possible for third parties to be granted custody in divorce, matrimonial or, at present, Guardianship of Minors Act proceedings, but this is dependent upon a spouse or parent taking the first step. The divorce court can also make orders about any child, apart from one boarded out by a local authority or voluntary organisation, who has been treated as a child of the family, but this will not affect the rights of a parent who is not a party to the proceedings.) Adoption of course normally requires the parents' agreement, and even if this is forthcoming, it may not always be in the child's best interests to sever all links with the natural family and establish artificial legal relationships. Even if rehabilitation of the natural family remains the ideal, the limitations of the choice, between the totality and finality (and often financial sacrifice) of adoption on the one hand and total insecurity on the other hand, were increasingly criticised, not least because it seemed that in some cases unrealistic assumptions about the possibility of rehabilitation had led to children waiting in a limbo of insecurity when they might have been found permanent homes (*Rowe and Lambert*, 1973).

The solution could simply have been to amend section 9 of the Guardianship of Minors Act so as to allow anyone to apply for custody, and to trust the courts to make orders only where this was genuinely best for the child. The courts would then have had to abandon their reluctance to interfere in cases where the child was in care, for otherwise the problem of the long term local authority foster parent would have remained untouched (including, of course, the case of Maria Colwell), while relatives and private foster parents acquired much better rights. But to do this would not only have given the courts unprecedented powers of reviewing the merits of local authority decisions, but would also have had dramatic implications for the nature of fostering and the confidence of parents in the child-care service.

The result has been a compromise. The new procedure, when in force, will allow application (although of course this may not succeed) to the local magistrates' court or county court, or to the High Court, for an order vesting legal custody in a non-parent, whether a relative or private or public foster parent, but only if the applicant has been looking after the child for some time. In keeping with the general attitude of the law, the required period can differ between relatives and non-relatives, and in keeping with the fears expressed about the implications for the nature of fostering and parental confidence, it differs even more significantly according to whether a person already having legal custody (usually of course the parent) agrees to the application being made.

(a) The applicants

The applicant or applicants must be "qualified" in one of three ways (Children Act 1975, s.33(3)). (i) A relative or step-parent with whom the child has had his home for at least the three months before the application is made is qualified to apply if he has the consent of "a person having legal custody" of the child. (ii) For anyone else applying with similar consent, the qualifying period is a total of 12 months, which may be in separate periods provided that it includes the past three months. (iii) If there is no such consent, the qualifying period for all applicants is a total of three years, including the past three months (but the Secretary of State will have power, with parliamentary approval, to prescribe a different period).

Several further points should be noted. (i) There is no requirement, as there is in adoption and in the Boarding-out Regulations, for joint applicants to be married to one another. (ii) Step-parents' applications will usually relate to illegitimate or orphaned children, because the step-parents of children involved in divorce are expressly excluded unless the parent other than the one they married has died or disappeared (s.33(5) and (8)); otherwise they can always apply to the divorce court for custody. (iii) Only the consent of "a" person having legal custody is required for the shorter periods to apply; thus if both parents have custody only one need consent; but is a local authority with parental rights under a care order or section 2 resolution a "person" with legal custody? (iv) If no one has legal custody, or the applicant himself has it, or the person with it cannot be found, the shorter periods apply without the need for consent (s.33(6)). (v) There is no way of dispensing with consent, save by the roundabout means of applying to adopt (see below).

(b) Custodianship as an alternative

The court can direct that certain other applications be treated as if they were for custodianship. (i) If the necessary agreements to adoption have been given or dispensed with, the court can nevertheless direct that the application be treated as one for custodianship if it thinks that this would be more appropriate (s.37(2)). In the case of adoption applications by relatives or step-parents (again excluding step-parents of children involved in divorce) this is a positive duty, provided that the court is satisfied that the child's welfare would not be better safeguarded by adoption than by custodianship (s.37(1)). This again reflects the growing disapproval of adoptions which distort rather than replace existing relationships. (ii) If mother or father apply for custody under the Guardianship of Minors Act and the court thinks that custody should be given to a third party, it may direct the application to be treated as a custodianship application by that party (s.37(3)). This is simply a roundabout way of preserving the present power of the courts to grant custody to third parties in such cases.

The courts can make these directions even though the applicant would not have been "qualified" to apply for custodianship in the first place (s.37(4)). Thus again the desire to restrict the right to apply is reconciled with the desire to provide a less drastic alternative to adoption.

(c) Protection against removal of the child

Removal of the child is prohibited while an application is pending, but only if the child has had his home with the applicant for a total of at least *three years* (s.41(1)). In most other cases, the person with legal custody will have consented and is thus unlikely to remove the child, although a change of mind is always possible and occasionally there will be someone else who has a right to remove the child and has not consented. If the prohibition applies removal will still be possible if the applicant agrees or with leave of a court, or by way of arrest, or under some statutory authority; but a local authority will not be able to remove a child who was in its care before going to the applicant and who remains in its care, except with the applicant's consent or the leave of a court (s.41(2)).

Contravention of section 41(1) is a criminal offence (s.41(3)). The courts may also direct a particular person not to contravene it if there is reasonable ground to think that he intends to do so (s.42(2)). If the child is unlawfully removed, the courts may order his return (s.42(1)), and if this is not done, they may authorise a court officer (High Court and county court) or police officer (magistrates' court) to search premises for the child and return him (s.42(3) and (4)).

(d) Reports

Notice must be given to the local authority by the applicant within seven days of making the application (s.40(1)), unless it is a case which the court itself has directed shall be treated as custodianship (s.37(4)). The authority must then investigate and produce a report in accordance with regulations to be made by the Secretary of State (s.40(2) and (3)). The section expressly mentions matters such as the wishes and feelings of the child, the means and suitability of the applicants, information relating to the members of the applicant's household, and the wishes and means of the natural parents. These are all, apart perhaps from means, matters which would normally be included in a welfare officer's report, and the court has a further power to ask either the local authority or a probation officer for a report on specific matters (s.39). Both types of report are covered by the provisions of the Guardianship Act relating to welfare officers' reports and must thus be disclosed to the parties. However, section 40 ensures that there will be an investigation and report in every case, even if it is not contested, and thus has affinities with the present role of the guardian ad litem in adoption cases. The section also recognises that the local authority may be actively involved in many cases.

(e) Effect of the order

A custodianship order, if made, vests "legal custody" of the child in the applicant, or one or more of them (s.33(1)). The right of anyone else to custody is for the time being suspended (s.44(1)), unless the custodian is married to the person already having custody, in which case they have it jointly (s.44(2)). There would thus seem to be no scope for splitting custody and care and control between applicant and natural parent as there is in other custody jurisdictions. "Legal custody" means all those parental rights and duties which relate to the child's person as opposed to his property (s.86), and thus encompasses most of the powers of parenthood, including the right to decide whether the child can marry under the age of 18 (Marriage Act 1949, s.3 as amended). The custodian will thus have almost complete control over the child's upbringing (and any dispute between joint custodians can be referred to a court as can disputes between parents, s.38), but there are signficant differences from adoption. (i) The custodian cannot arrange for the child's emigration (s.86). (ii) The child remains in his natural family for such purposes as inheritance and the devolution of property. (iii) The natural parent retains the right to decide whether the child shall be legally adopted. (iv) Most importantly perhaps, the link with the natural family is preserved by the possibility of ancillary orders and later revocation.

The effect on care orders and section 2 resolutions remains obscure (see Chapter 9), but it is clearly contemplated that custodianship should be possible in such cases, and it will certainly give the custodian the right to bring up the child. Whether any rights remain with the local authority or whether they must automatically disappear depends upon the content of resolutions and care orders themselves.

(f) Ancillary and other orders

(i) The court may grant access to the child to his natural mother or father or to anyone in relation to whom he has been treated as a "child of the family" (s.34(1)(*a*)). Access orders may be later varied or discharged at the request of the person granted access or the custodian (s.35(3) and (4)). (ii) The court may order the child's mother or father or someone in relation to whom the child was treated as a child of the family to make periodical payments towards his maintenance (s.34(1)(*b*)). It can also revoke or vary maintenance orders made previously by other courts (s.34(1)(*c*) and (*d*)). In keeping with the law's usual practice it cannot make maintenance orders against the father of an illegitimate child (s.34(3)), but the custodian can make a separate application for an affiliation order (s.45) unless he is married to the child's mother. Maintenance orders may also be later revoked or varied at the request of the person paying or the custodian (s.35(3) and (4)). (iii) The court has the same power to make supervision or care orders as it has in ordinary custody cases (s.34(4); see Chapter 3).

Furthermore, local authorities are empowered to make contributions to a custodian towards the cost of the child's maintenance and accommodation (s.34(5)). Although this power is not limited to children who were previously in the local authority's care, it was obviously designed to help applicants who might otherwise be deterred by the loss of the boarding-out allowance.

(g) Revocation

A custodianship order may be revoked on the application of the child's custodian, mother, father, guardian or any local authority (s.35(1)), but there are limitations. (i) A person who has previously applied unsuccessfully for revocation cannot apply again unless either the previous court directed that he could do so or there has been a change in the circumstances or some other good reason for considering revocation again (s.35(2)). This is no doubt designed to spare custodians the anguish of repeated applications from parents, but they will still have to meet suggestions that there are now good grounds. (ii) Before revoking an order, the court is expressly told to discover who will have legal custody if it does so (s.36(1)). If there is no one, the court must make a care order (s.36(2)). Normally, however, it will be the person whose rights were suspended by the custodianship order (s.44(1)), and if the court has misgivings, it may either allow him to regain custody subject to a supervision order or instead make a care order (s.36(3)). The court must call for a local authority or probation officer's report on the desirability of returning the child, unless it already has sufficient information (s.36(4)).

3. *Principles*

Given that there are means short of adoption whereby a non-parent can ask a court to allow him to continue caring for a child, the problem remains of what attitude the court would adopt towards the merits of such claims. This in effect involves two questions. What is the relative weight to be given to the wishes and claims of natural parents and the welfare of the child? And how do the courts interpret the welfare of the child in such cases?

(i) *Parental rights*

Both the wardship and custodianship jurisdictions are governed by the now familiar principle in section 1 of the Guardianship of Minors Act 1971: "Where in any proceedings before any court ... the custody or upbringing of a minor ... is in question, the court shall regard the welfare of the minor as the first and paramount consideration ..." (see Children Act 1975, s.33(9)). Of course, in many custodianship cases, the natural parents will have consented to the application, so that if the court decides that the order is indeed in the child's best interests, no problem of conflict will arise. But in its wardship jurisdiction, the court has already had to balance the claims of parenthood against the welfare of the child, and has come to a very firm conclusion.

In 1958 a little boy was born to a Spanish couple who were working in England. The mother suffered from tuberculosis and so the baby was cared for by an English couple for some 10 months, until she came out of hospital. Later, the parents took him back to Spain, but the family was very poor, living in slum conditions in Madrid, where the climate did not suit the little boy and his health deteriorated. In 1961, through the foster parents' Spanish maid, who visited the family while on holiday in Madrid, it was arranged that the boy should come back to the foster parents. Nobody contemplated that this would be permanent, but no time limit was agreed. The boy was formally received into the care of the local authority and boarded-out with the foster parents. There he settled down and his health improved considerably. A proposal that the parents should return to work in England did not bear fruit, and the mother did not take up an offer to pay for her to visit the boy. In 1963 he started school, and the foster mother wrote a "tactless" letter to the mother, remarking how English he was becoming. The mother became worried, and after a request for him to spend a holiday in Spain had been refused by the foster parents, formally asked the local authority for his return. The foster parents countered with notice of their intention to apply to adopt. The local authority, feeling caught between the Children Act and the Adoption Act, made the child a ward of court in December 1963. It took until July

1965 for the case to be heard and the parents were not there, although the local authority put forward the arguments in their favour. The judge ordered that care and control should remain with the foster parents, but that the boy should remain a Roman Catholic and be brought up with a knowledge of his Spanish origins and the Spanish language. In 1967, the foster parents applied to change his religion so that he could be sent to an Anglican choir school and the parents countered with a renewed application for his return. By this time both their material circumstances and the mother's health were very much better, but the boy was now nine, had been in England since the age of three, had learnt to play cricket and spoke only "pidgin" Spanish. The case was heard by the judge in 1967, the Court of Appeal, and finally the House of Lords in 1968. All decided that he should stay with the foster parents but should not change his religion (*J.* v. *C.*, 1970).

The case raised very neatly the precise application of the "welfare principle" in such disputes. It could have been argued that the Act (which was originally the Guardianship of Infants Act 1925) had not displaced the common law's presumption in favour of the natural parents, but had simply allowed it to be overridden where the welfare of the child clearly demanded it. If that were so the natural parents might have succeeded, for apart perhaps from not taking up the offer to visit, they could hardly be criticised for letting the boy to to England and now had a satisfactory home to offer. If, on the other hand, the welfare of the child was the first as well as an overriding consideration, he should surely remain where he was happy and settled, whether or not the foster parents had deliberately manipulated the situation towards this end.

The House of Lords held that the section applied just as much to disputes between parents and "strangers" as it did between mother and father, and that it meant just what it said: the child's welfare was always the first and paramount consideration. The position of the natural parents was probably best summed up thus:

> "The natural parents have a strong claim to have their wishes considered, first and principally, no doubt, because normally it is part of the paramount consideration of the welfare of the infant that he should be with

them; but also because natural parents may themselves have strong claims to have their wishes considered as normally the proper persons to have the upbringing of the child they have brought into the world" (Lord Upjohn).

Thus the fact of parenthood is not only a factor in the child's welfare but it appears that the parent's wishes are also a secondary consideration in their own right; as such they might just tip the scale where the welfare considerations are more evenly balanced than they were in this case. This is supported by a statement in the case of *Re F.* already described (see page 155), which was a dispute between the child's father and maternal grandmother: "I have borne in mind throughout that the child's welfare is the first and paramount consideration. I am convinced that it is in the child's interests to stay with her father and step-mother. But I also bear in mind that the child's welfare is not the only consideration. Her father is her only surviving parent. To take her away from him for insufficient reason would not only be wrong from her point of view; it would also in my judgment be a grave injustice to the father" (Bridge L.J., 1976).

(ii) *The welfare of the child*

The courts' approach to their "first and paramount consideration" in disputes between mother and father has already been discussed in Chapter 3, but two aspects deserve special mention in the context of disputes between parents and non-parents. These are an assumption that it is normally in a child's best interests to be brought up by his "own" parents, and an awareness of the dangers of interfering in a situation which has apparently been working well for some considerable time.

These two assumptions do of course conflict, and often more strongly in the case of disputes between parents and non-parents than in disputes between recently separated spouses. The problem is amply illustrated by a case in 1926. The father of a little girl, whose mother died when she was a few months old, was unable to have her cared for at home and so arranged for her to be looked after by her uncle and aunt. He maintained contact with them and sent money and clothing, but when he remarried a few years later, allowed the child to remain where she was. When he had been married about three years, however, and the girl was six, he asked for her back (perhaps because his second marriage was childless). The judge may (as was said in *J*. v. *C*.) have applied the correct principle and put the child's welfare before her father's rights, but in assessing her welfare he gave little weight to the disruption of existing well-established ties. "It is said that the little girl will be greatly distressed and upset at parting from Mr. and Mrs. Jones. I can quite understand it may be so, but, at her tender age, one knows from experience how mercifully transient are the effects of partings and other sorrows, and how soon the novelty of fresh surroundings and new associations effaces the recollection of former days and kind friends, and I cannot attach much weight to this aspect of the case" (*Re Thain*, 1926).

A modern judge would certainly not express himself in those terms nor dismiss as "transient" the effects of "partings and other sorrows." It is usually suggested that today the actual decision would have been different. Certain recent decisions (*J*. v. *C*., above, among them) do indicate that this is so, but to date there have of course been relatively few cases of this nature. It is worth recalling that, *in the context of another jurisdiction*, a court ordered that Maria Colwell should be returned to her natural mother after six years with an uncle and aunt, and that this course was unopposed by the social workers concerned. No doubt the social workers' decision was partly coloured by their view of what the court was likely to do (and this was only shortly after the decision in *J*. v. *C*.), but it was also coloured by what they saw as Maria's long-term interests — rehabilitation with the natural family. The fairest comment is surely not to question that as an ideal, but to suggest that both courts and social workers should ask themselves *why* it is usually better for children to be brought up by their natural parents. When this is done it should become easier to distinguish those cases where the aim is realistic from those where it should be abandoned.

Thus it is far too simple to see these cases as conflicts between the "rights of parents" and the "welfare of the child." The welfare of the child in itself demands that very careful consideration be given to the natural parents' claims. But each case, each parent, each child and each situation is different; the purpose of recent changes has been at least partially to encourage both a more flexible approach and more realistic planning (see also *DHSS*, 1976).

Part IV
New Families

11 Adoption

Adoption is the virtually complete and irrevocable transfer of a child from one legal family to another. As such it goes far beyond long-term fostering, where the most important parental responsibilities are transferred without any corresponding parental rights, and also far beyond a custody order, which transfers most parental rights and responsibilities, but leaves the child a member of his original family for other purposes, and may of course be revoked or varied. Although adoption was well-known to ancient Roman law and the continental legal systems which are largely based upon it, it was not recognised by the English common law and was only introduced here by statute in 1926; and whereas in early systems its purpose was mainly to provide an heir to carry on the family's name, religious observances and sometimes political aspirations, in England its principal object has been to provide permanent and secure family care for a child whose natural parents are unable or unwilling to keep him. The typical adoption is thus imagined as the placement of a young baby with a childless couple who are complete strangers to the natural family. In practice, however, many adoptions take place in quite different circumstances, notably where a child is adopted by one natural parent and a step-parent; but the imagined stereotype has and continues to have an important influence on English law and practice, not least in the emphasis it places upon the involvement of social workers.

1. *The Court*

The first distinctive feature of English law is that adoption cannot take place without a court order. This may often seem a tiresome formality, when most of the important decisions and safeguards operate long before the case gets to court; but the law is always likely to require a formal order to make such a drastic change in status, affecting not only the parties but their families and indeed anyone who comes into contact with them; in future it may perhaps be prepared, as in many undefended divorces, to absolve both applicants from attending a formal hearing, but not yet.

Applications can be made either to the High Court or to the applicants' local county or magistrates' court. The High Court has to deal with cases where neither applicant is domiciled in this country, and only the High Court or county court can make provisional orders allowing the applicants to take the child abroad to be adopted. Both of these are outside the scope of this book. In practice, the High Court deals with only a handful of cases, usually where there are particular difficulties or it is already involved in some way, and the main choice lies between the cheaper and more convenient county or magistrates' courts. At present, magistrates' adoption cases are heard in the juvenile court, but the Children Act 1975 will eventually transfer them to the domestic court, where all other custody disputes are heard (s. 21(3)). The county court may be preferred because the case will be heard by one legally-qualified judge, usually in his room in a building where no criminal cases are ever tried; but the choice is often governed by the agency's convenience, as well as by its knowledge of local courts' attitudes and practices. There is some indication that step-parent adoptions of children involved in divorce ought not to be taken to magistrates' courts, but both the lower courts can refuse to deal with a case which is more suitable for the High Court.

2. *Qualifications to Adopt and be Adopted*

The principal purpose of English adoption law is reflected in the qualifications to adopt and be adopted, which make some attempt to reproduce a natural family structure. A person can only be adopted while still a child under 18 (Children Act 1975, s. 107(1)), and only then if he has never been married (1975 Act, s. 8(5)). Providing an heir or carrying on the family name does not require adoption in a country where one can usually leave one's property to whomsoever one likes and one can adopt whatever surname one chooses; adoption is thus concerned with providing homes for children.

Every applicant for an adoption order, whether related to the child or not, must now be at least 21 years old (1975 Act, ss. 10(1) and 11(1)). Thus a mother below that age can no longer adopt her own illegitimate child. There is no maximum age laid down, and while most agencies would be reluctant to place a young child with a childless couple over the normal age of child-bearing, fostering studies indicate that couples who have already successfully brought up their own children may be best suited to caring for the older, more difficult, child.

Applications may be made by one person or by two people together, but joint applicants must be married to one another (1975 Act, s. 10(1)) and the stability of their marriage is obviously a factor for both agency and court. A sole applicant must either be unmarried (that is, single, widowed or divorced) or, if married, must satisfy the court that his or her spouse cannot be found or is incapable because of physical or mental ill-health of making an application or that they are living apart and the separation is likely to be permanent (1975 Act, s. 11(1)). In the past, a married person could make a sole application even if these criteria did not exist, provided that the other spouse consented, and the exclusion of such cases again reflects the desire to reproduce a normal family. Applicants must attach medical certificates to their applications, unless one is the child's parent or the child is 16, for although the court is no longer specifically instructed to consider their health, it is obviously an important factor in the "need to safeguard and promote the welfare of the child throughout his childhood," to which the court must now give first consideration (1975 Act, s. 3).

The desire to reproduce a normal family is also reflected in two recent provisions (already discussed in the chapters on step-parents and unmarried parents) which are aimed at discouraging adoptions which will distort rather than replace normal family relationships. Thus the court must not grant an adoption to a natural parent and step-parent, or to a step-parent alone, where the natural parents have been divorced and the court considers that the matter might be better dealt with by a custody order in the divorce proceedings

(1975 Act, ss. 10(3) and 11(4)). Furthermore, when the custodianship provisions are in force, the court will have a positive duty to consider this less drastic alternative in other types of step-parent adoption application. Secondly, the court must not grant an adoption on the sole application of the child's natural mother or father, unless the other natural "parent" is dead or cannot be found or there is some other reason justifying his exclusion; and if such an adoption is granted, the reason must be recorded (s. 11(3)). This is obviously aimed against sole adoptions by the mothers of illegitimate children, but may give rise to some difficulty because the word "parent" does not normally refer to the father of an illegitimate child; presumably the courts will make an exception in this case, for the section was surely meant to refer to him.

In either of the above situations, the courts' rules now permit them to decline jurisdiction at the outset, so that a guardian ad litem need never be appointed and all the effort and worry involved in an application which the court will have to refuse in the end may be avoided.

On the other hand, the old rule which prohibited a man from making a sole application to adopt a female child unless there were special circumstances (and the fact that he was her father was not in itself enough) has now gone. Provided therefore that the mother can be excluded, it will now be possible for a man to adopt his own illegitimate child.

Another provision which reflects the traditional hope that adoption will supply the child with a completely new and normal family is the procedure for concealing the applicants' identity by a serial number. This was no doubt to protect them and the child from the problems which might arise should the mother regret her decision and try to trace them, but it seems strange that the mother does not have a reciprocal right.

Last, it should be noted that there will be no difficulty if the applicant, or one of the joint applicants, is domiciled (that is, very roughly, permanently settled) in any part of the United Kindgom, Channel Islands or Isle of Man (1975 Act, ss. 10(2)(*a*) and 11(2)(*a*)). If this is not the case, it may be possible to obtain what will be known as a convention adoption order (when section 24 of the 1975 Act is in force) or an order allowing the applicant to take the child abroad to be adopted (at present known as a provisional adoption order under section 53 of the 1958 Act, eventually to be replaced by section 25 of the 1975 Act). These cases will require specialist legal advice and are outside the scope of this book.

3. *Restrictions on Arranging Adoptions*

The law places various general limitations on arranging adoptions which are distinct from the requirements attaching to particular placements (discussed in the next section) and which have two main objects:

(i) *Prevention of "trafficking"*

The first object is to avoid any possibility that children are being bought or sold. Thus it is an offence to give or receive any payment or reward either for giving or for receiving a child for adoption or for making the arrangements (1958 Act, s. 50). Courts are specifically prohibited from making adoption orders in favour of people who have contravened this section (1975 Act, s. 22(5)). Contributions towards the expenses of an adoption agency are however excepted, as are payments specifically sanctioned by the court (1958 Act, s. 50(3)). In addition, the 1975 Act will eventually allow the Secretary of State to approve schemes submitted by agencies for payment by the agency of allowances to actual and prospective adopters (s. 32). This is designed to remove one obstacle to desirable, but hitherto neglected, adoptions, for example of whole families or of handicapped children, or of long-term foster children, where the added expense or the loss of the boarding-out allowance may be a deterrent. The scheme in no way detracts from the principle outlawing "trafficking" in children.

Similarly, it is an offence for either parents or prospective adopters to advertise their desire for adoption, or for anyone other than an adoption agency to advertise willingness to make adoption arrangements (1958 Act, s. 51). This may be contrasted with the position on fostering advertisements, which are at present only prohibited if they indicate willingness to undertake or arrange fostering without disclosing the person's name and address (Children Act 1958, s. 37). The 1975 Act will eventually allow the Secretary of State to make more comprehensive regulations covering who may advertise about fostering and in what circumstances (s. 97), but these are not thought as dangerous as adoption advertisements and at least for voluntary organisations and local authorities can provide a useful method of recruitment.

(ii) *Ensuring expert placement*

The law also increasingly recognises that in most adoptions the important decision is made not at the court hearing but when the child is actually placed. It therefore makes some attempt to secure that that decision is handled by suitably qualified and experienced people who are not acting for personal profit. Thus, apart from the rules just mentioned, the law provides that no body of persons may arrange adoptions apart from a local social services authority or registered adoption society (Adoption Act 1958, s. 29). Adoption societies must be charitable bodies (1958 Act, s. 30(3)) and apply for registration to the local social services authority for the area of their administrative headquarters (1958 Act, s. 30(1) and see Adoption Agencies' Regulations 1959, reg. 1 and Sched. 1), to which they must also send annual reports and accounts (reg. 3 and Sched. 2). Authorities can inspect the books and records of registered societies (1958 Act, s. 33) and can refuse or cancel registration on a variety of grounds (s.30(4) and (5)), but there is a right of appeal to the Crown Court (s.31).

These provisions are however far from adequate to produce the desired result. While all local social services authorities have power to act as adoption agencies (1958 Act, s. 28), this is not yet a duty, and some either do not offer a service at all or only offer it in limited types of case. Similarly, adoption societies may have limited geographical coverage or only cater for people of particular religious or other affiliations; and although one of the grounds for refusal or cancellation of registration is that an insufficient number of suitably qualified or experienced workers is employed, standards can vary considerably. The principal recommendation, therefore, of the Departmental Committee on the Law of Adoption (the Houghton/Stockdale Committee, whose report in 1972 was largely responsible for the passing of the Children Act 1975) was that a comprehensive adoption service of high quality should be established throughout the country, not only because of the unevenness of the present provision but also because many of its other recommendations would impose additional resonsibilities upon every agency.

The Children Act 1975 will therefore oblige every local social services authority to see that such a comprehensive service is provided in its area, but this may be done in co-operation with the adoption societies operating locally as well as in conjunction with its own social services in the child care field, "so that help may be given in a co-ordinated manner without duplication, omission or avoidable delay" (ss. 1 and 2). But so that authorities will not therefore feel tempted to register less-than-efficient societies in order to comply with this duty, or even feel any lack of confidence in dealing with large and perhaps more experienced societies which happen to be centred in their area, the approval of societies will be transferred to the Secretary of State (ss. 4 to 7). The intention is however to allow authorities and societies enough time to develop such a service and to bring it up to the standards which their new responsibilities will demand, and these sections will not be implemented until this is done.

The other main problem is that the present law does little to discourage private adoption placements, whether by third parties, such as doctors, solicitors or matrons of nursing homes, or by the family itself. Such legal controls as may operate over "protected children" (see 4(ii) below) are usually too little and too late. Some might wonder whether the law could ever hope to abolish this practice, or even whether it should seek to place further obstacles between children in need of a home and the people who are willing to give them one, particularly as some studies have found that children placed privately do no worse than children placed by supposedly expert agencies (see, for example, *Seglow, Kellmer Pringle and Wedge*, 1972).

However, the impression among workers who have later had

to supervise such placements suggests that there is often little in the way of choice; that there may be inadequate counselling and supervision of both sides; that the applicants may have been rejected as unsuitable by conventional adoption agencies; that the rules prohibiting payments may more readily be disregarded; and that potentially damaging contact between natural and adoptive families may more often result; but that whatever their doubts it is usually the lesser of two evils to allow it to continue. Hence the Children Act 1975, following the Departmental Committee's recommendation, will eventually attempt to prohibit the practice. It will become an offence for any person other than a local authority or approved adoption society to make arrangements or place a child for adoption, unless the proposed adopter is a relative of the child or the person is acting in pursuance of an order of the High Court (1958 Act, s. 29 as amended by s. 28 of the 1975 Act). It will also be an offence to receive a child for adoption in such circumstances. The words "any person" can cover the child's own mother as well as a third party, but arrangements within the family are exempted and of course some adoption applications are not the result of any adoption placement at all (for example, applications by step-parents or foster parents with whom the child is already living). In these cases, however, as well as in those where an application results from a placement which was in fact unlawful, additional preliminaries will be required which will not be necessary in standard agency placements. However, these provisions cannot realistically be brought into force or enforced until the official adoption service is improved.

4. *Placement*

(i) *Agency placements*

Apart from the experience and training of their workers, and the greater choice of both children and prospective adopters available to them, agency practice should be superior to private placement because it is subject to closer legal regulation. For example, the natural parents should have a clearer idea of what they are doing, because all agencies must obtain their signature to an explanatory memorandum before even accepting the child for placement (Adoption Agencies Regulations 1959, reg. 4 and Sched. 3). Again, the prospective adopters should be more carefully chosen, because before the child is placed, the agency must have discovered a long list of obvious but sensible particulars about both the child and the prospective adopters (reg. 5(*a*) and Sched. 4); the agency must also interview them (reg. 5(*c*)), inspect their home (reg. 5(*d*)) and enquire of their local authority whether anything is known against the proposed placement (reg. 5(*e*)). Again, the risk that the placement will break down should be diminished by the need for a full medical report on the child (reg. 5(*b*) and Sched. 5) before he is placed, although certain tests which are unreliable below the age of six weeks may be postponed until after placement (see reg. 6(3)). The report does not have to be satisfactory, but obviously it may affect both the adopters' and the agency's decision. (Similarly, the courts' rules about adoption cases require a medical report on the child to accompany all adoption applications, unless the child has reached 16 or one of the applicants is his natural parent, in order to help the court to decide whether the adoption will be in his interests.) The only problem with the need for a prior report in agency cases is that it may delay the child's placement unnecessarily, but the need is to balance the acknowledged desirability of early placement against the risks of breakdown.

Once the agency has obtained all this information, the society's case committee (see reg. 11) or the local authority must approve the particular placement (reg. 5(*f*)). However, although the regulations lay down a detailed procedure, they say little about the considerations and values which should govern this most vital of all adoption decisions. The 1975 Act does however contain two relevant provisions. The first requires all agencies in placing a child to have regard, so far as is practicable, to any wishes of his parents as to his religious upbringing (s. 13). This replaces the old parental right to insert a religious condition when giving consent to adoption. These conditions were not only unenforceable once the adoption had taken place but might also operate against the child's best interests, for example where a mother decided to insist on religion only after an incompatible placement had occurred, or where the condition prevented placement with the applicants who were most suitable in every other respect. The parents' wishes can usually be fulfilled either by choosing an agency with appropriate religious affiliations or by securing the agency's co-operation in choosing an appropriate placement, and the modern view would probably be that nothing more is either necessary or justifiable.

The second provision is a general instruction to both courts and agencies. When reaching *any* decision relating to the adoption of a child, they must give *first* consideration to the need to safeguard and promote his welfare throughout his childhood; they must also, so far as practicable, discover his own wishes and feelings about the decision, and accord them the weight appropriate to his age and understanding (s. 3). For agencies, the object must be to focus their attention away from providing prospective adopters with the babies they want to match the ones they were unable to have themselves, towards providing children of all shapes, colours and sizes with parents whose prime aim is to give a loving stable home to a child in need (see *Kellmer Pringle*, 1972). It is aims and attitudes, rather than detailed procedural rules, which must justify the claim that agency practice is so superior to private placement that the latter must be banned.

(ii) *Placement of "protected children"*

Nevertheless, direct and third party placements are not covered by the agencies' rules. The only legal control which could operate before the decision is made results from the fact that some children will become "protected children" when placed. If a child below the upper age of compulsory schooling (16) is placed for adoption with someone who is not his parent, guardian or relative, and another person who is not his parent or guardian takes part in the arrangements, he will become a protected child immediately on placement (1958 Act, s. 37(1)(*a*)), unless one of the exceptions in section 2(2) (3)(*b*)-(*e*), or (4) of the Children Act 1958 applies (s. 37(2); for these see pp. 31-32). The third party should therefore give written notice of the placement to the local authority, not less than two weeks beforehand, or, if it was made in an emergency, not more than a week afterwards (s. 40(1) (2) and (3)). Then, if neither a local authority nor an adoption society took part, the local authority to which notice is given can prohibit the placement if it would be detrimental to the child (s. 41). A "person aggrieved" (presumably prospective adopter, third party or indeed the child's natural parent) may appeal against such a prohibition to the juvenile court (s. 42); but in any event many notices are given, if at all, too late for prohibition to be effective. When direct and third-party placements become a criminal offence, these provisions will obviously be even less use than they are at present and will be repealed.

5. *The Probationary Period and Welfare Supervision*

However the child has been placed, no adoption order can be made unless he has been continuously in the "actual custody" of the prospective adopters for at least three months, disregarding the first six weeks of life (1958 Act, s. 3(1)). It is not entirely clear what sort of interruptions will prevent custody being continuous, for the 1975 Act defines actual custody as "actual possession of his person, whether or not that possession is shared with one or more other persons" (s. 87(1)). Problems can also arise if one of joint adopters has to be away from home for a while. The 1975 Act will eventually provide some help with both these difficulties, for it will instead require that the child has "had his home" with the applicants "or one of them" (s. 9(1)), and a child will "have his home" with the person who, disregarding absence at a boarding school or hospital or any other temporary absence, has actual custody of him (s. 87(3)). In cases where the child was placed by an agency or by order of the High Court, or where the prospective adopter or one of them is a parent, step-parent or relative of the child, the period will be much the same as it is now, namely 13 weeks but the child must be at least 19 weeks old (s. 9(1)). In all other cases, the required period when these provisions are in force will be at least 12 months (s. 9(2)); this will cover quite lawful private arrangements where non-relatives decide to apply to adopt a child who was not originally placed for adoption; it will also cover placements which are in fact unlawful but have been allowed to continue (although this will be a matter to be reported to the court).

The object of this probationary period is not only to give the
adopter and the child some time to decide whether they will
suit, but also in most (but not yet all) cases to give an
opportunity for social work supervision and assessment. Thus
in agency placements, the regulations require the agency to
ensure that the child is visited within a month of placement
and to make adequate arrangements for supervision until the
local authority takes over (Adoption Agencies Regulations
1959, reg. 6). At present, however, the main responsibility lies
with local authorities, which must visit all "protected children"
in their area, in order to satisfy themselves as to the children's
well-being and to offer any necessary advice to the prospective
adopters (1958 Act, s. 38). Their authorised officers also have
power to inspect any premises where a protected child is being
kept (s. 39). Refusal to allow visiting or inspection is not only a
criminal offence (s. 44), but also automatically grounds for
obtaining a search warrant under section 40 of the Children
and Young Persons Act 1933 (discussed in Chapter 5) (s. 45).
These warrants only enable the child to be removed if the fears
that he is being neglected, ill-treated or the victim of certain
criminal offences seem well-founded once the police officer
gains entry; but the local authority also has power to apply to a
juvenile court for an order to remove a protected child to a
place of safety on wider grounds connected with the suitability
of the placement (s. 43). The procedure, grounds and effects
of such orders are virtually identical to those relating to private
foster children (discussed in Chapter 2). Finally, in order that
the authority can perform these functions properly, the people
caring for a protected child must supply various particulars to
the authority and keep it informed of changes of address (s.
40(4)-(6)).

But who is a "protected child"? As already seen, it covers
children below 16 who are placed with unrelated people for
adoption where someone other than a parent or guardian takes
part in the arrangements. Such children are protected from
(or even before) placement, unless one of the exceptions in
sections 2(2)(3)(*b*)-(*e*) or (4) of the Children Act 1958 applies.
More importantly, perhaps, it covers *all* children once notice
of intention to apply to adopt them is given to the local

authority under section 3(2) of the 1958 Act (s. 37(1)(*b*)), unless they are in a home, school or institution mentioned in section 2(3) of the Children Act 1958 or subject to compulsory powers under the Mental Health Act 1959 (s. 37(3)). Section 3(2) of the Adoption Act 1958 requires all prospective adopters to give notice to the local authority at least three months before the case is heard (and thus this will usually be done before application is actually made to the court), unless the prospective adopter or one of them is the child's natural parent or the child is over compulsory school age.

The net effect of all this is that, while adoptions involving a natural parent or a child over 16 are not subject to welfare supervision at all, third party placements with non-relatives are supposedly covered immediately and all other cases are covered once mandatory notice has been given. In agency placements, this has been criticised as an unnecessary interruption and division of responsibility, causing confusion to the prospective adopter and running the risk that neither agency nor authority will be fully committed to seeing the case through. The 1975 Act will therefore eventually take all children placed by agencies out of the definition of "protected child" and remove the need for notice to the local authority. Instead, the court will have to be satisfied that the *agency* has had sufficient opportunity to observe the child, whatever his age, "in the home environment" with both applicants (s. 9(3)). The agency will also have to report directly to the court on the applicants' suitability and any other matters relevant to the prime duty to safeguard the child's welfare and to respect his wishes (s. 22(3)).

Local authorities will not then be absolved of all welfare supervision apart from their own placements. The 1975 Act will require three months' notice to be given to the authority in all cases where the child was not placed by an agency (s. 18(1)). This will cover applications involving a natural parent, or a child over 16, which are not at present covered at all, as well as applications which follow either lawful or unlawful private arrangements. Again, the court must be satisfied that the authority has had sufficient opportunity of observing the child with the applicants in the home environment (s. 9(3)), and the authority will have to report directly to the court, not only as above but also as to whether the child was unlawfully placed (s. 18(2) and (3)). This last will not prevent the court making the order (unlike cases involving unlawful payments) but it may well influence the decision. The children will also become "protected children" once the required notice has been given, and the authority's powers of supervision, inspection and removal will apply until the adoption or some alternative order is made or the application is withdrawn.

Thus, although these projected changes may seem to diminish the protection available to some children, they are designed to increase it, both by strengthening the responsibilities of the placing agency and by extending protection and supervision to a large class of children who are at present not covered at all.

6. *Parental Agreement*

(i) *The requirements*

No adoption order can be made unless the court is satisfied that each parent or guardian of the child, freely and with full understanding of what is involved, agrees unconditionally to the making of that order, unless there are grounds for dispensing with that agreement (1975 Act, s. 12(1)). This does not mean that the parent has to attend the hearing to give her agreement, although of course she must be notified of it and may attend if she wishes. Written evidence is admissible and usual, and the parent's signature will be accepted as genuine if it is witnessed by a magistrate, justices' clerk, or county court clerk (1958 Act, s. 6). This should normally be arranged before the prospective adopters make their application to the court, because the courts' rules require evidence of agreement to be attached to the application unless grounds for dispensing with it are alleged. This evidence is not however conclusive, for agreement may be withdrawn at any time before the order is made. Indeed, one of the duties of the guardian ad litem, who is appointed by the court after the application is made, is to satisfy himself that it is genuine. The 1975 Act, which may limit the cases in which a guardian ad litem need be appointed, will also provide for the appointment of "reporting officers" whose principal function will be to witness parental agreements (s. 20(1)). They are likely to be senior social workers, but must not be connected with the placing agency (s. 20(2)). They should thus replace the trip to the court's offices and the guardian ad litem's later probing with a single, earlier, and independent check on the genuineness of the agreement; perhaps then fewer agreements will subsequently be withdrawn.

"Parent" means both mother and father of a legitimate child, but only the mother of an illegitimate child, although if the putative father has custody under a court order he is now included in the definition of "guardian" and his agreement will also be required. Indeed, illegitimate children present two practical problems. The problem of the putative father without custody who wishes to object to adoption has already been discussed in Chapter 6. There is also the problem of the husband of a married woman who has an illegitimate child. He is not the father, and the mother may wish to conceal the birth from him, but as already seen, the law presumes that he is the father until evidence is adduced to the contrary. Courts vary in their willingness to accept the mother's word for this at the outset so that he need never be approached. The rules require the guardian ad litem to inform the court of a parent's spouse, so that he can be made a respondent if need be. To keep him in ignorance on her word alone is to deprive both him and the child of the possible benefit of the law's presumption. If however the rebutting evidence is relatively clear the court may be prepared to accept it without giving him notice.

A mother cannot give an effective agreement until the child is six weeks old (1975 Act, s. 12(4)), but this does not prevent the child being placed before then if she has already indicated her intentions. Indeed, because immediate contact between mother and baby seems to play an important part in forming their relationship, some would suggest that she should be discouraged from seeing him at all, but whether this would make a later refusal or withdrawal of agreement more or less likely can only be conjectured.

"Guardian" means a legally appointed guardian where one or both of the "parents" has died (see Chapter 7), and also the father of an illegitimate child who has custody under a court order. Other people or bodies to whom some parental rights have been transferred by court order or by resolution are not included, although if there is a care order or section 2 resolution that local authority must be notified and may give its views on the adoption. The fact that a parent has been deprived of some rights under such orders or resolutions does not affect his right to withhold agreement to the final step of adoption (although in some cases it may help the court to dispense with the need for that agreement). The one exception to this is of course a previous adoption order; the adoptive parents are then mother and father for the purposes of any new adoption and the natural parents are not involved at all.

(ii) *Dispensing with agreement*

The great majority of adoptions obviously have parental agreement, but one of the most difficult legal problems is how far it is proper to deprive parents of their right to decide. Adoption means the complete and final severance of all ties with the child they have brought into the world, yet the child's future well-being, happiness and security may sometimes be much better safeguarded by adoption, particularly as, until custodianship is introduced, it is almost the only way of establishing legally secure links with a substitute family. It seems generally agreed that the child's welfare should be the *first* consideration of courts and adoption agencies (1975 Act, s. 3), but those who have argued that it should also become their *paramount* consideration (see *Kellmer Pringle*, 1972) may not have appreciated that the parents' right to decide would then be in danger of disappearing completely once they had parted with possession of the child for any reason (compare the case of *J.* v. *C.*, 1970). Few people are yet ready for such a draconian solution, although the comparative success rates of adoption compared with long-term fostering, and of illegitimate children who are adopted compared with those brought up by their mothers alone, might indicate that it should be contemplated. Instead, the law allows the courts to dispense with parental agreement on one or more of the six grounds set out in section 12(2) of the 1975 Act, and some are by no means easy to interpret or to apply.

(*a*) That the parent or guardian cannot be found or is incapable of giving agreement.

"Cannot be found" normally means that all reasonable steps have been taken to find the parent, but without success. In one case, the applicants wrote to the mother's last known address, advertised in the press, and tried to trace her through the post office, all without success, and so the trial court dispensed with her consent and made the order. When the mother found out about it, she alleged that the applicants knew her father's address and that he was in touch with her, yet never approached him. The Court of Appeal allowed her to appeal, even though five months had now elapsed since the order, because all reasonable steps had not been taken to find her. (The case was sent back for rehearing, and her consent may have been dispensed with on other grounds, *Re F.(R.)* 1970.)

Exceptionally, a parent "cannot be found" if there are no practicable means of communicating with him to obtain his agreement, as where the child had illegally escaped to this country from a totalitarian regime and any attempt to communicate with his parents there would be very dangerous for them (*Re R.*, 1967). In that case, the parents were also "incapable" of consenting, but generally the word will refer to mental incapacity.

(*b*) That the parent or guardian is withholding his consent unreasonably.

It is this ground which has caused the most legal difficulty, for instead of focussing on the parent's absence or her behaviour towards the child, it asks the court to evaluate the reasonableness of her state of mind; and the court's views on the weight to be given to the child's welfare in making that evaluation have undergone a considerable change. The earlier cases tended to suggest that it was always prima facie reasonable for a parent to withhold consent to such a drastic step, and the fact that adoption would be better for the child did not of itself make this unreasonable (see, for example, *Re K., Rogers* v. *Kuzmicz*, 1953; *Hitchcock* v. *W.B.*, 1952). The parent might however be unreasonable if he had vacillated to an unusual degree or been to some extent culpable in his behaviour (see *Re W.*, 1965).

More recent cases, and in particular two decisions of the

House of Lords (*Re W.*, 1971; *O'Connor* v. *A. and B.*, 1971), have now established a rather different approach, which may be summarised thus. First, the court is not allowed simply to substitute its own decision for that of the parent; the question is still whether a reasonable parent in the circumstances of this particular case could withhold her agreement. Secondly, however, there is no need to accuse the parent of culpable behaviour or callous indifference; but although a reasonable parent is entitled to take her own feelings into account, she should undoubtedly give great weight to what will be best for her child's long-term welfare, including the advantages of adoption and the disadvantages of disrupting a settled and well-established placement.

"A reasonable mother surely gives great weight to what is better for the child. Her anguish of mind is quite understandable; but it still may be unreasonable for her to withhold her consent. We must look and see whether it is reasonable or unreasonable according to what a reasonable woman in her place would do in all the circumstances of the case." (*Re L.*, 1962).

It has recently been held that the court's new duty, in reaching any decision relating to the adoption of a child, to give first consideration to the need to safeguard and promote the child's long-term welfare (1975 Act, s. 3) has not affected its approach to the problem of dispensing with parental agreement (*Re P.*, 1977).

The problem arises in two quite different contexts. Most commonly a parent decides to place the child for adoption and then changes her mind. She may have received inadequate counselling from her social worker and been subject to considerable pressure from family and friends. Her circumstances may now have improved. She can scarcely be blamed for what has happened, but the child may have been with the applicants from an early age and be just at the point where a disruption of the normal process of forming relationships is most dangerous. *Re W.* (1971) presented all these features, while in *O'Connor* v. *A. and B.* (1971) the mother had since married the father, although there was some doubt about the stability of their relationship and the child had been with the applicants for two and a half years. In both cases, their

Lordships dispensed with the parent's consent.

These cases might be better described as unreasonable "withdrawal" of consent, but in some cases the parent may never have signified his agreement to adoption. This is most likely to arise where a divorced mother and her new husband apply to adopt the children in her custody, although as already seen the 1975 Act now discourages these applications; or where long-term foster parents apply to adopt children boarded-out or privately fostered with them; it is not always appreciated that this has always been possible, but the 1975 Act may have made it more likely by placing obstacles in the way of removing a child from foster parents who wish to adopt after looking after him for five years (see 7 below). In the first type of case, the courts have been most reluctant to dispense with the divorced father's consent : there is so much doubt about whether such adoptions are genuinely in the children's best interests that a father will rarely be held unreasonable if he sincerely wishes to maintain the relationship (see the cases discussed in Chapter 8), especially as there is little risk that the applicants will actually lose the child. In the latter type of case, the reasonableness of the parents' attitude may have to be judged against the quality of their links with the child, the added difficulty but now acknowledged possibilities of adoptions of older children, the security and added commitment which may very well be the reason why adoption is much more successful than long-term fostering, and the much greater likelihood of the child's removal if the adoption does not take place. The legal test is no doubt the same in every case, but its application may differ very substantially.

(*c*) That the parent or guardian has persistently failed without reasonable cause to discharge his parental duties.

This is a slight rewording of the old law, which referred to parental "obligations," The courts interpreted this to include the natural and moral obligation to show affection towards and maintain an interest in one's children, as well as the legal duty to maintain them financially (see *Re P.*, 1962). It would be unfortunate if the new reference to "duties" were interpreted in such a way that the courts could only take failure to perform one's legal duties into account.

This ground is most likely to be suggested in applications by step-parents or foster parents, for a parent who has placed her child specifically for adoption has every cause not to discharge her parental duties (indeed, once notice of intention to apply to adopt is given in relation to a child in the care of a local authority, parental contributions are no longer payable while the child remains with the prospective adopters; 1958 Act, s. 36(2)). The divorced father may readily be accused of such a failure, but the courts have said that it must be so great and so culpable that there is no value to the child in maintaining the relationship (*Re D.*, 1973). They may be prepared to take a less restrictive view where parents have lost touch with their fostered children, for the advantages of adoption may be greater and the parents' conduct less understandable than the natural estrangement and hostility of divorce. Nevertheless, it appears that little use has been made of this possibility in planning the long-term future of "children who wait," perhaps because far too many long-term cases are allowed to drift, in a vague but increasingly unrealistic hope of rehabilitation in the natural family.

(*d*) That the parent or guardian has abandoned or neglected the child; or (*e*) has persistently ill-treated the child; or (*f*) has seriously ill-treated the child, but in this case the rehabilitation of the child within that household must, for whatever reason, be unlikely.

These grounds will again not apply to a normal placement for adoption, for the parent will have had little chance to neglect or ill-treat the child, and placing a child for adoption is not abandonment in the technical sense. They may sometimes apply to a recalcitrant divorced father, and adoption may well have more solid advantages in such a case. More importantly, however, they would justify plans for adoption in serious cases of child abuse : once the child has been removed from home, and provided that each parent was involved, there is no legal obstacle to adoption. There must be many such children for whom the best solution would be a completely fresh start with a carefully chosen substitute family, yet as with ground (*c*) this possibility seems to have been remarkably neglected, perhaps because of lack of forward planning and perhaps because of a natural tendency to cling, however unrealistically, to hopes of rehabilitation. Perhaps the climate is now swinging again in the other direction.

(iii) *Freeing a child for adoption*

The risks and problems of withdrawal of consent might be substantially reduced if the parent could give her final agreement at an earlier stage. At present, she will often sign one form when setting the adoption process in motion; later she will sign her formal agreement; later still she will be questioned by the guardian ad litem; and even then she will be able to change her mind before the order is made. The resulting uncertainty can be damaging for her, the prospective adopters, and of course the child, and if there is then an application to dispense with consent the uncertainties will increase.

Hence the Departmental Committee recommended a procedure for "freeing a child for adoption," perhaps before he is even placed, but certainly before the case is ready to be heard. The 1975 Act provides for this, but the relevant provisions are not yet in force. The application will be made by the adoption agency, and the court must be satisfied that each parent or guardian either agrees fully and unconditionally to "an" adoption, or that if not his agreement can be dispensed with on one of the above grounds (s. 14(1)). But at least one parent will have to consent to the application (as opposed to agreeing to adoption), unless the agency wants the court to dispense with every parent's agreement and it already has the child in its care (s. 14(2)). Thus although the agency must be willing to apply, because it will have the responsibility once an order is made, the parent will usually have the right to choose between this procedure and the present method. Furthermore, the court will not be able to dispense with any agreement unless the child is already placed or the court is satisfied that placement is likely (s. 14(3)); it would be most unjust to deprive an unwilling parent of all rights unless adoption were virtually certain. The court will also have to satisfy itself that any person who claims to be the putative father of an illegitimate child and who does not already have custody, either has no intention of applying for it or if he did would be unlikely to succeed (s. 14(8)).

The rules will probably provide for a guardian ad litem for the child in all these applications (s. 20(1) and (2)), for the effect of the order will be to vest *all* parental rights and duties in the agency and to extinguish those of his former parents (ss. 14(6) and 8(2) and (3)). However, each parent or guardian who can be found must first be asked whether she wants any further involvement in the child's future (s. 14(7)). If she formally declares that she does not, that is the end of the matter; but if she makes no such declaration, she will have to be told after a year whether the child has been adopted or placed for adoption, and thereafter kept informed of developments unless she then decides to make a declaration (s. 15). Furthermore, a parent who did not make a declaration at the time will be able to apply for the order to be revoked after 12 months, if the child has neither been adopted or placed (s. 16(1)), and the child must not be placed while such an application is pending (s. 16(2)). If the order is revoked, parental rights will return to whoever had them before it was made, or if they were then in a local authority or voluntary organisation, to whoever had them before that (s. 16(3)). If the application is dismissed, however, the applicant cannot try again unless the court gives her special leave, and the agency will no longer have to keep her informed (s. 16(4) and (5)).

Agencies who use this procedure will obviously have to have facilities for caring for children whom they cannot place immediately, but this need not be a long-term problem, for two agencies will be able to apply jointly for the transfer of parental rights from one to the other (s. 23). The severance of links with the natural family would however be most undesirable if there were any substantial risk that the child would not be placed, for he would then remain in indefinite legal limbo. It will be interesting to see how many mothers do in fact wish to take advantage of the procedure when it is introduced.

7. *Return or Removal before the Hearing*

The ways in which a placement may be ended before any order is made depend upon who wishes to end it, the type of placement it was, and the stage which the proceedings have reached.

(i) *By the prospective adopters*

The prospective adopters may decide that they no longer wish to proceed. If the child was placed with them for adoption by an agency, they should give written notice of this decision to the authority or society, and must return the child within seven days of the notice (1958 Act, s. 35(1)(*a*) and (3)); they must also return the child within seven days of withdrawing an application which is already pending before a court (s. 35(3)). If in fact the child was and remains in the care of a local authority, there seems no reason why, if both parties want this, the child should not be boarded-out with the same couple as foster parents instead of prospective adopters. If indeed notice of intention to apply to adopt is given in respect of a child in care who was *not* originally placed for adoption, the same procedure applies, but the Act specifically states that the child need not be returned unless the authority so requests (s. 36(1)). In step-parent applications and private placements, the future of the child after an adoption plan has been abandoned will be governed by any previous court order or by agreement between the parties.

(ii) *By the agency or local authority*

The agency itself may decide that it wishes to end the placement. In agency placements for adoption where the court application has not yet been made, the agency may serve written notice on the prospective adopters who must then return the child within seven days (1958 Act, s. 35(1)(*b*) and (3)). Once an application has been made, the agency can only serve such a notice with leave of the court (s. 35(2)). Alternatively, if the child is in fact in the local authority's care and was simply boarded-out with the prospective adopters, the authority may wish to exercise its ordinary rights to remove children from their foster parents. However, once the prospective adopters have given notice of their intention to the local authority (and this should still be necessary when section 18(1) of the 1975 Act comes into force, for it will not be an agency placement *for adoption*), the authority can only recover the child by means of the agency procedure (see s. 36(1) and (2)), and this of course requires the court's leave once the application has actually been made. Thus if one local authority receives notice in respect of a child in the care of another authority the former must inform the latter. (For the position where the child has been with the prospective adopter for five years, see below.)

(iii) *By the natural parents*

Last the natural parent may wish to recover the child. In general, as she retains parental rights until the order is made (or, once the procedure is in force, until the child is freed for adoption), she can simply ask for or take him back; but there are some important exceptions. First, once an actual adoption application has been made, a parent who has signified her agreement to adoption is no longer entitled to remove the child from the applicants against their will, except with the court's leave (1958 Act, s. 34(1), substituted by 1975 Act, s. 29). This will of course apply to the great majority of cases once the application is made, for it must usually be accompanied by evidence of parental agreement. The second exception is not yet operative because it relates to pending applications to free a child for adoption; it will prevent any parent who did *not* consent to the application from removing the child from the people with whom he is living, except again with the court's leave (1958 Act, s. 34(2), added by 1975 Act, s. 29); this will not apply to a parent who *did* consent to the application but has since changed her mind, nor will the first exception apply to her because no adoption application will yet be pending. However, this provision will enable an agency to "freeze" the situation even though parental agreement to adoption has not been obtained and may have to be dispensed with, and this will be a new and important departure.

The third exception is another step in that same direction, but although it is already operative it is limited to children who have had their home with the prospective adopters for a continuous period of five years. Such children cannot be removed against the prospective adopters' will, not only once an actual adoption application has been made (s. 34A(1)), but also once notice of intention to apply to adopt has been given to the local authority (s. 34A(2)); in the latter case, however, the prospective adopters cannot "freeze" the situation for ever, for the prohibition will lapse after three months unless an actual application is made before then, and once lapsed, it cannot be renewed by giving a fresh notice within the next 28 days, which would give plenty of time to remove the child if this were appropriate. These prohibitions apply to anyone who might otherwise remove the child, the only exceptions being the child's arrest, some statutory authority (such as a place of safety order), or the court's leave to remove him. If the child is in fact in the care of a local authority, the authority would normally have statutory authority to remove him, and so the section specifically provides that it may only do so in accordance with sections 35 and 36 of the 1958 Act or with the court's leave; thus while it was necessary to make this clear in the new provisions, they appear to add nothing to the existing position regarding *all* children in care once notice of intention to apply to adopt them has been received; they can be removed after seven days' notice until the actual application is made, after which the court's leave will be required.

The purpose of this new five-year rule is to make it easier for long-term foster parents to apply to adopt without prior parental agreement, for they will be able to retain the child while seeking agreement or alleging grounds for dispensing with it. However, once custodianship is in force, they will be able to forestall removal by making a custodianship application after only three years, and could then perhaps couple this with an alternative adoption application.

If removal of the child is prohibited on any of the three grounds above, not only will it be a criminal offence (ss. 34(3) and 34A(6)), but a court will be able to order the child's return and to authorise a court officer (in the High Court or country court) or a police officer (in the magistrates' court) to enter specified premises, search for, and return the child. A court may also prohibit a suspected removal in advance, which might not only be more of a deterrent, but would also give that court the power to punish for disobedience to its orders (1975 Act, s. 30).

8. *The Guardian ad litem*

At present, whenever a court proceeds with an adoption
application it must appoint a guardian ad litem, who is the
child's representative in the litigation and has the general duty
of safeguarding his welfare, together with some specific tasks
laid down in the courts' rules (1958 Act, s. 9(7); see Adoption
(High Court) Rules 1976, rr. 12, 13 and Sched. 2; Adoption
(County Court) Rules 1976, rr. 10, 11 and Sched. 2; and
Magistrates' Courts (Adoption) Rules 1976, rr. 9, 10, and
Sched. 2). These are almost, but not quite, identical.

(i) *Who may be appointed*

In the High Court, the guardian is normally the Official
Solicitor, unless he declines or the applicants ask for some
other suitably qualified person. In other courts, it is either a
local authority social worker (provided that the authority
agrees), or a probation officer, or if neither is practicable or
desirable, some other suitably qualified person; but no one
may be appointed if he or his agency either has parental rights
and duties over the child or, more importantly, has taken part
in the adoption arrangements. Subject to this, however, there
is nothing to prevent the same worker undertaking both
welfare supervision and guardian's duties.

(ii) *His duties*

The first prescribed task is to interview the applicants and
learn something about them. This includes obvious information about the membership of their household, their
accommodation, their means and any property the child
might stand to gain, any serious illnesses or family history of
tuberculosis, epilepsy or mental illness, and their religion. It
concentrates, however, on why they want to adopt the child,
whether they understand the full consequences of adoption,
the stability of their marriage, why (if this is so) only one of a
married couple is applying, whether if natural mother or
father is applying alone there is anything to justify excluding
the other, and on anything else, including an assessment of the
personalities of both applicants and child, which may affect

the suitability of the proposed adoption. He must also follow up their references, which are required unless either is a parent or relative, and he must give them some obvious information about the child — the date and place of any baptism, any immunisations, any property he stands to lose or retain if adopted, and any insurance against his funeral expenses. If it seems to the guardian that a sole applicant or both of joint applicants may not be domiciled in the United Kingdom, he must immediately inform the court, for this will affect its jurisdiction profoundly.

The second task is to discover whether the child is able to understand adoption. If he can, this must immediately be reported to the court, and the guardian must try to discover his wishes and feelings about the decision. The court has a duty to take these into account (1975 Act, s. 3) and in the lower courts a child who is old enough to understand must attend the hearing unless there are special circumstances making this unnecessary. It is thus hard to see how an adoption can be concealed from an older child, although there may sometimes be good reasons for doing so.

The next task is to investigate the views of the other people or bodies involved. He must interview all individuals who seem to have taken part in the adoption arrangements or who must be made respondents to, or be notified of, the application. The latter obviously include every person whose agreement to the adoption is required, and the guardian must satisfy himself that any agreement is given freely and with full understanding of what is involved. The other individuals are anyone liable by court order or agreement to maintain the child (such as a putative father or step-parent) and the spouse of a married applicant who is applying alone. The court can make anyone else a respondent if it wishes. Thus the guardian must inform the court if he hears of anyone who is or has been married to the child's mother or father (see the discussion on page 239); and of anyone who claims to be the father of an illegitimate child and is not already involved as a guardian or a person liable to maintain but who wishes to be heard; and of any relative of a deceased parent of the child who similarly wishes to be heard — such a relative may well have very valid objections to the child leaving his family, but will otherwise have no means of preventing it; the guardian does not have any duty to search these people out, but he must not forget to mention those about whom he knows. Similarly, the guardian must obtain any relevant information (usually in the form of written reports) from any local authority or adoption agency which took part in the arrangements, any local authority which was responsible for welfare supervision, and any local authority or voluntary organisation which has the child in its care or has parental rights.

The object of all this is to gather all the relevant information and interested parties together, so as to ensure that nothing is overlooked and an independent check is made. In part, this should secure that the law is complied with; the guardian has to discover who has been looking after the child for the whole of his life, and for how long each person has done so; this will reveal whether the probationary period has been completed, and may well bring to light any unlawful placement. More importantly, the guardian will be expected to pass the arrangements made by others under a critical eye, in order to help the court to decide whether the adoption is indeed in the child's best interests.

Having done all this, the guardian must prepare a confidential written report for the court hearing (although he may make an earlier interim one if he needs guidance or there are matters which the court should know immediately). This need not be shown to the parties unless the court sees fit (compare the rules about home surroundings reports discussed in Chapter 4), but the guardian is not entitled to a private oral hearing and should not retire with the magistrates (*Re B.*, 1975).

(iii) *Changes to come*

The central function of the guardian ad litem is quite distinct from both placement and welfare supervision. He is an independent expert appointed by the court to check and evaluate the work done by others and his only client is the child himself. In practice, however, a great deal of the work required duplicates that already required in the Adoption Agency Regulations. Furthermore, although in society placements the guardian ad litem is likely to be the same authority which was responsible for welfare supervision, and a local authority can usually supervise its own placements so that only the guardian need be different, it is not impossible for three separate workers to be involved in one case. This can be confusing to the prospective adopters, and while some work can be unnecessarily repeated other things may be overlooked altogether. Particular problems obviously arise from the need to approach the natural parents yet again, although particular solutions have been suggested for this (see 6 above).

The Departmental Committee suggested that a guardian ad litem should no longer be necessary in every case. The 1975 Act will therefore allow new rules of court to prescribe when a guardian must be appointed and what his duties will be (s. 20(1)). The duties may not differ very much from those at present, although they will clearly depend on the sort of cases in which an appointment will be required and this is not yet known. The Committee thought that in agency placements this function could safely be replaced by making the agency itself directly responsible to the court (as indeed it will be under section 22(3) of the 1975 Act), unless perhaps there were a problem about parental agreement or an application to free the child for adoption. Thus in most cases the present tripartite division of responsibility could be replaced by the sole continuing responsibility of the placing agency, although the reporting officer would provide an independent check upon parental agreements. Despite the shortcomings of the present system, some have wondered whether this will provide adequate protection for the child, particularly now that we are increasingly conscious of the divided loyalties of caseworkers, so that the tendency is to increase rather than decrease provision for the separate representation of children. Certainly any such change will place a much heavier burden on agencies and lend special point to their "first" duty under section 3 of the 1975 Act. It is not suggested that the guardian would be dispensed with in family and private placements, but for these of course welfare supervision will also be necessary and the two may be combined.

9. *At the Hearing*

The hearing will be in private. In the lower courts, the rules require all applicants to be present, unless one spouse has verified a joint application by sworn evidence; and if the child is old enough to understand he should also be there. There are no corresponding rules in the High Court. Any of the people or agencies who must be notified or made respondents (see 8(ii) above) may attend, although this will obviously be unusual unless there is a dispute. If, for example, the natural mother does attend and the applicants have chosen to conceal their identity by a serial number, the hearing has to be conducted in such a way that she does not see them or learn their names without their consent. After the hearing, the court has a number of things which it may do.

(i) *Granting the adoption order*

The court cannot do this unless it is satisfied that all the necessary parental agreements have been given or can be dispensed with, that the child has been with the applicants for the required probationary period, that where necessary three months' notice has been given to the local authority, and that the applicants have not made or received unlawful payments for the adoption. Provided that all this is clear and the guardian ad litem's report favourable, most adoptions are likely to go through without difficulty, but the final decision always rests with the court. It has to make an independent decision as to whether the order should be made, first consideration being given to the child's long-term welfare and appropriate consideration being given to his own wishes (1975 Act, s. 3). Some courts may have quite decided views on certain types of case, and although an unfavourable decision can always be appealed to a higher court, agencies will probably try to discover the local court's views, so that they can either be taken into account in placement or, if the agency disagrees with them, the case may be taken to a different court. For example, some judges have been reluctant to allow baptised Christian children to be brought up by non-Christian adopters, others may have doubts about racial differences between child and adopters, or about the suitability of older applicants to care for a young child, and so on. Certain doubts which the courts have already voiced are now built into the law, for the restrictions on granting adoptions to certain step-parents, or to natural parents applying alone have already been mentioned. There are also several things which can be done instead of granting an adoption, and a refusal will not always result in the applicants' losing the child. Thus the particular and drastic consequences of an adoption order (see 10 below) should be an important factor in whether the application is granted.

(ii) *Alternative orders*

(a) An interim order

Provided that the necessary agreements have been given or dispensed with, and that where necessary notice was given to the local authority, a court which is still not satisfied that adoption is the right solution may make an interim order (1958 Act, s. 8). This leaves the child with the applicants, but instead of the full parental rights of adoption, they will only have custody, and the court may make ancillary orders about the child's supervision and maintenance if it wishes. The order lasts for a fixed period of up to two years (and if originally fixed for less may be extended up to a maximum of two years), after which the applicants or failing them the guardian ad litem should bring the case back to court. No doubt normally the order is made in the hope that at the end of that time any doubts will have been resolved so that a full order can be made. Interim orders are not common, but could be supported in placements which carry a higher risk of breakdown, in effect to extend the probationary period. However, they can be used in cases where the court thinks that adoption is not the appropriate solution but that the child ought to remain with the applicants for the time being. This solution was upheld in the case of an illegitimate child whose mother's rights were vested in the local authority by section 2 resolution and whose foster parents had applied to adopt. The judge thought that on balance she should eventually be brought up by her father, but that a gradual transition could be accomplished by leaving her with the applicants under an interim order providing for supervision by the local authority and access by the father. The local authority appealed, largely because the order would interfere with its normal rights over the children in its care; but the Court of Appeal not only held that this did not prevent the court making an interim order, but also that this power could be used for other purposes than assessing the suitability of the applicants (*S.* v. *Huddersfield Borough Council*, 1975). However, once custodianship is in force, it may provide a more appropriate means of achieving the same object.

(b) Custodianship and other custody orders

When the custodianship provisions of the 1975 Act (discussed in Chapter 10) are in force they will enable the courts to consider an order vesting legal custody in the applicants as an alternative to adoption in almost every case. It will not then matter that the applicants would not have been "qualified" to apply for custodianship in the first place, but all the necessary agreements to adoption must have been given or dispensed with. As custodianship does not involve the complete severance of links with the natural family, it may be particularly appropriate where those links are valuable to the child or where adoption would distort rather than replace natural relationships. Thus the court will have a positive duty to use it in applications involving step-parents where it is satisfied that adoption would be no better for the child.

This will not normally apply to the step-parents of children involved in divorce, however, for they can instead apply to the divorce court for a custody order, but this will of course require a separate application to a different court. Such people are not in much danger of losing the child should the adoption be refused, whereas a principal purpose of custodianship is to give a measure of legal security to people who can only otherwise obtain it by adopting the child.

(c) Supervision and care orders

If the court does not make an adoption order, and the child is under 16, it may make either a supervision or a care order (1975 Act, s. 17). The grounds upon which these may be made, and their effects, are equivalent to those in ordinary custody disputes (see Chapter 3). Obviously, if an adoption order is refused and the child cannot remain with the applicants, but it is equally impracticable for him to go to his natural parent, the sensible course is to commit him to the care of the local authority. A supervision order may be appropriate if the child is to remain with the applicants on some other basis, but is perhaps more likely to be used where the child is to go to the natural parent : some difficulty may surely be anticipated if she has withdrawn her agreement after the child has been with the prospective adopters some while but the court is not prepared to hold her unreasonable.

(iii) *When must the child go back?*

If an adoption application is refused and no alternative order made, the legal position varies with the type of placement. In a conventional agency placement for adoption, an order will presumably have been refused either because of doubts about the applicants' suitability or because the mother has withdrawn her consent. Thus the child must be returned to the agency within seven days of the refusal (1958 Act, s. 35(3)), but the court may now extend that period to up to six weeks (1958 Act, s. 35(5A), added by 1975 Act, s. 31). This is presumably to give the agency extra time to make alternative arrangements for a child who is not to go to his natural parents.

If the child was not placed for adoption by an agency, the refusal may have resulted from doubts about the suitability of adoption in itself, instead of doubts about the applicants or lack of parental agreement, and the refusal is much less likely to lead to their losing the child (even if no custodianship order is made). Thus if a child was and is in the care of a local authority, the refusal of an adoption order may not affect the suitability of the fostering placement, and the child need only be returned if the authority insists (1958 Act, s. 36(1)). Similarly, if one of the applicants already has parental rights as a natural parent or under a court custody order (which the court hearing the adoption should in any event be wary of disturbing), the refusal will not affect these and the child will stay where he is. Last, in private and family arrangements, the court may feel particularly tempted to make a care or supervision order if adoption is refused, but if no order is made the child's future will depend on the arrangements made between the parties themselves.

However, if an adoption application is refused, no court can hear a later application by the same people for the same child unless either the first court exempted them from this rule, or the second court finds a change in the circumstances or some other special reason for allowing them to try again (1975 Act, s. 22(4)). One such reason might of course be a change of heart on the part of a natural parent who was not previously willing to agree.

10. *The Effects of Adoption*

As already seen, an adoption order effects a virtually complete and irrevocable transfer of the child from one family to another. There are however three aspects to this, a few exceptional points, and some qualifications to the principle of irrevocability.

(i) *The transfer*

First, from the moment the order is made, all parental rights and duties relating to the child vest in the adoptive parents (1975 Act, s. 8(1)). The court has power to impose such terms and conditions as it sees fit, on making the order (s. 8(7)), but as such conditions are difficult to enforce and likely to detract from the purpose of adoption, they are rare. One recent example is a condition allowing access to the putative father, but this was exceptional. The abolition of the parents' right to impose religious conditions may result in more courts imposing them, but if agencies respect their duty in section 13, this should be unlikely. The adoptive parents will thus normally have an unfettered right to bring the child up, decide his education and religion, and whether he should emigrate, marry under the age of 18, or even be adopted again. They will also have full responsibility for looking after him properly, educating him and maintaining him.

Secondly, although the order has no effect on parental rights and duties so far as they relate to any period before it is made (s. 8(2)), once made it extinguishes the parental rights and duties of anyone other than the adopters, whether these arose naturally or by court order (s. 8(3)(*a*)). Care orders and section 2 resolutions also cease. The natural parents will have no right to keep in touch with the child (unless the court has made this a condition) and no duty to maintain him. Thus although arrears owing under a maintenance agreement or order may be recovered, once an adoption order is made, no further liability can accrue (s. 8(3)(*b*)) and of course no new orders can be made. This is a change from the previous law, which allowed affiliation orders to continue, and indeed to be applied for, if the mother was sole adopter of her own illegitimate child; now if she wishes for the benefits, she must accept the full consequences of adoption. (There are two minor exceptions, for maintenance agreements which constitute a trust, or which expressly provide for continuing despite adoption, s. 8(4); thus a natural parent may deliberately set out to provide for a child who is to be adopted.)

However, an adoption order does not merely transfer and extinguish parental rights and duties, for this would simply be a drastic form of custody order. For almost every legal purpose, adoption removes the child from one family and places him in another. Thus as regards anything which happens after the adoption, the child is to be treated as the legitimate child of the adoptive parents' marriage (or, if there is only one adopter, as his legitimate child, but not of course the child of any particular marriage); and he is *not* to be treated as the child of anyone else (1975 Act, Sched. 1, para. 3). The Act somewhat unnecessarily declares that this prevents an adopted child from being illegitimate. The main effect, however, is that any reference to a child or indeed to any other relationship in any statute or legal document now automatically includes an adopted child or a relationship traced through adoption, unless the contrary intention is expressed.

This in fact changed the law relating to dispositions of property and so only applies to dispositions which take effect on or after January 1, 1976. For those which took effect before then, an adopted child could only claim property if he was adopted *before* the disposition (for example a settlement or will, or a distribution occurring because someone has died without making a will). The person who had died or disposed of his property was presumed only to want to benefit children who had already been adopted and whom he would thus have a chance of specifically excluding. But many dispositions of property can benefit children who have not yet been born, and under the new rule the person making such a disposition (or dying without making one) is presumed to want to benefit future adopted children as well as future natural children; if he wishes to exclude them, he must say so. If entitlement depends upon a child's date of birth, an adopted child is taken to be born on the date of the order, so that if a man leaves property to his "eldest grandchild," an ordinary grandchild who was born before another grandchild's adoption will take, even though the adopted child may in fact be older (there are however rules for preserving the priority of an illegitimate child who is then adopted by his natural parent, for the adoption will not affect his existing rights of succession from that parent's family). If, on the other hand, the grandfather left his property to be divided between all his grandchildren when they reached 21, the adopted child would reach 21 on the anniversary of his birth rather than his adoption. Further explanation of these complicated rules is outside the scope of this book, and they are unlikely to affect many adopted chldren, whereas the general principle will.

(ii) *The exceptions*

There are a few exceptions to the general principle. The most important reiate to marriage, nationality and peerages. Thus there are certain people to whom one is so closely related either by blood or by marriage that one is not allowed to marry them (basically, any blood relation closer than first cousin, and parents-in-law, step-parents, children-in-law and step-children). It is expressly provided that an adopted person remains in his natural family for this purpose. Thus not only can he not marry his natural mother, grandmother, sister, aunt or niece, which may be eugenically sensible, but neither can he marry a step-mother whom his father married after he was adopted, which is surely neither eugenically nor socially undesirable. This rule of course raises the problem that an adopted child will normally have no means of knowing who his natural relatives are, but the Children Act has now made it possible for him to discover this (see below). An adopted person is also prohibited from marrying his adoptive parent, for this might indeed introduce a damaging ambiguity into the relationship, but he is not prevented from marrying his other adoptive relatives. There is of course no eugenic reason why he should be, but some have argued that the possibility of marriage between adopted siblings may distort normal family life.

An adopted person is not automatically his adoptive parents' child for any purpose connected with British nationality, United Kingdom citizenship, or immigration control. This is doubtless to prevent evasion by adoption abroad (for the general principle applies to all recognised adoptions wherever they take place). However, a child who is adopted *here* either by a married couple of whom the husband is a United Kingdom citizen, or by a sole adopter of either sex who is a United Kingdom citizen, will automatically gain citizenship if he does not already have it (1958 Act, s. 19).

Adoption does not affect succession to peerages and other titles, or to any attached property, for these still depend on blood relationship. Nor need it affect entitlement to certain social security death benefits, to a pension already being paid to the child when he is adopted, or to an insurance policy against the child's funeral expenses (but nothing more) which is transferred to the adoptive parents. Otherwise, however, the general principle holds good.

(iii) *Irrevocability*

With one exception an adoption order is irrevocable, but this statement does require some explanation and qualification. The exception relates to children who are adopted by one natural parent alone and who are subsequently legitimated by his or her marriage to the other parent. The court may on their application revoke the adoption order (1958 Act, s. 26) so that the child becomes the legitimated child of both instead of the adopted child of one and step-child of the other. (This exception also applies to natural parents whose marriage did *not* legitimate the child before 1959, because one was married to someone else at the time of his birth, and who therefore adopted the child after their marriage, see Adoption Act 1960.)

Adoption orders may sometimes be appealed to a higher court, High Court and county court orders to the Court of

Appeal, and magistrates' court orders to the Family Division of the High Court. An appeal is however more likely if the application is refused than if it is granted, except where a parent objects to the court's decision to dispense with her agreement. There are normally only six weeks in which to appeal, after which the order can certainly be considered final, although the appeal court could in an exceptional case grant leave to appeal out of time (for an example, see page 241).

There is of course nothing to prevent an adopted child being adopted again by different applicants. The first adoptive parents will then be in the position of natural parents, and the natural parents will have nothing to do with it. It is perhaps most likely to happen where one adoptive parent remarries after the other's death or divorce rather than in a totally new placement.

Finally, an adopted child may now be able to discover something of his origins. When an adoption order is made, it is recorded in the Adopted Children Register and a "birth" certificate based on that entry may be obtained (the short form certificate now in common use will not of course reveal that the child is adopted). At the same time, the record of his birth must be marked "adopted" and the Registrar-General must have some means of tracing the connection between the two. However, until recently in England, that connection could only be revealed under a court order, whereas in Scotland there was no such prohibition. A Scottish study (*Triseliotis*, 1973) revealed that while few adopted children embarked upon the search, those who did were usually unhappy and lonely people, whose adoptive relationship had not been satisfactory, or who had learned of their adoption in a distressing or negative way, and who desperately needed to know "who they were." The implications of this for agency practice are clear, but in addition the study supported the suggestion that the Scottish practice should be adopted here. The 1975 Act thus gives an adopted person who has reached 18 the right to obtain his original birth certificate (and someone under 18 who is intending to marry is entitled to ask whether the marriage would be prohibited) (1958 Act, s. 20A, added by the 1975 Act, s. 26). However, the Registrar General and every adoption agency must establish counselling services for people who wish to obtain their original birth certificates, although only those adopted before the 1975 Act was passed will be obliged to take advantage of the service. This provision recognises that the searchers may well be insecure young people whose experience of adoption has not been as happy as might be hoped and who may need more help than simple knowledge of their origins can give. It may also enable the counsellor to explore the implications for the natural parents. Although it may be that many adopted people are merely looking for background geneological information rather than a meeting, the natural parent will have no right to object to the disclosure of the original birth certificate, and the counsellor should surely point out the damage which a refusal to meet or an unsatisfactory meeting could do to them both.

It would seem, however, that this sort of identity crisis causes fewer problems amongst adopted children than it does amongst those in long term care. It is no doubt better to have substitute legal parents than, in effect, none at all, but what implications should this have both for the law and for child care practice?

Adoption Act 1976: Comparative Table

[Note: The Adoption Act 1976 is unlikely to be brought into force in the near future. Hence, references in the text are to legislation currently in force.]

Table of Derivations
The following abbreviations are used in this Table:

1958 = The Adoption Act 1958
    (7 & 8 Eliz. 2, c. 5)
1960 = The Adoption Act 1960
    (1960 c. 59)
1964 = The Adoption Act 1964
    (1963 c. 57)
1968 = The Adoption Act 1968
    (1968 c. 53)
1975 = The Children Act 1975
    (1975 c. 72)

ADOPTION ACT 1958

1958	1976	1958	1976
s. 9 (3) (4)	s. 66 (1) (2)	s. 26 (1)..........	s. 52 (1)
	(6)	(2)..........	Sched. 1
(5)...........	66 (5)		para. 6
19	40 (1) (2)	(3)	s. 52 (4)
20	50	27	Sched. 1,
20A	51		para 5 (1)
21 (1)	Sched. 1,	29 (1)	s. 11
	para. 1 (1)	(2A).......	11
(4)—(6)	Sched. 1, para.	(3)—(5) ..	11
	1 (3)—(5)	32 (1)..........	9 (1) (2)
24 (1)—(3)	Sched. 1, para.	(1A).......	9 (1) (2)
	4 (1)—(3)	(2)..........	9 (4)
(4)	Sched. 1, para.	(3)..........	9 (3)
	2 (1)	(4)..........	67 (5)
(6)	Sched. 1 para.	33.................	10
	4 (4)	34.................	27
(7)	Sched. 1 para.	34A	28
	4 (6)	(7)	67 (3)

ADOPTION ACT 1958

1958	1976
s. 35	s. 30
36 (1)	31 (1)
(2)	31 (2) (3)
(3)	22 (4)
37 (1)	32 (1) (2)
(3)	32 (3)
(4)	32 (4)
38	33 (1)
39	33 (2)
40 (4) (6) ...	35 (1)
(5)	35 (2)
43 (1)—(4) ..	34
44 (1) (*a*) (*b*)	36 (1) (a) (*b*)
(*d*)....	36 (1) (*c*)
(2)	36 (2)
45	37 (1)
46	37 (2)
47	37 (4)
48	37 (3)
50	57
51	58
52	56
54 (1)	68
55	69
56 (1)	67 (1) (2)
(2)	67 (6)
57 (1)	72 (1)
(2)	72 (3)
(4)	72 (4)
Sched. 5,	
para. 5	Sched. 2, para. 8
para. 6	Sched. 2, para. 5 (2) (3)
para. 7	Sched. 2, para. 5 (4)
para. 10	Sched. 2, para. 4

ADOPTION ACT 1960

1960	1976
s. 1 (1)	s. 52 (2)
(3)	52 (4)

ADOPTION ACT 1964

1964	1976
s. 1 (5)	s. 59 (3)
2	60
3	Sched. 1, para. 2 (2)—(5)

ADOPTION ACT 1968

1968	1976
s. 4 (3)	72 (2)
5 (1)	59 (1)
6 (1)	53 (1)
(3)—(5)	53 (2)—(5)
7	54
8 (1)	Sched. 1, para. 1 (2)
(2)	Sched. 1, para. 3
(4)	Sched. 1, para. 5 (2)
9 (1)—(4)	s. 70
(5)	40 (3)
10 (1)	71 (2)
11 (1)	ss. 71 (1), 72 (1)
(2)	s. 72 (4)
12 (2)	67 (1) (2)
(3)	67 (4)
(4)	67 (5)

CHILDREN ACT 1975

1975	1976
s. 1	s. 1
2	2
3	6
4	3
5	4
6	5
7	8
8 (1)—(5)	12 (1)—(5)
(7) (8)	12 (6) (7)
9	13
10	14
11	15
12	16
13	7

CHILDREN ACT 1975

1975	1976	1975	1976
s. 14	18	Sched. 1,	
(6)	59 (2)	para. 1 (6)	s. 46 (3)
15	19	para. 2	46 (1) (2)
16	20	para. 3 (1)	
(3) (c)	59 (2)	(2)	39 (1) (2)
17 (1)—(3)	26	(3)—	
18	22 (1)—(3)	(6)	39 (4)—(6)
19	25	para. 4	41
21 (1)—(3)	64	para. 5	Sched. 2,
22 (1) (2)	66 (3) (4)		para. 6
(3)	23	(3)	46 (4)
(4) (5)	24	para. 6 (1)—	
23	21	(6)	42
24	17	para. 7	47
25	55	para. 8	48
30 (1)—(5)	29	para. 9	39 (3)
32	57	para. 10	44 (1)
100 (1) (2)	62 (1) (2)	para. 11	49
(4) (a)		para. 14 (1)	
(5)	62 (3) (4)	(3)	43
(6)	62 (6)	para. 15	45
(8)	62 (5)	para. 16	44 (2) (3)
101	63	para. 17	46 (5)
102 (1) (a)		Sched. 3,	
(2)	61	para. 22	66 (1) (2)
106 (1)	67 (1) (2)		(6)
(3)	67 (4)	para. 34	57
107 (1)	72 (1)	para. 35	58
Sched. 1,		para. 37	69
para. 1 (1) (2)	38 (1)	para. 61	Sched. 1,
(4)	38 (2)		para. 2
			(2)—(5)

Index